ONE-MAN GUITAR JAM

How to Use Riffs, Bass Lines, and Rhythm Parts for Self-Accompaniment While Soloing

BY TROY NELSON

To access audio visit:
www.halleonard.com/mylibrary

Enter Code
4602-4676-2838-8422

ISBN 978-1-4803-5409-8

HAL•LEONARD®
CORPORATION
7777 W. BLUEMOUND RD. P.O. BOX 13819 MILWAUKEE, WI 53213

In Australia Contact:
Hal Leonard Australia Pty. Ltd.
4 Lentara Court
Cheltenham, Victoria, 3192 Australia
Email: ausadmin@halleonard.com.au

CONTENTS

INTRODUCTION

Picture this: You walk into a music store, ready to test-drive some of their shiny new guitars. The place is packed with other guitarists—one's playing "Stairway to Heaven," one's playing "Enter Sandman," and another is butchering a blues lick that he just learned at last week's guitar lesson. Each is competing for sonic space, yet no one is really distinguishing himself. Or this: Your relatives are visiting for the holidays. They heard you've been taking guitar lessons and want to hear you play. Or perhaps you're hanging out with a group of friends and want to impress them with your chops. The question in each of these scenarios is this: What are you going to play? How do you stand out among the din of the guitar shop? How do you dazzle your relatives or peers?

We've all experienced these types of scenarios, and there really is no right or wrong thing to play. If your audience is fellow guitarists, shreddin' a few licks always goes over well. Strumming your way through a pop or rock tune will probably impress relatives and friends. But if you *really* want to stand out—particularly if you're at a music store, surrounded by a bunch of guitar players—nothing turns heads more than a guitarist who can switch back-and-forth between rhythm and lead, moving effortlessly between the two techniques within the structure of a song—a guitarist who is able to accompany himself while outlining the chord changes with his lead phrases.

Self-accompaniment is a technique that lends sophistication to one's playing above and beyond what is attainable from playing lead or rhythm individually. Most people associate this type of playing—sometimes referred to as "solo guitar"—with jazz, and rightfully so. However, self-accompaniment is not solely limited to jazz. In fact, self-accompaniment can be applied to *any* musical style, and that's exactly what you'll find in *One-Man Guitar Jam*. This is not a solo-guitar book in the traditional sense, as the focus is not on a group of songs. Instead, the book focuses on five different genres—blues, rock, jazz, country, and funk—and introduces several popular rhythm styles (accompaniment) in each—25 total.

No song melodies are involved; the focus here is strictly rhythm and lead playing and how to incorporate the two techniques into a cohesive performance, played over a set of chord changes—whether a simple 12-bar blues or more complex progressions like Coltrane Changes or Rhythm Changes, all of which are featured in *One-Man Guitar Jam*. That's not to say that the lessons and musical examples in this book don't translate to traditional solo guitar (they do!); however, the focal point of the book is the myriad benefits of learning how to accompany oneself, including performing within the parameters of song structure, memorizing and internalizing a set of chord changes, keeping proper time, transitioning from lead to rhythm (and vice versa) "on the fly," and implying harmonies via your lead phrases, among others. In short, self-accompaniment will take your playing to a whole new level.

The skill level required to perform the musical examples ranges from intermediate to advanced, with the music genres determining the level of difficulty more so than the book's content, which is pretty consistent throughout. Naturally, the jazz examples are more challenging than, say, the country or blues figures, but with dedicated practice, all of the examples are playable. Consequently, you can jump into the book at any point, letting your musical interests determine how you proceed. If blues is your thing, you can start in Section I and work your way through the book's first six chapters, which touch on everything from blues-based shuffles and bass lines to riffs and fingerpicking. If you're interested in learning some funk, go ahead and jump to Section V, where you can choose from a riff-based figure (Chapter 24) or a "skank" groove (Chapter 25). And, in between, you'll find six rock styles (Chapters 7–12), seven jazz styles (Chapters 13–19), and four country styles (Chapters 20–23) from which to choose.

Each of the 25 chapters is subdivided into six "Jams"—150 in all! The first Jam of each chapter introduces both the rhythm style (riff, bass line, picking pattern, etc.) and the song form, including the number of measures, the chord progression, and, if applicable, the sections. The second Jam of each chapter continuously alternates one bar of lead and one bar of rhythm. In the third Jam, the alternations are extended to two bars. Then, in the fourth Jam, the order is reversed, resulting in a rhythm/lead sequence, and the alternations are, once again, played as one-bar intervals. Like the lead/rhythm sequence, the fifth Jam extends the rhythm/lead alternations to two bars. Finally, in each chapter's sixth Jam, the alternations are arranged randomly. Think of the random Jams as the desired outcome from practicing the structured one- and two-bar alternations. After all, the goal of self-accompaniment is to alternate between rhythm and lead parts spontaneously, rather than in predetermined one- or two-bar intervals. By practicing the alternations in all of these configurations, you will naturally begin to make the transitions "on the fly."

Also included in each chapter is a Resources section, where you'll find chord frames and scale diagrams. The chord frames are simply the chords that are utilized in the rhythm figure, or, in the case of the bass lines, the underlying shapes. Chord frames are a five-fret "snap shot" of the neck and can assist with fingerings and the performance of the examples, especially instances where the full chords are not struck (e.g., bass lines, fingerpicking patterns). Meanwhile, the scale diagrams represent the scales from which the lead phrases are derived. Like the chord frames, the diagrams help to visualize the scales' construction and neck locations. They are also included as a resource for creating your own solo passages. Once you're able to play the phrases in each Jam, you can use the diagrams to manipulate the passages and create your own improvisations (see "Creating Your Own Lead Phrases").

One-Man Guitar Jam is a performance-centric book. Sure, the instruction, chord frames, and scale diagrams will help, but it's the music examples that are going to transform you into a more sophisticated guitarist. The only way to truly learn self-accompaniment is to practice self-accompaniment, and that's what you'll be doing as you play through the various configurations of the lead/rhythm alternations. While you learn to alternate the two approaches, you'll simultaneously learn new rhythm-guitar techniques and increase your lick vocabulary exponentially.

Once you're able to perform the Jams as written, the next step is to accompany yourself while you improvise your own solos. The following sections present several topics to help you in that regard, as well as to help you better understand the content of the forthcoming Jams.

ABOUT THE AUDIO

To access the audio examples that accompany this book, simply go to **www.halleonard.com/mylibrary** and enter the code found on page 1. This will grant you instant access to every jam track. The jam tracks are marked with an audio icon throughout the book.

MEMORIZING AND INTERNALIZING CHORD PROGRESSIONS

If you've ever witnessed a guitarist solo over a chord progression without the benefit of a pianist or fellow guitarist backing him with the changes, you probably noticed how focused his lines were and how he was able to effectively imply the chord changes solely with his lead phrases. He is able to accomplish this by playing within the confines of song structure, mentally noting the changes as they occur and adjusting his lines accordingly. In a solo setting, playing to a predetermined set of chord changes prevents your solos from rambling. Compare this approach to those music-store guitarists who wander aimlessly from lick to lick, often playing out of time and with no particular key or chord in mind.

To "play through the changes" effectively while accompanying oneself, memorizing and internalizing the chord progression and song form is imperative. The progression encompasses the qualities and sequence of the chords, while form refers to the song's length (number of measures), structure (number of sections), and, in some case, where certain chords occur. For example, a 12-bar blues, the song form used predominantly in *One-Man Guitar Jam*, tells us that the tune is 12 bars long and contains one section, which can be repeated indefinitely. A 12-bar blues also involves specific placement of the I, IV, and V chords. In Jam #1, a 12-bar blues in the key of E, the I chord (E7) occupies bars 1–4, 7–8, and 11–12. The IV chord (A7) occupies bars 5–6 and 10, and the V chord (B7) appears in bar 9 and the second half of bar 12. A few variations exist, but this standard 12-bar structure is the heart and soul of countless rock, blues, and jazz tunes.

It's not enough to simply memorize the progression and song form; you must *internalize* the changes. When a progression is internalized, lead phrases flow out almost naturally, with little thought given to the individual chords—the guitarist *feels* the changes. To achieve that level of familiarity with a progression, begin by playing through the changes (rhythm only) several times, playing along to a metronome set to a slow tempo. For example, Jam #1 has a tempo of 100 beats per minute (bpm). A good initial tempo for this example would be somewhere in the range of 50–60 bpm, depending on your skill level. Once you're able to play the blues shuffle cleanly in this range, bump the tempo up to the 56–66 bpm range, playing the rhythm pattern several more times until you can perform it flawlessly at this new tempo. Continue to increase the tempo incrementally until you reach the target tempo of 100 bpm. By this time, you should have a good handle on when/where the I, IV, and V chord changes occur. This is the first step toward internalizing the progression. The next step is illustrated in Jams 2–6, where one-bar, two-bar, and random alternations are introduced, requiring you to make the changes while fluctuating between lead and rhythm parts—in time!

TEMPO, RHYTHM, AND GROOVE

In addition to melodic (lead) and harmonic (rhythm/chords) responsibilities, the solo performer must play the role of time keeper—a role usually reserved for the drummer. As de facto drummer, it's your responsibility to ensure the tempo remains consistent. Wild, random fluctuations in tempo can ruin a performance; therefore, when initially learning the Jams, utilizing a metronome is imperative. Starting slowly and increasing your tempo incrementally (as explained in the previous section) will strengthen your internal clock, resulting in consistent tempos, as well as accurate rhythms.

Once you're able to play a Jam up to tempo with a metronome, you're ready to fly solo. Some guitarists—including yours truly—tap a foot to simulate the click/beep of a metronome. This technique is really helpful with regard to keeping a steady tempo, as well as with feeling some of the rhythmic subdivisions. For example, in 4/4 time, the foot makes contact with the floor on each downbeat, while a rising foot represents the upbeats. Using the blues shuffle as an example, the sequence is illustrated below.

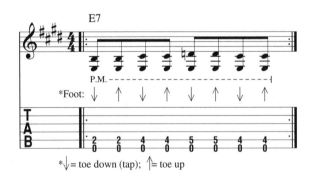

As you can see, the toe taps in a quarter-note rhythm, representing the pulse of the music, while the foot's ascension subdivides the beat into eighth notes. Again, the foot taps the floor on each downbeat, while the upbeats are represented by the foot's recoil.

If some of the rhythms give you problems, don't hesitate to employ counting prompts, either aloud (in practice sessions only!) or mentally. The time signature featured predominantly in *One-Man Guitar Jam* is common time (4/4), with a few Jams played in either 3/4 or 12/8. (*Cut time* is featured in the country section. This is simply a variation of 4/4 time, whereby half notes represent the pulse, rather than quarter notes.) To help you tackle the rhythms that you'll encounter in the book, from simple to complex, counting prompts for all three meters are provided on pages 7–8.

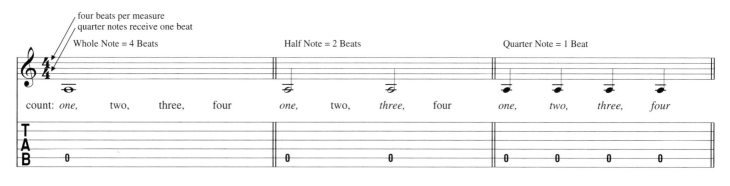

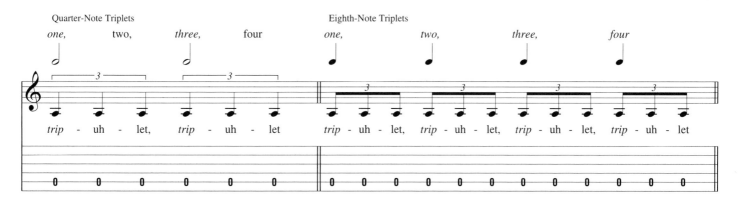

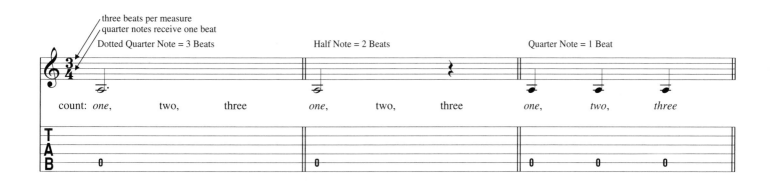

7

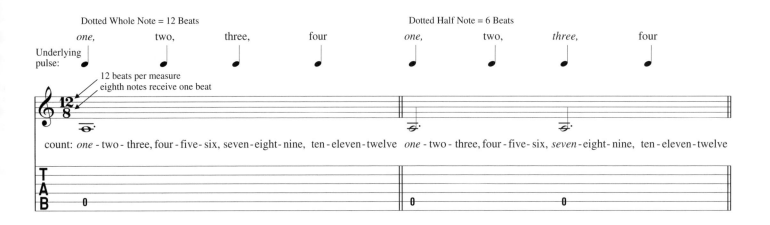

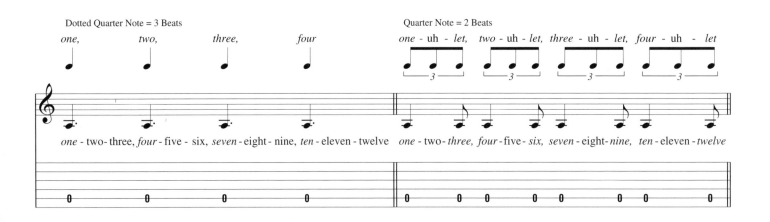

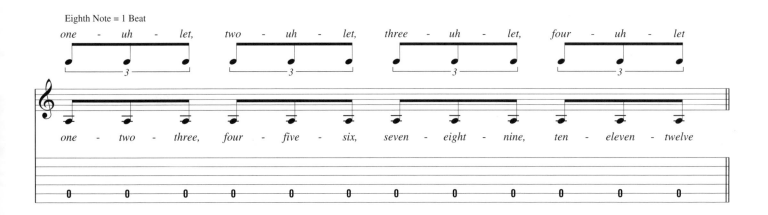

As a one-man rhythm section, a steady tempo and accurate rhythms aren't your only concerns; just as important is establishing a genre-specific "groove." For example, when performing the Jams in the jazz section, you must swing the eights notes, playing the first eight note of each eighth-note pair slightly longer than the second. More specifically, the first eighth note has the same rhythmic value as the first two notes of an eighth-note triplet, while the second eighth note is held for the same duration as the third eighth note of an eighth-note triplet. Swung eighth notes are indicated after the tempo marking ($\sqcap = \sqcap^3\!\!\downarrow$). Also, keep in mind that the swing feel revolves around the drummer's hi-hat, which steadily crashes on the backbeat (beats 2 and 4). You can get a good sense of this feel by listening to the audio demonstrations of the gypsy-jazz Jams in Chapter 15. Notice how the chord attacks on the backbeat are played slightly louder than the attacks on beats 1 and 3.

Similarly, when performing the funk examples in Chapters 24–25, you want to play "in the pocket." Playing in the pocket essentially means establishing a steady groove. Because it's funk, you'll want to establish a groove that feels *slightly* behind the beat. If your playing drifts ahead of the beat, your groove will suffer. One technique that helps to establish a funk groove is to perform quarter and eight notes in staccato (short/clipped) fashion. You can hear this to great effect in the funk riff in Chapter 24 (Jams 139–144), where staccato lends the single-note lines additional punch. Further, watch out for syncopation, which can throw off your entire jam. Syncopation is a vital component of funk but can be a challenge to perform accurately, especially when attempting to establish a groove in a solo setting. So, for the sake of your groove, spend some extra time on these passages.

Similar to funk, the blues has a laidback feel, so its groove should fall slightly behind the beat, as well. That's not to say the blues Jams should drag; on the contrary, they should have a steady tempo, with each note or chord attack falling slightly behind the beat. Like the jazz examples, the blues Jams feature swung eighth notes. If you can swing eighth notes, then the laidback, behind-the-beat groove should come more easily.

CREATING YOUR OWN LEAD PHRASES

Once you've learned the lead phrases presented in the Jams, the next step is start improvising your own passages. The 150 Jams that comprise *One-Man Guitar Jam* are merely an entry point into the world of self-accompaniment. The ultimate goal is to be able to pick a musical style, decide what progression you're going play, and start alternating the rhythm-guitar part with lead lines that are created spontaneously (i.e., improvised).

EVERYTHING OLD IS NEW AGAIN

One place to start is to simply manipulate the phrases that are presented in the Jams. Let's use the one-bar phrase that opens Jam #2 as an example. This phrase is a pretty straightforward, open-position Delta blues lick that implies the E7 chord with notes from the E composite blues scale (E–F♯–G–G♯–A–B♭–B–C♯–D).

This first variation maintains the minor-to-major (G-to-G♯) hammer-on of the original lick but eliminates the first eighth-note triplet in favor of six continuous eighth notes. Also, the half-step bend of the original is now performed as a slide/pull-off figure.

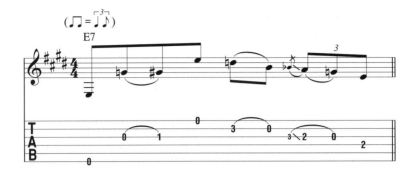

This next lick *opens* with the half-step bend that capped the original phrase. Note the inclusion of the minor-to-major (G-to-G♯) hammer-on, which is a signature sound of the original passage.

This last variation is fueled by eighth-note triplets, which occupy three of the lick's four beats. The phrase kicks off with the signature minor-to-major (G-to-G♯) hammer-on, moves on to a juxtaposition of open treble strings and fretted pitches, and closes with the half-step bend that closed the original phrase.

Now let's take a look at how more linear, scale-and-arpeggio-type phrases can be manipulated in a similar fashion. Let's use the one-bar phrase that opens Jam #80 as an example. This jazzy passage opens with a pickup note, F♯, and outlines the G7 harmony with pitches from the G Mixolydian mode (G–A–B–C–D–E–F).

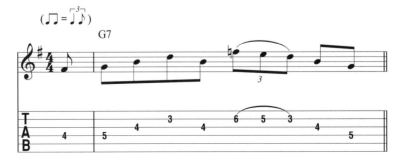

This first variation retains the F♯ pickup note but quickly segues to a string skip (beat 1), moving from the fourth-string root (G) to the D note at fret 3 of the second string. On beat 2, the three-note (F–D–E) pull-off figure from the original phrase appears, although it arrives one beat earlier. The lick then concludes with a jagged sequence of chord tones (B, D, and G, respectively), reversing the string skip from beat 1.

This next variation also includes the F♯ pickup note and, like the previous example, features a string skip. However, this time the jump moves from string 3 to string 1 and starts on the upbeat. This lick also substitutes a hammer/pull figure, played here on beat 3, in place of the three-note pull-off. Note that the defining ♭7th tone, F, is present, as well; it's just been moved to beat 4.

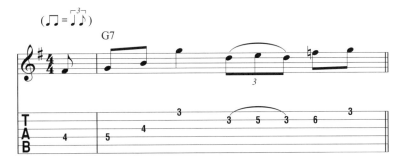

This next lick is the most heavily altered of the three variations. Rather that begin with the F♯ pickup note, the lick commences with a hammer/pull figure that moves back-and-forth between the root (G) and the 9th (A). The next three notes—F, E, and D—are borrowed from the pull-off figure from the original lick, only they're played here as eighth notes rather than as a triplet. The phrase concludes with a bluesy, grace-note hammer-on from the minor 3rd (B♭) to the major 3rd (B).

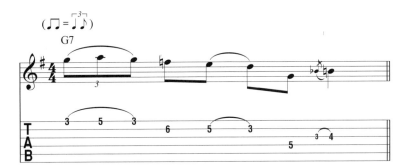

SIMPLICITY IS BLISS

Altering the Jams' phrases is just one approach to creating your own improvisations. A couple of additional approaches include incorporating your own licks into the Jams or using the scale diagrams in the Resources sections as templates for creating brand new passages. If you choose the former, just be mindful of the chord changes, adjusting your phrases accordingly. If transposing licks to new keys is new to you, use the scale diagrams to point you in the right direction. As long as you know where the roots are located in your licks, simply use the diagrams to locate the roots of the new keys.

If you choose to improvise new lead phrases, the scale diagrams are a good place to start. When learning to alternate rhythm and lead parts, one of the biggest obstacles to overcome is keeping a steady tempo while getting in and out of phrases. To mitigate this problem, start basic—that is, keep your lead rhythms simplistic and stick to chord tones exclusively. For example, if the Jam you're working on is in 4/4 time, use a quarter-note rhythm, playing chord tones on each beat. For major chord changes, play the root, major 3rd, 5th, and major 7th (1–3–5–7) of any major scale. (If the major 7th doesn't exist in the scale that you're using, substitute the major 6th, or simply repeat one of the other chord tones.) For minor chords, play the root, minor 3rd, 5th, and minor 7th (1–♭3–5–♭7) of any minor scale. And, for dominant chords, play the root, major 3rd, 5th, and minor 7th (1–3–5–♭7) of any dominant scale. (*Note:* The nine-note composite blues scale, the scale most often used in *One-Man Guitar Jam*, contains all three qualities—major, minor, and dominant—although it's primarily used over dominant chords.)

Let's put this concept into practice over the first seven chords (bars 1–4) of Coltrane Changes (Chapter 18). The progression, Bmaj7–D7–G6–B♭7–E♭maj7–Am7–D7, contains all three qualities (major, minor, and dominant), with six of the seven changes occupying just two beats. The entire phrase is comprised of quarter notes, with each change outlined with the root and 3rd of its associated scale. For the one chord that occupies four beats, E♭maj7, all four chord tones (1–3–5–7) are played.

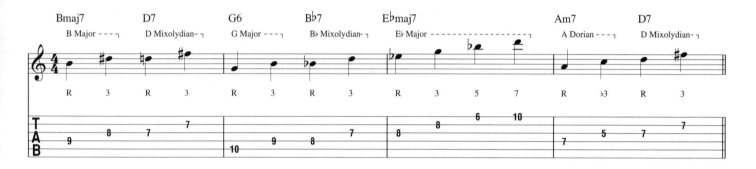

Now let's add a bit more rhythmic complexity to the phrase. The following example introduces eighth notes to beats 1 and 3 of each measure while sticking exclusively to chord tones.

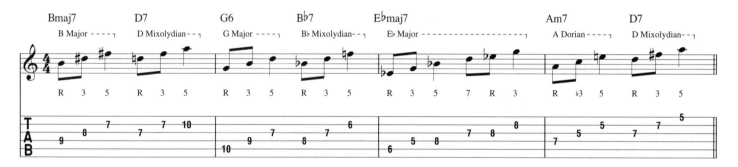

Finally, begin to incorporate non-chord tones (i.e., passing tones) into your lines. As you become more comfortable with improvising your own phrases, continue to increase their rhythmic complexity, vary their direction (ascending or descending), and start some of them on chord tones other than the root. The following example illustrates each of those concepts.

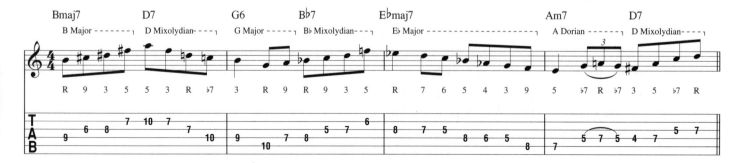

If the more advanced rhythms trip you up, go back to quarter notes or eighth notes. Simple rhythms make it easier to hear and feel the beginning of a new measure and/or chord change. When more complex rhythms are introduced, it requires more complex counting, making hearing/feeling the rhythmic pulse more difficult. When finding beat 1 becomes problematic, your phrases either get truncated or start to meander—or both. As a result, your lead/rhythm transitions suffer.

YOU ARE WHAT YOU PLAY

As a self-accompanying soloist, you must not only be cognizant of *what* scale tones you play but also *where* you play them. Unless your intent is to imply a chord substitution, chord tones must be played on the downbeats. Without the aid of a pianist or fellow guitarist to provide the harmony, you and your lead phrases are tasked with outlining the chord changes.

The most effective method for implying chord changes with your lead phrase is to play the root on beat 1 and follow it with chord tones on the downbeats of beats 2–4. The notes in between are mostly inconsequential. Other chord tones can be played on beat 1, but the root is the most effective tone for driving home the harmony. Although playing chord tones on the downbeats is not a hard-and-fast rule—exceptions are plentiful—you will be a more effective solo performer if it becomes a natural part of your lead playing. Play through the next few examples to hear how displacing a phrase by merely a half beat can drastically alter its tonality.

Set your metronome to a moderate tempo—say, 100 bpm—and then strum the open C major chord. On beat 1 of the second measure, play the C major scale (C–D–E–F–G–A–B) in the indicated eighth-note rhythm, followed in measure 3 by another iteration of the C chord. Note that chord tones (circled) fall on the downbeats of all four beats of measure 2.

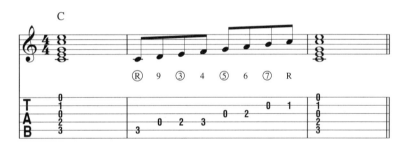

Use the same approach as you play through this next example. Here, the C major scale begins a half beat earlier—on the "and" of beat 4 of the first measure—placing non-chord tones (circled) on the downbeats. The one exception is the upper-octave root, which falls on the downbeat of beat 4.

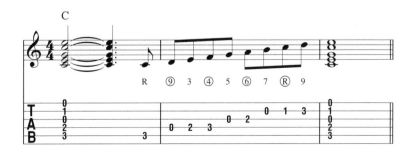

13

Notice how drastically different the two phrases sound. Even though the same notes are played, by voicing chord tones on weak beats (i.e., upbeats), the tonality changes from C major to D minor:

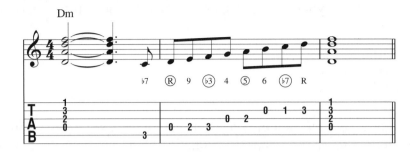

Remember: You are the *only* harmonic source, so the way you phrase your lead passages will determine what chords your audience hears. If your intent is to substitute Dm for the C major harmony, then the latter phrase works well. However, if your goal is to outline a C major chord, then be sure to emphasize chord tones on the downbeats.

ALWAYS HAVE A PLAN!

Unless your goal is free-form improvisation, with expansive lead phrases, tight and focused lines are preferable. For that to occur, the self-accompanying soloist must engage in some planning. Some of the decisions that must be made include: 1) what scales will be used, 2) where will the phrases be played, and 3) what transitional devices will be employed to move in and out of lead passages, as well as from chord to chord.

The rhythm pattern that you use will help determine which scales/licks you will play and where you will play them. For example, if you're playing a Delta blues fingerpicking pattern like the one in Chapter 6, most of your lead phrases will be relegated to open position for authenticity and practicality purposes. Jumping all over the fretboard doesn't make much sense if your entire rhythm figure is played near the nut (like the Delta blues pattern). Therefore, getting acclimated to the scale types and patterns available in open position for the changes that you'll be playing over—in the case of Chapter 6, E7, A7, and B7—is wise. In the Resource section of Chapter 6, several options are available, including the E composite (E–F♯–G–G♯–A–B♭–B–C♯–D), A composite (A–B–C–C♯–D–E♭–E–F♯–G), and B composite (B–C♯–D–D♯–E–F–F♯–G♯–A) blues scales, as well as the A Mixolydian mode (A–B–C♯–D–E–F♯–G).

TRANSITIONAL DEVICES

Extended Pentatonic Scales

If you do decide to move some of your phrases up the fretboard, you'll need to determine what options are available to help you transition seamlessly from rhythm to lead. One option is to use the extended forms of various pentatonic-based scales, such as the B major pentatonic scale (B–C♯–D♯–F♯–G♯) illustrated in Chapter 6. These patterns are great tools for transitioning from one position to another, especially when targeting a higher-register scale for a new chord change.

The following example represents bars 7–12 of a 12-bars blues in the key of E, using the Delta blues fingerpicking pattern from Chapter 6. After two bars of I-chord (E7) fingerpicking, the V (B7) chord is outlined with the extended form of the B major pentatonic scale, which also relocates the fret hand to fifth position, where an A composite blues scale phrase implies the IV (A7) chord.

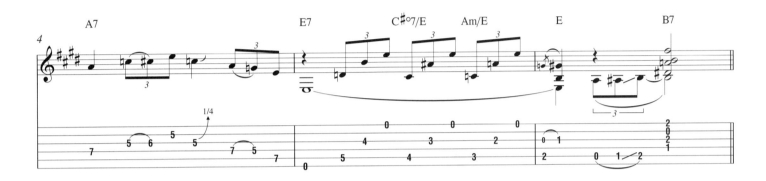

Open Strings

Another option available for making quick shifts up or down the fretboard is open strings. Guitar-based music is ripe with songs in the keys of E, A, D, and G, which, not coincidentally, represent the bottom four strings of the guitar. These keys enable certain open strings to be incorporated into the song without falling outside of the key. In a solo setting, these open strings can come in handy when transitioning from rhythm to lead (or vice versa), especially when making a large jump up or down the fretboard.

This next example represents bars 1–4 of a 12-bar blues in the key of E, with the "quick change" (the IV chord, A7) occurring in bar 2. To demonstrate how helpful open strings can be when transitioning between rhythm and lead parts, the blues shuffle from Chapter 1 is offset by one-bar lead phrases.

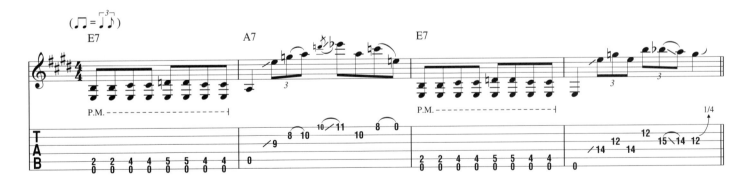

The open A and open E strings enable fret-hand shifts to eighth position and 12th position, respectively, while simultaneously emphasizing the E7 and A7 harmonies. Similarly, at the end of measure 2, the A blues scale lick concludes with a pull-off to the open E string, which, in addition to being part of the scale, enables time to reposition the fret hand for the forthcoming shuffle pattern (measure 3).

Leading Tones

Leading tones are another method for segueing from rhythm to lead and a favorite of jazz guitarists. A *leading tone* is the note located one half step (semitone) below the tonic (root) of the scale or lick. Leading tones are so effective because they have a strong desire to resolve upward to the tonic. For example, the leading tone in the key of C major (C–D–E–F–G–A–B) is B, the major 7th.

Leading tones are diatonic to major keys but non-diatonic to minor and dominant keys, whose 7ths are minor in quality and, therefore, located a *whole step* below the tonic. For example, in D Dorian (D–E–F–G–A–B–C), the leading tone is C♯, but the seventh degree of the scale is C *natural*. Further, in G Mixolydian (G–A–B–C–D–E–F), the leading tone is F♯, but the seventh degree of the scale is F *natural*. In short, either note can function as the leading tone, but semitone (half-step) movement is most effective.

To hear the difference between diatonic and non-diatonic leading tones, play through the following examples, which employ both tones to transition from gypsy-jazz comping (see Chapter 15) to one-bar lead phrases.

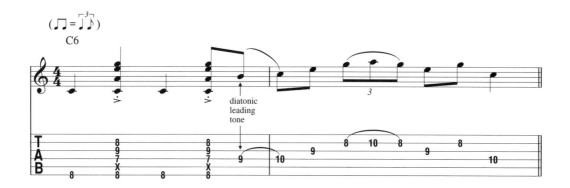

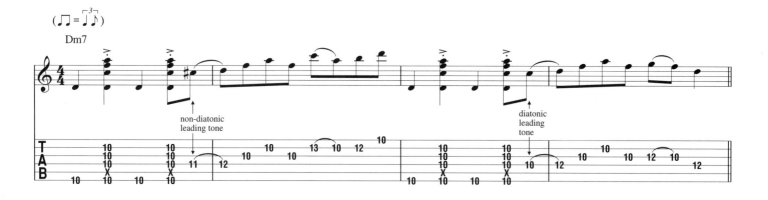

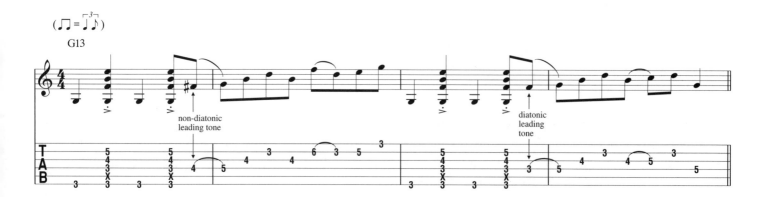

Rests

Of course, making smooth transitions between lead and rhythm parts isn't always about *what* you play; sometimes it's what you *don't* play. Often, a simple, strategically placed eighth- or quarter-note rest is all that's needed to effectively segue to/from a lead phrase. When using rests, be mindful that the longer the pause, the more difficult it is for your audience to follow along. Also, the inclusion of rests doesn't mean that you get to take a break; on the contrary, you must be even more diligent about your counting.

To hear how brief, eighth- and quarter-note rests affect rhythm-to-lead transitions, play through the following four examples, incorporating foot-tapping and the eighth-note counting prompt for assistance. All four examples employ the blues shuffle from Chapter 1 for the I (E7) chord, followed by a one-measure lick over the IV (A7) chord.

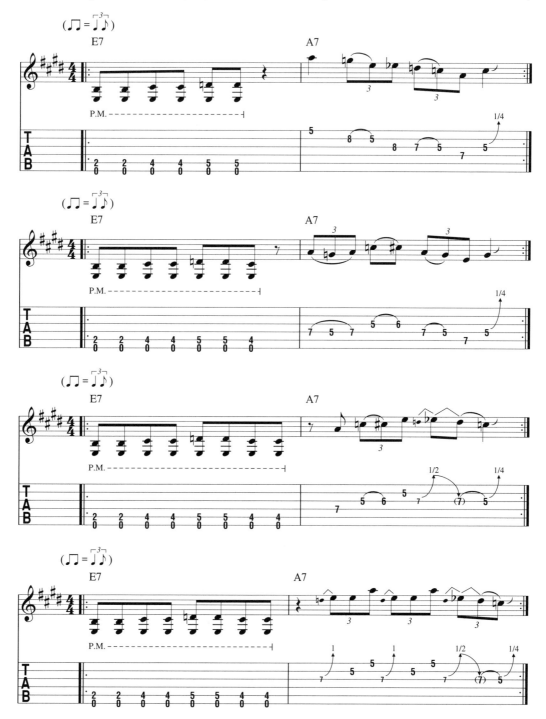

Although the duration and location of the rest are varied in each example, each pause enabled enough time to reposition your fret hand to fifth position for the IV-chord lick. In fact, the pauses are so brief, they're barely noticeable; the jam continues to move right along. Again, the key to incorporating rests is to count diligently.

Chord Variations and Transposition

If you have a good handle on chord inversions and transposition, you can use these skills to your advantage. Just because you learn an accompaniment pattern in one position doesn't mean that you're relegated to that position alone. On the contrary, inversions, transposition, and entirely new voicings can be implemented to minimize fretboard jumps. The next three examples put these concepts into practice.

The first example alternates the blues shuffle from Chapter 1 and one-bar lead phrases. The figure begins with the open-position E7 (I chord) shuffle before jumping up to fifth position for a phrase that outlines the A7 (IV) chord. Then, rather than jumping back down to open position, the E7 shuffle is recreated with a pattern that has been transposed up one octave yet retains the low end of the original by incorporating the low E string. As a result, the subsequent lead phrase (measure 4) can be played in the higher register without necessitating a large jump back up the fretboard.

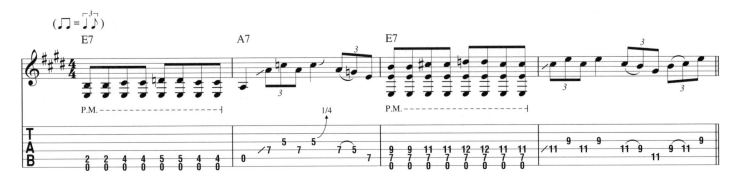

The next example represents the first four bars of the gypsy-jazz comping Jams (Chapter 15). The pattern commences with a seventh-position voicing of an F6/9 chord, followed in measure 2 by a run up the extended form of the F major pentatonic scale (F–G–A–C–D). Rather than jump back down to seventh position in measure 3, an alternate, 12th-position voicing of the F6/9 chord is implemented, putting the fret hand in an advantageous position for the subsequent lead phrase (measure 4).

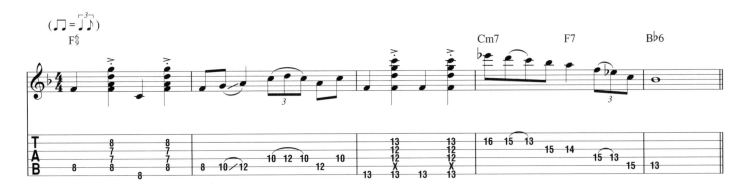

The bluegrass strumming pattern from Chapter 20 provides the rhythm part for this next example. Following a three-note (G–A–B) pickup, alternating bass notes (C and G) offset eighth-note chord strums. In measure 2, the extended form of the C major pentatonic scale (C–D–E–G–A) moves the fret hand to eighth position, where a sixth-string C major barre chord handles the second repetition of the strumming pattern. Like the previous examples, the subsequent lead phrase can be played in the higher register without requiring a large fret-hand jump.

18

Voice Leading

Voice leading is the way the individual notes (voices) of a chord transition to the notes of a subsequent chord. Although most often associated with chord progressions, voice leading is also an important component of lead playing. Effective voice leading is especially important in a solo setting and, in many ways, will determine the success—or failure—of your solos. Good voice leading results in lines that flow smoothly from chord to chord and make your progression sound like a cohesive unit, rather than a disjointed set of changes. In short, voice leading is the difference between playing *through* the chord changes (preferred) and playing *over* the changes.

In this book, we're going to analyze voice leading from a couple of perspectives: 1) the distance (interval) the last note of one phrase travels to arrive at the first note of the subsequent phrase, and 2) the relationship between the notes and their associated harmonies (chord changes). As a soloist, clearly indicating when chords are changing within the context of your solos is immensely important, and strategic voice leading helps tremendously in that regard. Again, good voice leading leads to fluid lead phrases.

The next 11 examples represent only a handful of the voice-leading options that are available. While each of them resolves in descending order and move to the root of each subsequent chord, voice leading works in ascending order and can target chord tones other than the root, as well. (*Note:* Any note has two intervallic relationships with another note—one ascending and one descending. For example, moving upward from C to D is a major 2nd interval, but moving downward from C to D is a minor 7th). You'll encounter several alternative voice-leading options as you play through the Jams.

Each of the following licks is played in a jazz-blues style over a I–IV–I progression in the key of G (G7–C7–G7). Scale/ chord relationships are provided between the notation and tab staves. When two numbers are separated by a forward slash, the note to the left of the slash represents the note's relationship to the harmony (chord) of that measure, whereas the note to the right of the slash represents the note's relationship to the impending chord change. (*Note:* Scale/chord relationships are provided throughout the book to give you greater insight into what notes are being played at a given time, how various notes sound over certain chords, and what voice-leading concepts are being used.)

For reference, here's a list of all of the symbols that you'll encounter and what they represent:

R = Root
9 = Major 2nd/9th
♭9 = Diminished 9th
♯9 = Augmented 9th
♭3 = Minor 3rd
3 = Major 3rd
4 = Perfect 4th
5 = Perfect 5th
♭5 = Diminished 5th (Tritone)
♯5 = Augmented 5th
6 = Major 6th
♭7 = Minor 7th
7 = Major 7th

Unison

In this first example, each chord change is implied a half beat early. In measure 1, the C note on the "and" of beat 4 functions as both the 4th in the key of G and the root in the key of C (measure 2). Similarly, the G note at the end of measure 2 functions as both the 5th in the key of C and the root in the key of G.

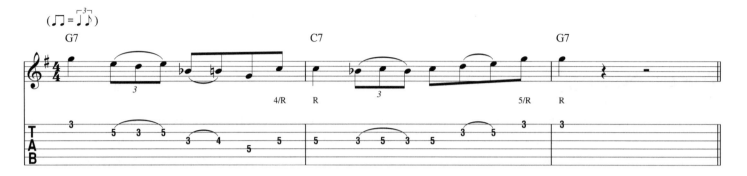

Major 2nd (Whole Step)

The voice leading in this next example resolves to each new chord via a whole step (a major 2nd). At the end of measure 1, the D note functions as both the 5th of G7 and the 2nd/9th of C7. At the end of measure 2, the A note functions as both the 6th of C7 and the 2nd/9th of G7. (*Note:* Technically, the 6ths and 9ths are not part of the dominant-seventh harmonies, but they are found in the chords' relative scales. In this context, they imply chord extensions: dominant 9ths and dominant 13ths.)

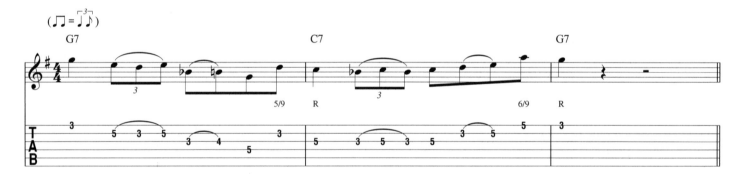

Minor 3rd

The descending minor 3rd interval is quite effective as a voice-leading option, especially when moving from the IV chord to the I chord—in this case, C7 to G7. You'll notice that the B♭ note functions as both the ♭7th of C7—*the defining tone of a dominant seventh chord*—and the ♭3rd of G7. Although G7 is comprised of a *major* 3rd, B, the B♭ imparts the minor-against-major sound that is so prevalent in blues and jazz.

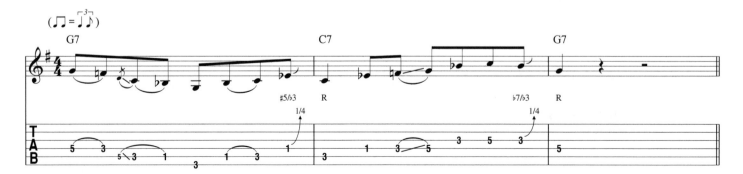

Major 3rd

In this next example, the phrase resolves to each new chord via a major 3rd interval. At the end of measure 1, the E note functions as both the 6th in the key of G and the major 3rd in the key of C. Interestingly, the B note at the end of measure 2 functions as the *major* 7th over C7—a *dominant* seventh chord. But, because the next chord is G7, where B functions as the major 3rd, it works.

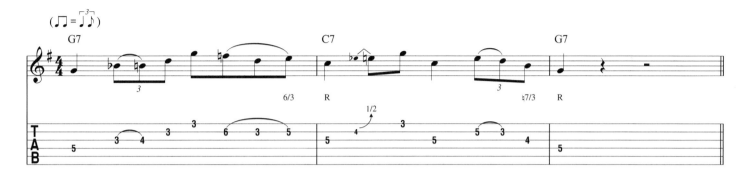

Perfect 4th

The perfect 4th is not quite as effective at resolution as some of the other intervals, but it works nevertheless. Although the initial tones in this example function as non-chord tones (4ths) relative to the target chords, they *do* function as chord tones within their respective measures (♭7th and root, respectively).

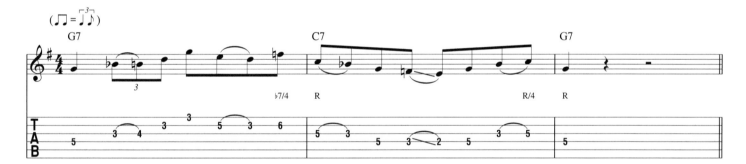

Perfect 5th

In this next example, the lick resolves to the IV and I chords via a perfect 5th interval. At the end of measure 1, the G note functions as both the root of G7 and the 5th of the impending C7 chord. Similarly, at the end of measure 2, the D note functions as both the 9th of C7 and the 5th of G7.

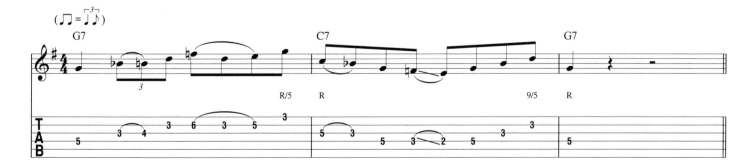

Major 6th

Although you won't encounter major-6th resolutions as often as some of the other intervals, it does impart a colorful sound. In this example, the phrase jumps from a first-string A note to a third-string C note. The A note functions as the 9th of G7, whereas it functions as the 6th of C7. A similar move occurs at the end of measure 2, where an E note functions as the 3rd of C7 and the 6th of G7.

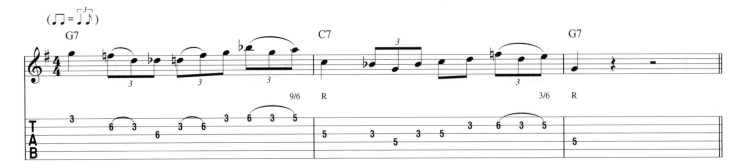

Minor 7th

Although a wide interval (five whole steps), the minor 7th has a surprisingly strong desire to resolve to the root. Similar to the major 6th intervals, the minor 7th jumps in this example require a string skip. At the end of measure 1, a first-string B♭ note jumps to a third-string C note, the root of the C7 chord. The same type of jump occurs at the end of measure 2, although it's been shifted down one string. Note that the B♭ note in measure 1 functions as both the ♭3rd of G7 and the ♭7th of C7. Meanwhile, the F at the end of measure 2 functions as the 4th of C7, whereas it functions as the ♭7th of G7.

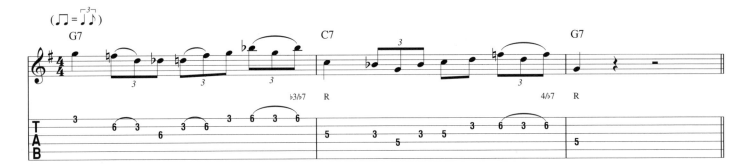

Chromaticism (ascending)

Another effective voicing-leading method is chromaticism. In this next example, the root of each subsequent chord is approached via chromatic pitches. In measure 1, the C7 chord is targeted with the notes B♭ and B, which function as the minor and major 3rds of G7 and the minor and major 7ths of C7, respectively. Similarly, the G7 chord is approached by the chromatic pitches E, F, and F♯.

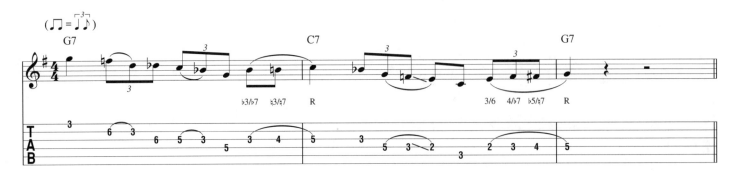

Chromaticism (descending)

Chords can also be approached chromatically in descending fashion. In the following example, the C7 and G7 chords are targeted with pitches that are located a whole- and half-step away. The D–D♭–C figure at the end of measure 1 is a bluesy phrase, while the A–A♭–G movement at the end of measure 2 is straight out of a jazz guitarist's playbook.

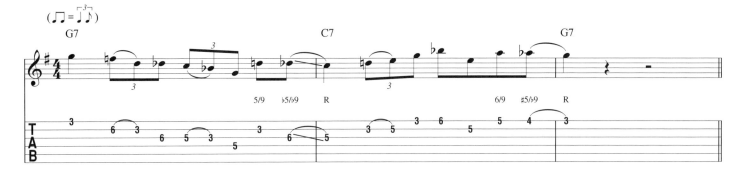

Minor 3rd to Major 3rd

This last voice-leading tactic, moving from the minor 3rd to the major 3rd, is one that you'll encounter frequently as you work your way through the book. It's a favorite of country, blues, and jazz players, no doubt due to its strong desire to resolve to the root of the target chord. It's also extremely versatile, as it can be executed with a hammer-on, slide, or bend. In the following example, the C7 chord is preceded by an E♭-to-E bend—the minor 3rd and major 3rd of C7. A similar maneuver is used at the end of measure 2, although a hammer-on is used in lieu of a bend.

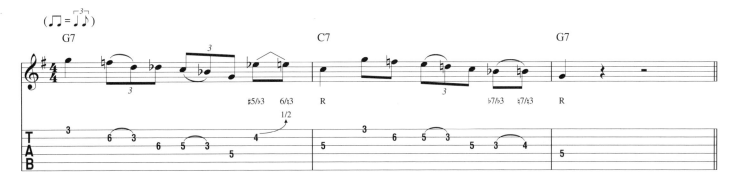

FINAL THOUGHTS BEFORE GETTING STARTED

As you memorize the chord changes to each Jam, spend some extra time mentally visualizing the changes. This is part of the internalization process. The goal is to be able to anticipate the changes; that is, as you're playing rhythm or lead over one chord, your mind is already thinking ahead to the next chord—you're strategizing your next move. The more you play through the changes, the more this concept will become a natural part of your playing. Until that time, however, you must force yourself to literally envision the progression as it unfolds.

If any segment of a Jam gives you trouble, don't hesitate to isolate that section of the music and practice is several times along with your metronome, independent of the rest of the Jam. This approach can help smooth out some of the lead/rhythm transitions (or vice versa). For example, you might choose to isolate each of the lead/rhythm transitions of a Jam—whether of the one-bar or two-bar variety—before stringing them all together.

Lastly, don't overlook the fact that the rhythm parts are introduced in the first Jam of each chapter, including the audio examples. If you're having trouble with any of the lead phrases, simply pull up the audio track and play along. Use the audio demonstrations as your personal backing tracks!

 TUNING NOTES

SECTION I: BLUES

CHAPTER 1: BLUES SHUFFLE

THE RESOURCES

CHORDS

E5

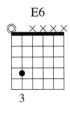
E6

E7

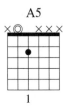
A5

A6

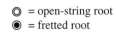
◎ = open-string root
⦿ = fretted root

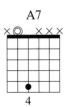
A7

B5

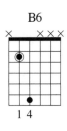
B6

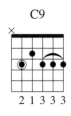
C9

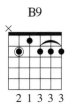
B9

SCALES

E Composite Blues Scale:
E–F♯–G–G♯–A–B♭–B–C♯–D
(1–2–♭3–♮3–4–♭5–♮5–6–♭7)

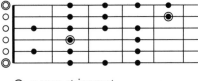

A Composite Blues Scale:
A–B–C–C♯–D–E♭–E–F♯–G
(1–2–♭3–♮3–4–♭5–♮5–6–♭7)

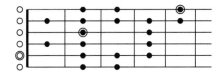

B Composite Blues Scale:
B–C♯–D–D♯–E–F–F♯–G♯–A
(1–2–♭3–♮3–4–♭5–♮5–6–♭7)

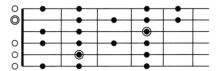

◎ = open-string root
⦿ = fretted root

 JAM #1: THE 12-BAR FORM

Harmonically, this shuffle, or "boogie," pattern is based on standard 12-bar blues changes: four bars of the I chord, two bars of the IV chord, two bars of the I chord, one bar of the V chord, one bar of the IV chord, and a I–V turnaround in the final two bars. The result is an E7–A7–E7–B7–A7–E7–B7 progression, with the C9 chord functioning as a transitional chord that moves chromatically to B9 (substituted for a dominant seventh voicing). Rhythmically, the figure is comprised exclusively of shuffled eighth notes, with root/5th, root/6th, and root/♭7th dyads (i.e., two-note chords) relative to each chord implying the changes.

MEASURES 1–4: To outline the I (E7) chord in measure 1, E5 (E/B) dyads are shuffled on beat 1, followed by E6 (E/C♯) and E7 (E/D) dyads on beats 2 and 3, respectively, before returning to E6 to close out the measure. This figure is repeated in measures 2–4.

MEASURES 5–8: For the IV (A7) chord change in measures 5–6, the shuffle pattern is shifted from strings 5–6 to strings 4–5, where A/E (root/5th), A/F♯ (root/6th), and A/G (root/♭7th) dyads are employed. Measures 7–8 mark the return of the original pattern for the I (E7) chord.

MEASURES 9–12: While open strings represent the root notes for the E7 and A7 changes, no such luxury exits for the B7 change in measure 9. Therefore, the shuffle pattern is moved to second position, where the index finger plays the B note on fret 2 of the fifth string, and the ring and pinky fingers handle the fourth-string notes of the B5 (B/F♯) and B6 (B/G♯) dyads, respectively (note that, ironically, the B7 dyad has been omitted for the B7 chord change). Measures 10–11 mark a return to the shuffle patterns for the IV (A7) and I (E7) chords, respectively, leading to the chromatic C9–B9 turnaround on beat 2 of measure 12.

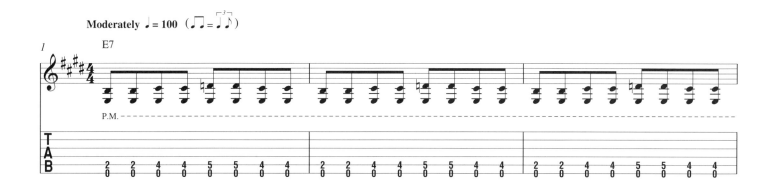

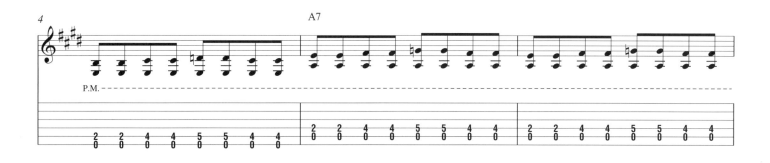

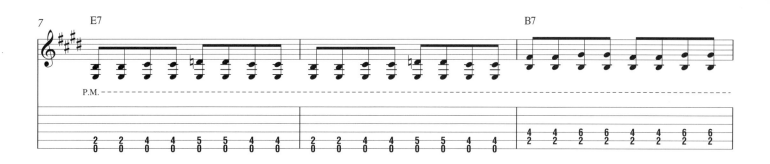

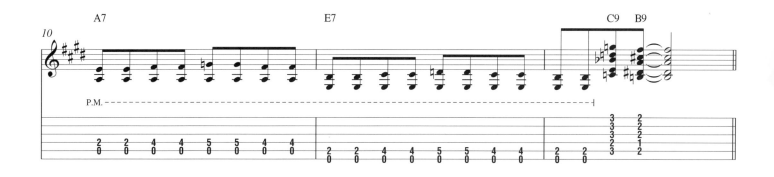

JAM #2: ONE-BAR LEAD/RHYTHM ALTERNATIONS

This Jam alternates one bar of lead playing and one bar of the shuffle pattern throughout its 12 bars. All of the lead lines are played in open position and derive their notes from the E, A, and B composite blues scales for the E7, A7, and B7 chord changes, respectively.

MEASURES 1–4: Measure 1 introduces a rhythmic and melodic motif that is carried through the entire 12-bar form. The notes are derived from the E composite blues scale (E–F♯–G–G♯–A–B♭–B–C♯–D) and are played in a rhythm that pairs eighth notes and eighth-note triplets. The motif is altered in measure 3—specifically, on beats 3–4— resulting in a "call and response" phrase, a staple of the blues. Notice the notes that lead back into the shuffle patterns in measures 2 and 4: G (♭3rd) and E (root), respectively. Both notes have a strong urge to resolve to the root of the E7 chord. In the case of the latter note, E, the root simply arrives a fraction of a beat early.

MEASURES 5–8: Although the phrase in measure 5 differs from the original motif, melodically, the eighth-note triplet on beat 2 is a remnant of the motif's rhythm. On beat 4, a half-step bend from the minor 3rd (C) to the major 3rd (C♯) offers a strong lead-in to the shuffle pattern for the A7 chord. Measure 7 marks the return of the original motif but, like measure 3, has been altered after the initial low E string attack and third-string hammer-on figure.

MEASURES 9–12: The phrase in measure 9 borrows notes from the B composite blues scale (B–C♯–D–D♯–E–F– F♯–G♯–A) to recreate the original motif over the new chord, B7. The phase ends on the note E, which happens to be a chord tone—specifically, the 5th—of the forthcoming A7 chord (measure 10). The lead/rhythm trade-offs conclude with a standard blues turnaround phrase (measure 11) and a chromatic approach to the V (B9) chord (measure 12), which signals a return to the top of the 12-bar form (i.e., the I chord).

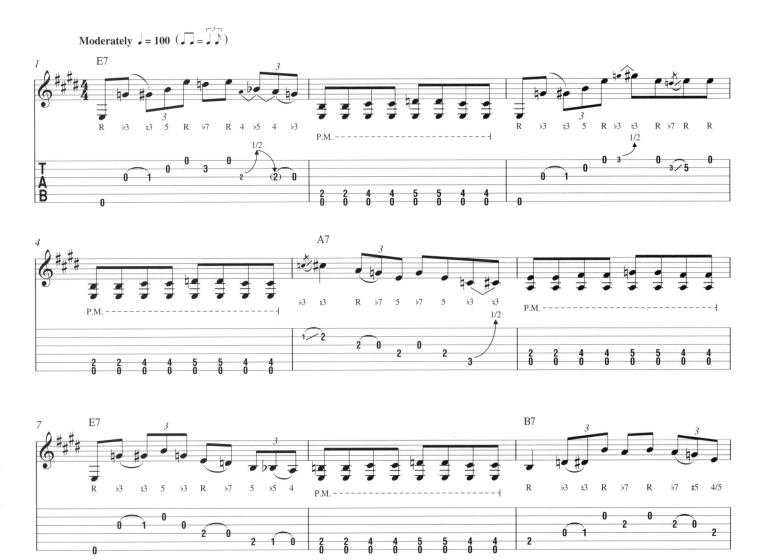

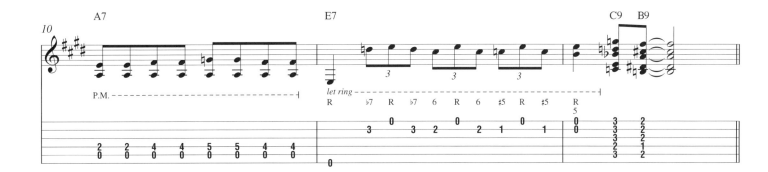

JAM #3: TWO-BAR LEAD/RHYTHM ALTERNATIONS

This Jam juggles two bars of lead playing with two bars of the blues shuffle, alternating the two approaches throughout the 12-bar form. Like Jam #2, the lead phrases are derived from either the E composite, A composite, or B composite blues scale, depending on the harmony being implied at the time (E7, A7, or B7).

MEASURES 1–4: Measures 1–2 feature an ascending/descending phrase that contains all but two notes (F♯ and C♯) of the nine-note E composite blues scale (E–F♯–G–G♯–A–B♭–B–C♯–D). The rhythmically diverse line, which is comprised of quarter notes, eighth notes, eighth-note triplets, and a 16th-note triplet, concludes with a minor-to-major (G-to-G♯) bend that resolves to the root of the E5 chord on beat 1 of measure 3.

MEASURES 5–8: Following two measures of the E7 shuffle pattern (measures 3–4), a two-measure phrase is launched in measure 5. This line is derived from the A composite blues scale (A–B–C–C♯–D–E♭–E–F♯–G) and closely mirrors the line that opened the 12-bar form, lending continuity to the Jam. Like the end of measure 2, a half-step (G-to-G♯) bend resolves the phrase and leads into two more bars of the E7 shuffle pattern (measures 7–8).

MEASURES 9–12: In measure 9, a short motif is created via half-step bends from the minor 3rd (D) to the major 3rd (D♯) of the B composite blues scale (B–C♯–D–D♯–E–F–F♯–G♯–A), which is transposed down one whole step, to the key of A, for the A7 change. Here, hammer-ons have been substituted for the bends, and the phrase resolves to the root note (A) on beat 3, which receives a touch of vibrato for good measure. The Jam concludes with a return to the E7 shuffle pattern (measure 11) and a half-step (i.e., chromatic) chordal move to the V (B9) chord.

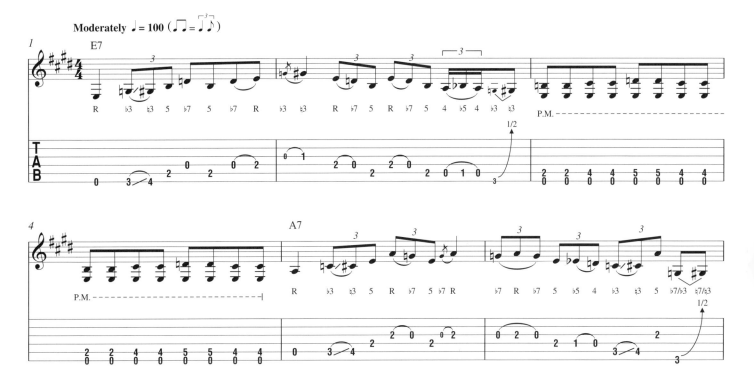

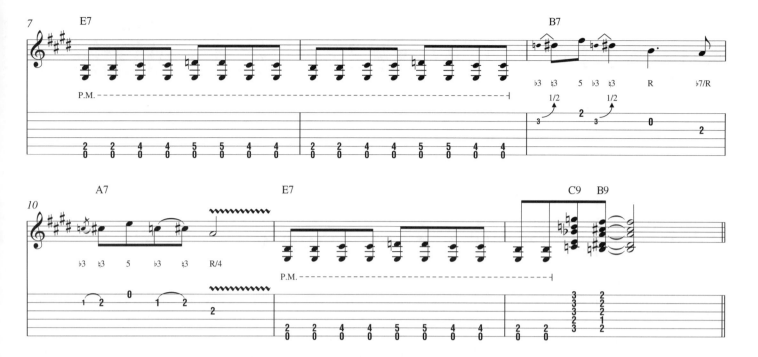

 # JAM #4: ONE-BAR RHYTHM/LEAD ALTERNATIONS

In this Jam, the sequence of the lead/rhythm alternations from Jams 2–3 is reversed. Here, the shuffle pattern is employed in measures 1, 3, 5, 7, 9, and 11, whereas lead phrases comprise measures 2, 4, 6, 8, and 10 (measure 12 contains a combination of the two). Like the previous two Jams, the lead lines are composed of notes from the composite blues scales relative the chord changes: E composite, A composite, and B composite.

MEASURES 1–4: Following one measure of the E7 shuffle pattern, a melodic and rhythm motif is carved from the E composite blues scale (E–F♯–G–G♯–A–B♭–B–C♯–D). After returning to the shuffle pattern in measure 3, the motif from measure 2 is restated in measure 4 (albeit modified on beats 3 and 4), lending continuity to the Jam.

MEASURES 5–8: The final note of measure 4, B, creates a smooth, scalar (B is the 2nd/9th of the A composite blues scale) segue to the A7 shuffle pattern in measure 5. In measure 6, the shuffle pattern is retained for one beat (beat 1) before giving way to a lick that is rooted in the A composite blues scale (A–B–C–C♯–D–E♭–E–F♯–G). Notice that, even though the notes are different, this phrase's rhythm is identical to the motif from measure 2—again, giving the Jam a sense of cohesion. Following another measure of the E7 shuffle pattern (measure 7), the original motif returns in measure 8, with a more rhythmically sophisticated deviation appearing on beats 3 and 4. Notice the seamless, chromatic transition that occurs during the lead/rhythm transition at the end of measure 8, where a B♭ note segues to the B7 shuffle pattern (measure 9).

MEASURES 9–12: The shuffle pattern of measure 9 leads to a second-position lick derived from the A composite blues scale (measure 10). Since your index finger is already located at fret 2 (for the B7 shuffle), no fret-hand shift is required. The E7 shuffle pattern is reprised in measure 11, transitioning to a short turnaround lick that begins on beat 2 of measure 12.

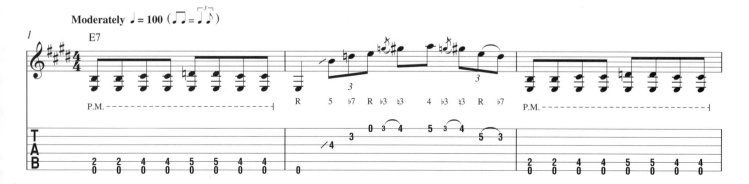

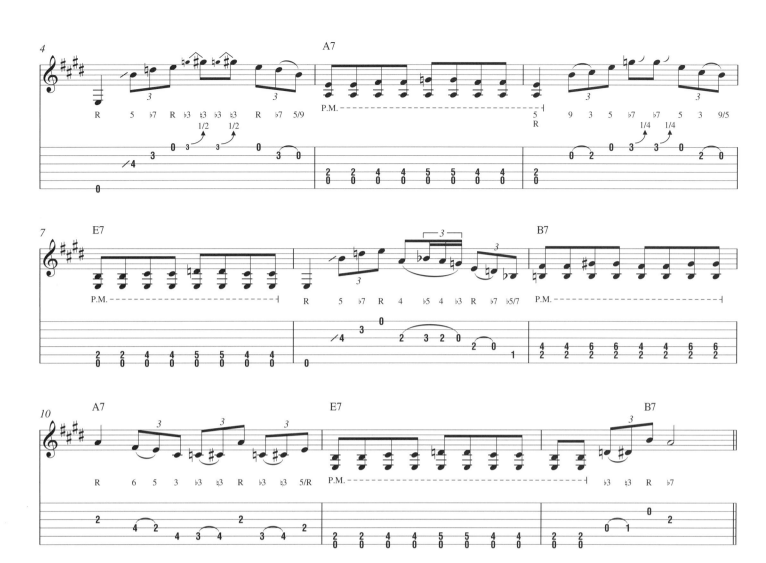

JAM #5: TWO-BAR RHYTHM/LEAD ALTERNATIONS

For this Jam, the rhythm and lead figures have each been extended by one measure apiece. The result is two bars of rhythm continuously alternating with two bars of lead throughout the 12-bar form. Like previous Jams, the lead lines are derived from the E composite and A composite blues scales (no lead phrases are played over the B7 chords).

MEASURES 1–4: After the rhythmic foundation is laid down in measures 1–2 via the E7 shuffle pattern, a two-bar lead line commences in measure 3. Derived from the E composite blues scale (E–F♯–G–G♯–A–B♭–B–C♯–D), the phrase contains a rhythmic and melodic motif (see the triplet figures on beats 2 and 4 of measure 3) that is reprised throughout the 12-bar form (continuity!). The pair of half-step bends that occur on beat 4 of measure 4 effectively transition to the A7 shuffle pattern that follows, as the notes represent the minor 3rd (C) and major 3rd (C♯) of the new harmony (A7).

MEASURES 5–8: Following two measures of the A7 shuffle pattern (measures 5–6), a two-bar lead phrase commences with the same motif that was established at the beginning of measure 3. On beat 3, however, the lick deviates from the original phrase, fueled by a string of eighth-note triplets. On beats 3–4 of measure 8, a half-step (D-to-D♯) slide segues to measure 9's B7 shuffle pattern (in the key of B, D and D♯ are the minor 3rd and major 3rd, respectively), a voice-leading tactic similar to the one used at the end of measure 4.

MEASURES 9–12: In measures 9–10, the shuffle pattern outlines the B7 and A7 changes before a conventional blues turnaround figure commences in measure 11. Allow the open low E string to ring out as you move the major 6th shapes down strings 3 and 5 chromatically.

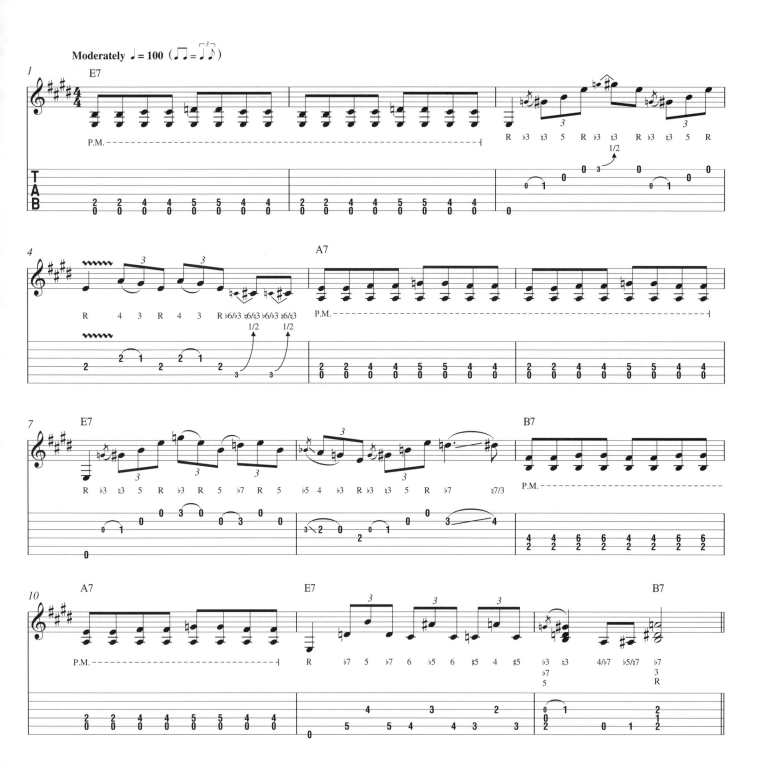

🔊 JAM #6: RANDOM RHYTHM/LEAD ALTERNATIONS

While Jams 1–5 were arranged in interval-specific lead/rhythm alternations (every bar, every two bars, etc.), this Jam randomly switches between the two techniques, resulting in a more "organic"—and less "composed"— approach to solo-guitar playing. It's that outcome you should be striving for as you work through *One-Man Guitar Jam*: transitions that sound both seamless and unpredictable.

MEASURES 1–4: After the shuffle rhythm is established in measure 1, a one-bar lead phrase, derived from the E composite blues scale (E–F#–G–G#–A–Bb–B–C#–D), is played in measure 2. A rhythmic and melodic motif, composed of a whole-step bend and arpeggiations of the open B and high E strings, kicks off the phrase. In measure 3, the shuffle pattern returns for one measure before giving way to a two-measure lead phrase that seamlessly connects the E7 and A7 harmonies. Notice that the phrase kicks off with a restatement of the motif from measure 2.

MEASURES 5–8: The lead line that connects measures 4 and 5 effectively signals the A7 chord change via a chromatic line: G–G♯–A. For the E7 harmony, G and G♯ represent the minor 3rd and major 3rd, respectively, whereas A is the root of the new chord (A7). Following one measure of the A7 shuffle pattern (measure 6), another lead phrase commences with a restatement of the motif from measure 2. This line is played exclusively in open position and borrows a transitional technique from Jam #5 to move from E7 to B7: a half-step, minor 3rd (D)-to-major 3rd (D♯) slide.

MEASURES 9–12: The melody that is created over the B7 chord (measure 9) is transposed down one whole step for the A7 harmony (measure 10). To signal the arrival of the E7 chord in measure 11, a half-step (G-to-G♯) bend is implemented at the end of measure 10 (again, in the key of E, G and G♯ are the minor 3rd and major 3rd, respectively). The Jam concludes with a return to the E7 shuffle pattern and chromatic chordal movement to the V (B9) chord.

CHAPTER 2: CHICAGO BLUES BASS LINE
THE RESOURCES

CHORDS

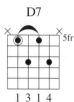

SCALES

G Composite Blues Scale:
G–A–B♭–B–C–D♭–D–E–F
(1–2–♭3–♮3–4–♭5–♮5–6–♭7)

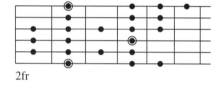

2fr

G Major Pentatonic (Extended Form):
G–A–B–D–E
(1–2–3–5–6)

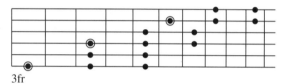

3fr

C Mixolydian (2nd Position):
C–D–E–F–G–A–B♭
(1–2–3–4–5–6–♭7)

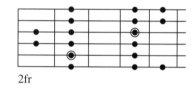

2fr

C Mixolydian (5th Position)

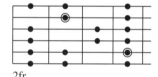

5fr

D Mixolydian (2nd Position):
D–E–F♯–G–A–B–C
(1–2–3–4–5–6–♭7)

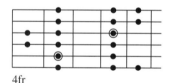

2fr

D Mixolydian (4th Position)

4fr

D Major Pentatonic:
D–E–F♯–A–B
(1–2–3–5–6)

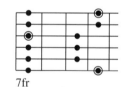

7fr

 # JAM #7: THE 12-BAR FORM

This bass line is most commonly associated with Chicago blues of the '60s—particularly Windy City legend Buddy Guy, who built entire songs around the riff. The beauty of this bass line is that it transfers easily to guitar and is relatively easy to get into and out of while weaving lead lines into the 12-bar form. Like Jams 1–6, the eighth notes in this example are shuffled. However, this figure is played in the key of G, resulting in a new set of changes: G7 (I chord), C7 (IV chord), and D7 (V chord).

MEASURES 1–4: This 12-bar form differs slightly from the one employed in Jams 1–6, with a "quick change" occurring in measure 2. Rather than four measures of the I (G7) chord, the IV (C7) chord makes an appearance in measure 2 before the progression returns to the I chord for measures 3–4. The bass line itself is built from the following chord tones: root, root (octave), ♭7th, and 5th. Over the G7 chord, the result is G–G–F–D; for C7, the bass line is C–C–B♭–G. Make sure to shuffle the notes and play them in staccato (i.e., short/clipped) fashion.

MEASURES 5–8: Measure 5 marks the return of the IV (C7) chord bass line, which is played for two measures. At measure 7, the I (G7) chord bass line is reprised and played for two more measures. To transition between the G7 and C7 bass lines, simply shift the pattern from strings 6–4 to strings 5–3. Although the strings change, the pattern remains intact.

MEASURES 9–12: Measure 9 marks the first appearance of the V (D7) chord bass line, which is comprised of the notes D, D (octave), C, and A. In measures 10–11, the C7 and G7 patterns return for one measure apiece before a chromatic (C–C♯–D) walk-up to the V (D7) chord, which is positioned on the "and" of beat 2 of measure 12.

🔊 JAM #8: ONE-BAR LEAD/RHYTHM ALTERNATIONS

This Jam starts with a measure of lead before giving way to a continuous stream of one-bar lead/rhythm alternations. The lead phrases played over the G7, C7, and D7 chord changes are derived from the G composite blues scale (G–A–B♭–B–C–D♭–D–E–F), C Mixolydian mode (C–D–E–F–G–A–B♭), and D Mixolydian mode (D–E–F♯–G–A–B–C), respectively. For the sake of finger efficiency, all of the phrases have been arranged in third position.

MEASURES 1–4: The Chuck Berry–style lick that opens the Jam is a melodic motif that is reprised is measures 3, 5, 7, and 11, lending continuity to the 12-bar form. At the end of measure 1, the bluesy lick concludes with a three-note chromatic line (B♭–B–C) that implies the forthcoming C7 chord changes a half beat early. After a measure of the C7 bass line, measure 3 features a variation of the opening lick. Notice the G note that concludes the phrase, which allows for a seamless transition to the G7 bass line in measure 4.

MEASURES 5–8: Despite the new chord, C7, the melodic motif from measure 1 opens the phrase in measure 5; however, to reinforce the new C7 harmony, the lick emphasizes the chord's 3rd (E) by holding it a bit longer than the other notes of the phrase (see the tie that connects beats 2 and 3). On beat 4, the chromatic, Bb–B–C line from measure 1 is reprised for the transition to the C7 bass line (measure 6). A variation of the opening lick is performed in measure 7. Notice, however, that instead of a Bb–B–C line to close the phrase, a C–Bb–B line is created (preceded by a half-step bend). This line effectively sets up the return to the G7 bass line in measure 8, as Bb and B are the minor 3rd and major 3rd of the G7 harmony.

MEASURES 9–12: In measure 9, a relatively simple lick is carved from the D Mixolydian mode to outline the V (D7) chord, using a heavy dose of chord tones (D, F♯, A, and C). Following a measure of the C7 bass line (measure 10), a variation of the opening lick is played to indicate a return to the G7 harmony. Notice that, due to the articulation of the sixth-string root (played by the thumb) on beat 1, the Chuck Berry–style lick has been displaced by one beat. The phrase works its way down the G composite blues scale before landing on the root of the V chord, D, signaling a return to the beginning of the form.

34

JAM #9: TWO-BAR LEAD/RHYTHM ALTERNATIONS

In this Jam, both the lead phrases and the bass lines are two bars long, alternating in this fashion throughout the 12-bar form. For the lead phrases, the same scales types that were utilized in Jam #8 are employed here: G composite blues scale (G–A–Bb–B–C–Db–D–E–F), C Mixolydian mode (C–D–E–F–G–A–Bb), and D Mixolydian mode (D–E–F#–G–A–B–C). The C composite blues scale (C–D–Eb–E–F–Gb–G–A–Bb) makes a brief appearance in measure 6, as well, courtesy of the half-step, minor-to-major (Eb-to-E) bend.

MEASURES 1–4: The Jam opens with a two-bar phrase that is derived from the G composite blues scale and commences in sixth position before employing a first-string slide to transition to third position. The lick concludes with a minor-to-major (Bb-to-B) hammer-on to resolve to the root of the G7 bass line (measure 3), which is played for two measures.

MEASURES 5–8: In measure 5, a two-bar lick, rooted (mostly) in the C Mixolydian mode, mimics the opening G7 phrase. To outline the new C7 harmony, emphasis is placed on chord tones—particularly the quarter-step bend of the b7th (Bb), the vibratoed root (C) that is tied across measures 5–6, the half-step bend of the minor 3rd (Eb) to the major 3rd (E), and the vibratoed root (C) on beat 3 of measure 6. To signal a return to the G7 bass line (measures 7–8), a triplet figure featuring a minor-to-major (Bb-to-B) hammer-on and a first-string root note (G) is played on beat 4 of measure 6.

MEASURES 9–12: In measure 9, a chord-tone-heavy phrase, derived from the D Mixolydian mode and featuring second- and first-string slides, is played over the V (D7) chord. A variation of the phrase, transposed down one whole step, handles the IV (C7) chord. Notice that the latter phrase signals a return to the G7 bass line (measure 11) via vibratoed root notes (G) on beat 4 of measure 10 (G also is the 5th of C7). The Jam concludes with a chromatic (C–C#–D) walk-up to the root of the V chord.

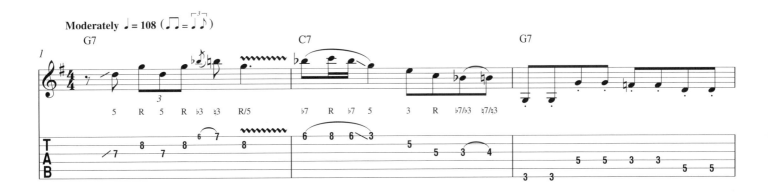

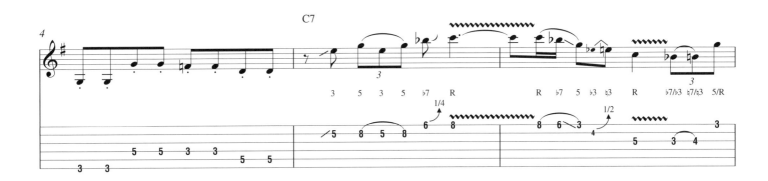

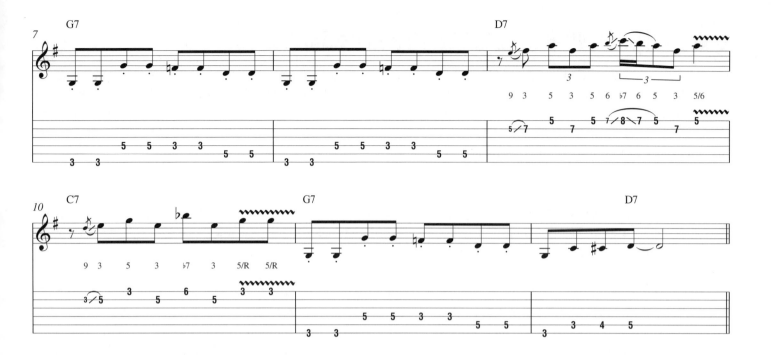

🔊 JAM #10: ONE-BAR RHYTHM/LEAD ALTERNATIONS

In this Jam, the sequence and length of the lead/rhythm alternations are modified. Here, one bar of the bass line is alternated with one bar of lead playing throughout the 12-bar form. While the bass line itself remains unchanged, the single-note soloing that dominated previous Jams has been replaced by "sliding 6ths."

MEASURES 1–4: Following one bar of the G7 bass line, sliding 6ths are employed in measure 2 to (mostly) target C7 chord tones. Specifically, the 6ths on beats 2 and 4 consist of the notes B♭ and D (♭7th and 9th) and G and B♭ (5th and ♭7th), respectively. Measure 4 features a similar approach, only the harmony is now G7 and the sliding 6ths shift from strings 1 and 3 to strings 2 and 4 for the second half of the measure. Pluck the bottom notes of the 6ths with your pick and the top notes with your middle finger.

MEASURES 5–8: In measure 5, the bass line handles the change in harmony (C7) before giving way to another sliding-6ths figure that targets chord tones. The bass line and 6ths are transposed to the key of G to outline the G7 harmony in measures 7–8.

MEASURES 9–12: The bass line returns for the V (D7) chord in measure 9 before giving way to a 6ths lick (the descending version of the lick from measure 6) that resolves to the notes B♭ and D, which function as the ♭7th and 9th of C7 and ♭3rd and 5th of G7, the forthcoming harmony. The Jam comes to an end with a return to the G7 bass line (measure 11) and a C–C♯–D walk-up to the root of the V chord (measure 12).

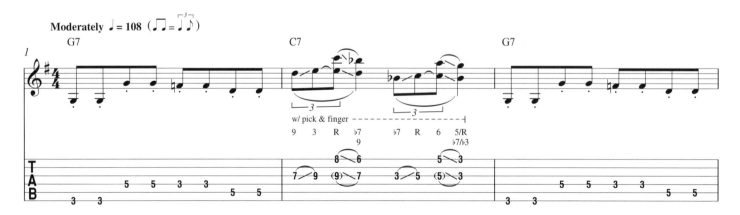

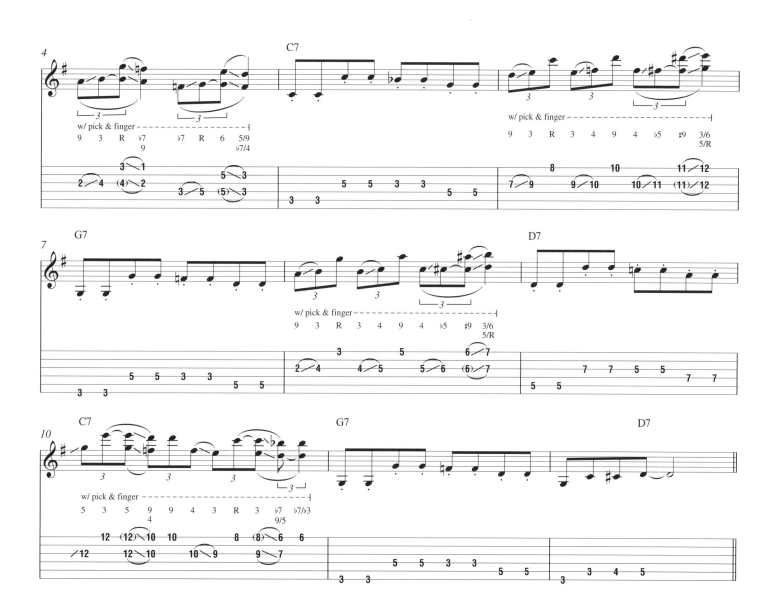

JAM #11: TWO-BAR RHYTHM/LEAD ALTERNATIONS

The rhythm/lead alternations from Jam #10 have been extended in this example. Now, two bars of the shuffled bass line are continuously alternated with two bars of lead playing. As you can see, due to the inherent location of the chord changes within the 12-bar form, the lead lines in this Jam are only played over the G7 change, using notes from the G composite blues scale (G–A–B♭–B–C–D♭–D–E–F) and the extended form of the G major pentatonic scale (G–A–B–D–E).

MEASURES 1–4: After the bass line outlines the G7 and C7 changes in measures 1–2, a bluesy two-bar phrase, derived from the G composite blues scale, handles the restatement of the G7 harmony in measures 3–4. The line is played entirely in third position and features a handful of hammer-ons and pull-offs.

MEASURES 5–8: The bass line returns in measure 5 to outline two measures of the IV (C7) chord before a variation of the original lick is implemented for the return of the I (G7) chord in measure 7. Notice that the first two beats are identical to the original lick, and both phrases share similar contours. On beat 4 of measure 8, an F-to-F♯ hammer-on (in the key of D, the minor 3rd to major 3rd) signals the arrival of the V (D7) chord (measure 9).

MEASURES 9–12: The bass line returns for the V–IV (D7–C7) change in measures 9–10, leading to a run up the extended G major pentatonic scale in measure 11. In measure 12, the scale reverses course and settles on the D note at fret 7 of the third string to signal the arrival of the V chord.

JAM #12: RANDOM RHYTHM/LEAD ALTERNATIONS

The alternations that occur in this Jam are arranged randomly, which is a less structured, more "organic" approach to self-accompaniment. To outline the chord changes, the bass line from James 7–11 is used for the "rhythm" measures, while the lead phrases make liberal use of double stops. Once again, the G composite blues scale (G–A–Bb–B–C–Db–D–E–F) is the scale of choice for the G7 changes, while C Mixolydian (C–D–E–F–G–A–Bb) and D major pentatonic (D–E–F#–A–B) handle the C7 and D7 changes, respectively.

MEASURES 1–4: A double-stop phrase opens the Jam and outlines the G7 harmony. In measure 2, the phrase is altered slightly to target chord tones of the new C7 harmony, resolving to the G note at fret 5 of the fourth string, which serves as both the 5th of C7 and the root of the forthcoming G7 chord (measure 3). The G composite blues scale phrase continues throughout measures 3–4, leading to an F-to-E slide that signals a change in harmony (F is the b7th of G7, and E is the 3rd of C7).

MEASURES 5–8: Measure 5 features a C dominant seventh arpeggio (C–E–G–Bb) to outline the C7 chord, leading seamlessly into the first appearance of the bass line (measure 6). The bass line continues for two more measures, effectively outlining the G7 harmony in measures 7–8.

MEASURES 9–12: A repetitive double-stop figure, derived from the D major pentatonic scale, is launched in measure 9 to outline the V (D7) chord and then transposed down one whole step to handle the IV (C7) chord. The phrase in measure 11 is borrowed from measure 3, lending continuity to the Jam, and resolves to the D note at fret 5 of the fifth string, which functions as the root of the V chord.

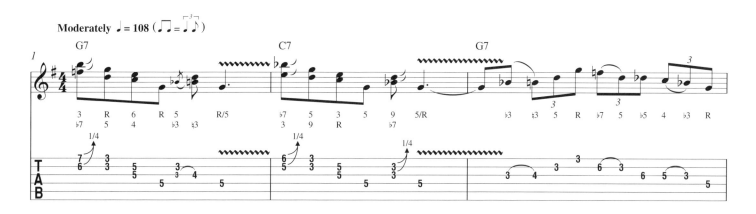

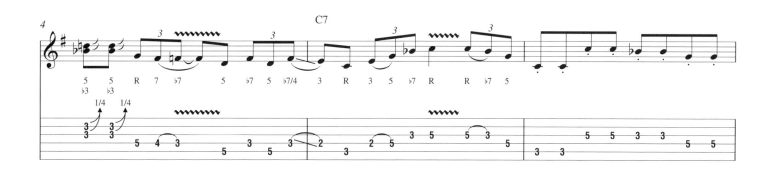

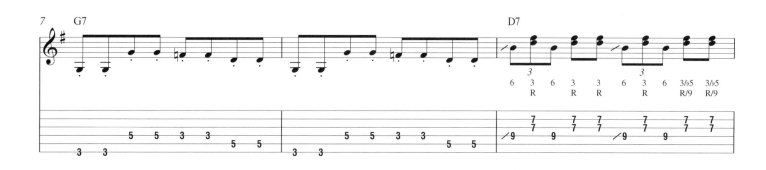

CHAPTER 3: TEXAS BLUES RIFF
THE RESOURCES

CHORDS

  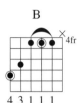 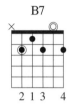

SCALES

E Composite Blues Scale:
E–F♯–G–G♯–A–B♭–B–C♯–D
(1–2–♭3–♮3–4–♭5–♮5–6–♭7)

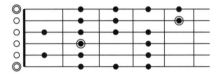

E Composite Blues Scale (Extended Form)

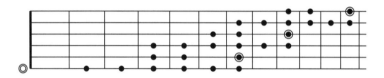

E Blues Scale:
E–G–A–B♭–B–D
(1–♭3–4–♭5–♮5–♭7)

12fr

A Composite Blues Scale (Open Position):
A–B–C–C♯–D–E♭–E–F♯–G
(1–2–♭3–♮3–4–♭5–♮5–6–♭7)

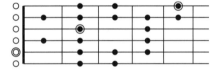

A Composite Blues Scale (4th Position)

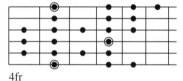

4fr

B Composite Blues Scale:
B–C♯–D–D♯–E–F–F♯–G♯–A
(1–2–♭3–♮3–4–♭5–♮5–6–♭7)

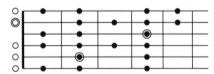

B Major Pentatonic (Extended Form):
B–C♯–D♯–F♯–G♯
(1–2–3–5–6)

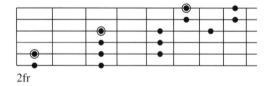

2fr

 JAM #13: THE 12-BAR FORM

This Texas blues riff is reminiscent of Stevie Ray's Vaughan's "Pride and Joy," with bass notes occurring on the downbeats (plucked with the pick) and chord strums articulated on the upbeats (plucked with the remaining fingers). Played in isolation, the bass notes form a standard boogie bass line, with the chord strums further enhancing the harmony. The structure of the Jam is a standard set of 12-bar blues changes played in the key of E: E (I chord), A (IV chord), and B (V chord). While the I- and IV-chord changes are played in open position, the V-chord riff is played in fourth position and requires a bit more practice to perfect.

MEASURES 1–4: The boogie riff that outlines the I (E) chord in the opening four measures is based on an open-position E major triad. While the index finger frets the G♯ note at fret 1 of the third string, use your middle, ring, and pinky fingers to voice the bass notes on frets 2, 3, and 4, respectively.

MEASURES 5–8: Similar to the E chord, the boogie riff that outlines the IV (A) chord is based on an open-position A triad. While the index finger barres the notes on fret 2, use your middle and ring fingers to voice the bass notes on frets 3 and 4, respectively. At measure 7, the E-chord riff returns for restatement of the I chord.

MEASURES 9–12: A position shift is required for the arrival of the V (B) chord in measure 9. The B-chord riff is modeled after an open-position G triad, with the open strings of the latter replaced with a fourth-fret index-finger barre for the former. As your pinky voices the bass note on fret 7 of the sixth string, use your middle and ring fingers to voice the bass notes at frets 5 and 6, respectively. At measure 10, the first half of the A-chord riff outlines the IV (A) chord before the E-chord riff returns for the turnaround (measures 11–12). The Jam concludes with a chromatic (A–A♯–B) walk-up to an open-position voicing of a B7 chord on beat 3 of measure 12.

JAM #14: ONE-BAR LEAD/RHYTHM ALTERNATIONS

This entire Jam is fueled by a single motif, which is introduced in measure 1 and then restated every other measure, alternating with the Texas blues riff. The original motif is derived from the E composite blues scale (E–F♯–G–G♯–A–B♭–B–C♯–D), while the A- and B-chord licks are derived from the A composite (A–B–C–C♯–D–E♭–E–F♯–G) and B composite (B–C♯–D–D♯–E–F–F♯–G♯–A) blues scales, respectively.

MEASURES 1–4: The opening lick revolves around two notes, B and D (the 5th and ♭7th, respectively), implying a dominant seventh (E7) harmony. The phrase resolves to the root (E) before giving way to the E-chord boogie riff in measure 2. The motif is restated in measure 3, albeit with an alternate ending. Notice that the phrase ends on the ♭7th (D), which results in a smooth transition to the root of the E-chord riff in measure 4.

MEASURES 5–8: Although the motif has been melodically altered to fit the new A major harmony in measure 5, the rhythm and legato phrasing remain intact. Again, a chord tone (C♯, the 3rd) concludes the phrase, giving the lick a strong urge to resolve to the root of the A-chord riff (measure 6). Measure 7 features a note-for-note reproduction of the original lick, imparting the Jam with strong continuity before segueing to another bar of the E-chord riff (measure 8).

MEASURES 9–12: The motif is reconfigured in measure 9 to outline the B major harmony. Although the lick differs slightly from the original motif, both melodically and rhythmically, it retains enough of the original elements to preserve the musical idea. After a bar of the A-chord riff (measure 10), the original lick is played for a third time (measure 11) before giving way to a turnaround phrase that is comprised of an ascending chromatic line (A–A♯–B) and alternations of the root (B) and ♭7th (A) of the B7 harmony.

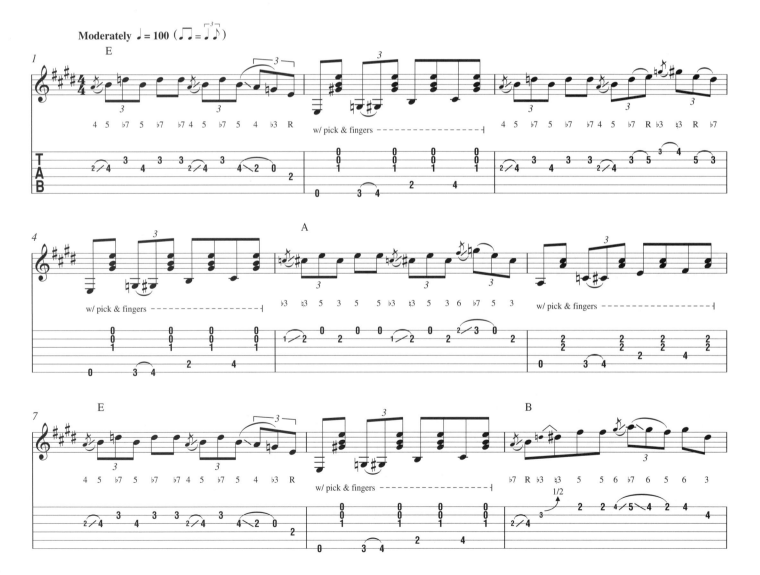

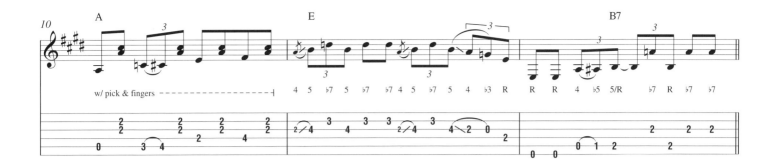

JAM #15: TWO-BAR LEAD/RHYTHM ALTERNATIONS

For this Jam, the lead/rhythm alternations have been lengthened to two bars. Like Jams 13–14, the Texas blues riff is utilized here for the rhythm parts, while the lead phrases for the E, A, and B chord changes are crafted from the E composite blues scale (E–F♯–G–G♯–A–B♭–B–C♯–D), A composite blues scale (A–B–C–C♯–D–E♭–E–F♯–G), and the extended form of the B major pentatonic scale (B–C♯–D♯–F♯–G♯), respectively.

MEASURES 1–4: The opening phrase is played exclusively in open position and travels across all six strings. On beat 4 of measure 2, a sixth-string minor-to-major (G-to-G♯) bend resolves to the E-chord riff, which is played throughout measures 3–4.

MEASURES 5–8: At measure 5, a Chuck Berry–style bending phrase mimics the slides that kicked off measure 1, lending some cohesion to the Jam. The phrase is played in fifth position until beat 4 of measure 6, where it transitions to second position to set up the fret hand for a return to the E-chord riff (measures 7–8).

MEASURES 9–12: The entire phrase that is employed for the B chord in measure 9 is derived from the extended form of the B major pentatonic scale, starting from fret 2 of the fifth string. The phrase ends on the scale's sixth degree, G♯, which sets up a strategic half-step transition to the note A (fret 7, fourth string), the root of the A major harmony (measure 10). The E-chord riff returns in measure 11, leading to a chromatic (A–A♯–B) walk-up to the turnaround chord, B7.

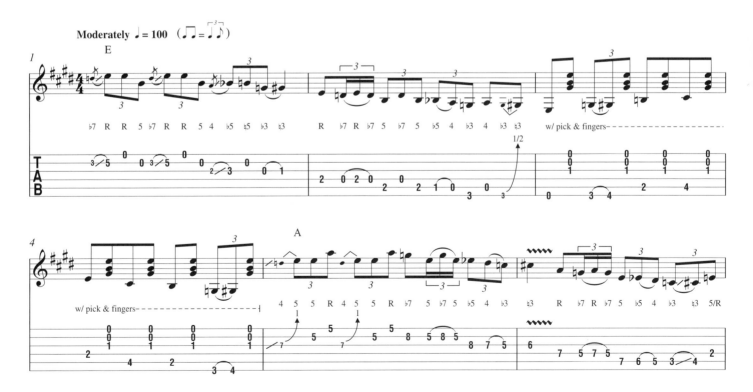

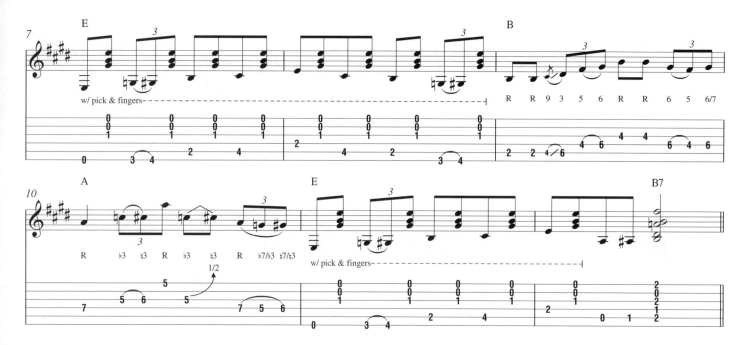

🔊 JAM #16: ONE-BAR RHYTHM/LEAD ALTERNATIONS

In this example, the sequence of the lead/rhythm alternations from the previous two Jams has been reversed. Now, one bar of the Texas blues riff is alternated with one bar of lead playing throughout. The leads are rooted in the E composite (E–F♯–G–G♯–A–B♭–B–C♯–D) and A composite (A–B–C–C♯–D–E♭–E–F♯–G) blues scales for the E and A chord changes, respectively (no lead is played over the B chord).

MEASURES 1–4: Following a bar of the shuffle riff, a bluesy open-position lick is carved from the E composite blues scale and features several legato techniques (slide, hammer-on, pull-off, etc.) and a half-step bend, which sets up the return to the E-chord riff in measure 3. In measure 4, the opening lick is transposed up an octave; however, on beat 4, the half-step bend has been replaced by a slide from C to C♯, which represent the minor 3rd and major 3rd of the forthcoming A major harmony, respectively.

MEASURES 5–8: The A-chord riff is played in measure 5 before giving way to a restatement of the opening lick (measure 6), only it's been transposed to the key of A to fit the chord change. Notice that the half-step bend at the end of the phrase has been retained from the original, as the notes (G–G♯) have a strong urge to resolve to the root of the E major harmony in measure 7. After another measure of the E-chord riff, measure 8 features a variation of the original lick and concludes with the open B string, which just so happens to be the root of the B major harmony in measure 9.

MEASURES 9–12: After the B-chord riff is played for a measure, a descending lick, derived from the A composite blues scale, outlines the A major harmony and segues to the E-chord riff in measure 11. Again, notice the inclusion of the notes G and G♯ (this time, in the form of a hammer-on) at the end of the phrase, signaling a return to the I (E) chord. The Jam ends with a chromatic (A–A♯–B) walk-up to a standard B7 chord voicing, which functions here as the V chord.

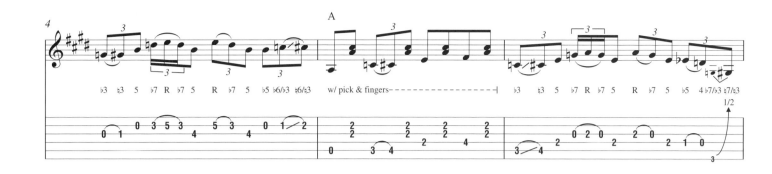

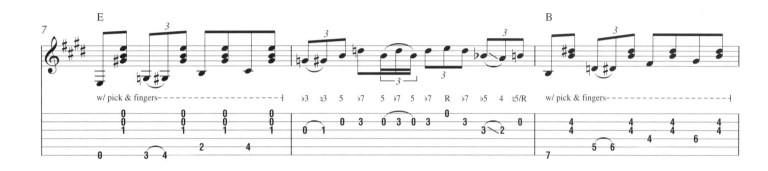

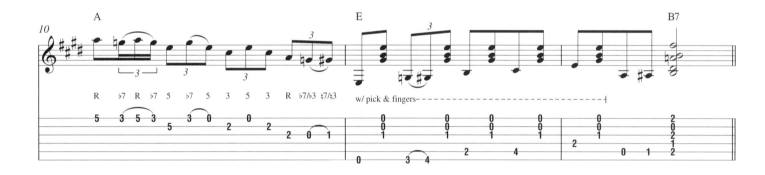

JAM #17: TWO-BAR RHYTHM/LEAD ALTERNATIONS

Two bars of the Texas blues riff and two bars of lead playing are alternated throughout this Jam's 12 bars. All of the lead phrases occur over the I (E) chord and are derived from the E composite blues scale (E–F#–G–G#–A–Bb–B–C#–D), with most of the lines rooted in the extended form of the scale.

MEASURES 1–4: Following two bars of the E-chord riff, the open low E string launches an ascending lick that is played in two octaves. At the end of measure 4, a G–G# hammer-on leads to the IV(A) chord riff, creating a three-note (G–G#–A) chromatic line.

MEASURES 5–8: Two measures of the A-chord riff are followed by a two-measure phrase derived from the E composite blues scale, which effectively outlines the return to the I (E) chord. Notice the quarter-step bends in measure 7, which are a nod to the first phrase and create cohesion in the Jam. Similar to the end of measure 4, a three-note (A–A#–B) chromatic line is played to transition from the E chord to the B chord (measure 9).

MEASURES 9–12: The boogie riff is employed for the V and IV (B and A) chord changes in measures 9 and 10 before yielding to a descending lick that is derived from the E composite blues scale. This phrase leads to another three-note chromatic passage (A–A#–B), which, along with articulation of the B7 chord's b7th (A, fret 2 of the third string), signals the turnaround.

JAM #18: RANDOM RHYTHM/LEAD ALTERNATIONS

To give you a "real world" approach to swapping lead and rhythm, the alternations in this Jam have been arranged in random fashion. The boogie riff is a holdover from Jams 13–17, while the lead phrases are derived from the E blues (E–G–A–B♭–B–D) and E composite blues (E–F♯–G–G♯–A–B♭–B–C♯–D) scales for the I (E) chord changes, the A composite blues scale (A–B–C–C♯–D–E♭–E–F♯–G) for the IV (A) chord, and the extended form of the B major pentatonic scale (B–C♯–D♯–F♯–G♯) for the V (B) chord.

MEASURES 1–4: The Jam commences with two measures of the E-chord riff, enabling the listener to get accustomed to the feel of the rhythm before lead work takes over in measures 3–4. Here, repetitions of the open low E string reinforce the E major harmony, followed by a fairly common 12th-position E blues scale lick.

MEASURES 5–8: In measure 5, the riff is reintroduced to signal a change to the A chord and keep the Jam moving along. After one measure of the A-chord riff, theA composite blues scale provides the pitches for a chromatic-laden phrase that moves seamlessly to a two-bar lick outlining the return to the I (E) chord. Again, notice the repetitions of the open low E string to reestablish the E major harmony, which is followed by an open-position lick derived from the E composite blues scale.

MEASURES 9–12: At measure 9, the extended form of the B major pentatonic scale is employed to outline the V (B) chord, with the minor 3rd (D, fret 5 of the fifth string) included for a touch of chromaticism. The phrase, which originally began in measure 6, continues in measure 10 with a lick that swiftly shifts from second to fifth position to outline the IV (A) chord before yielding to the E-chord riff and an open-position B7 chord for the Jam's turnaround.

CHAPTER 4: 12/8 SLOW-BLUES RIFF
THE RESOURCES

CHORDS

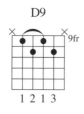

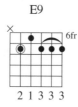

SCALES

A Composite Blues Scale (4th Position):
A–B–C–C♯–D–E♭–E–F♯–G
(1–2–♭3–♮3–4–♭5–♮5–6–♭7)

A Composite Blues Scale (Extended Form)

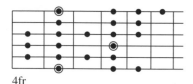

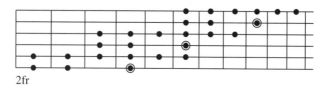

D Composite Blues Scale (4th Position):
D–E–F–F♯–G–A♭–A–B–C
(1–2–♭3–♮3–4–♭5–♮5–6–♭7)

D Composite Blues Scale (6th Position)

D Composite Blues Scale (9th Position)

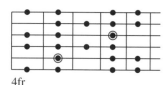

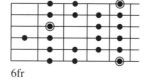

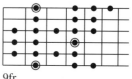

D Major Pentatonic:
D–E–F♯–A–B
(1–2–3–5–6)

E Composite Blues Scale (6th Position):
E–F♯–G–G♯–A–B♭–B–C♯–D
(1–2–♭3–♮3–4–♭5–♮5–6–♭7)

E Composite Blues Scale (11th Position)

E Major Pentatonic:
E–F♯–G♯–B–C♯
(1–2–3–5–6)

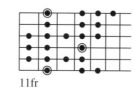

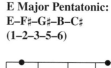

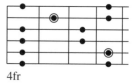

 JAM #19: THE 12-BAR FORM

The next six Jams employ "sliding 9ths" for their rhythm parts. This is a common blues technique, especially for slow blues played in 12/8 meter (as is the case here), and involves sliding a three-note ninth-chord voicing—comprised of the chord's ♭7th, 9th, and 5th, low to high—up a whole step before returning to its original location. When slid up a whole step, the resultant chord consists of the root, major 3rd, and 6th—a major-sixth voicing! In each measure, the root note precedes the chordal slide and is articulated with an open string. For these changes (A9, D9, and E9), the open A string is the root of the I chord, the open D string is the root of the IV chord, and the open low E string is the root of the V chord.

MEASURES 1–4: The first four measures of this slow-blues Jam contain a "quick change," which means the IV (D9) chord is played in measure 2 (rather than four measures of the I chord). At measure 3, the progression returns to the A9 chordal slide for two more measures.

MEASURES 5–8: In measure 5, the D9 chordal slide makes a second appearance and is played for two measures before transitioning back to the I (A9) chord for measures 7–8. Be careful with the slides—the first slide of each pair receives no rhythmic value, whereas the second slide is played in a shuffle rhythm.

MEASURES 9–12: For the Jam's final four measures, the E9, D9, and A9 chordal slides are played sequentially, leading to the turnaround, which involves a chromatic walk-up (D–D♯–E) to a common E9 (V) chord voicing. Use your middle finger to fret each of the three chromatic notes; that way, it's already in position to voice the E9 chord.

JAM #20: ONE-BAR LEAD/RHYTHM ALTERNATIONS

This Jam juggles one bar of lead playing with one bar of sliding 9ths, alternating the lead/rhythm dichotomy throughout the 12-bar form. The lead phrases feature a Chuck Berry–style string-bending motif and borrow their notes from the A composite (A–B–C–C♯–D–E♭–E–F♯–G), D composite (D–E–F–F♯–G–A♭–A–B–C), and E composite (E–F♯–G–G♯–A–B♭–B–C♯–D) blues scales to outline the A9, D9, and E9 chord changes, respectively.

MEASURES 1–4: The jam kicks off with the Chuck Berry–style string-bending motif, which leads to a double-stop slide/pull-off passage and a pair of hammer-ons. Notice that the last note of the lick, F♯, is the major 3rd of the forthcoming D9 (IV) chord, creating a strong desire to resolve to the new harmony. After a measure of sliding 9ths (measure 2), the opening lick is restated nearly note for note, with beat 4 being the only exception. Here, the C-to-C♯ hammer-on is followed by resolution to the root, A, maintaining the A9 harmony for measure 4, where sliding 9ths make another appearance.

MEASURES 5–8: In measure 5, the Chuck Berry–style bends are shifted to 10th position, where they help to outline the D9 harmony. This phrase is an exact replica of the lick from measure 3, only it's played here in the key of D. Measure 6 features an iteration of the D9 chordal slides, followed by a restatement of the lick from measure 3 and another measure of A9 chordal slides (measures 7 and 8, respectively).

MEASURES 9–12: For the arrival of the V (E) chord, a slippery E composite blues scale lick is played along strings 1–3. The phrase ends on F♯ to facilitate a strong transition to the D9 harmony in measure 10, where sliding 9ths outline the change. The turnaround (measures 11–12) is handled by a phrase that is a variation of the A9 licks used earlier in the Jam, coming to rest on the E note at fret 5 of the second string, which functions as the root of the V chord (i.e., the turnaround chord).

JAM #21: TWO-BAR LEAD/RHYTHM ALTERNATIONS

The lead/rhythm alternations from Jam #20 have been lengthened to two bars in this example. The lead phrases are derived from the composite blues scales respective to the chord changes and feature oblique bends, slides, hammer-ons, and pull-offs, among other techniques. These lines are offset by repetitions of the sliding 9ths.

MEASURES 1–4: An oblique double-stop bend commences the Jam, effectively outlining the A9 harmony with the chord's root and 3rd—A and C♯, respectively—before descending the strings and resolving to the root of the D9 (IV) chord on beat 1 of measure 2. Here, chord tones (D, F♯, A, and C) are used predominantly to emphasize the D9 harmony. At the end of the lick, a C-to-C♯ hammer-on pulls the listener's ear to the root of the A9 chordal slides in measure 3, which are repeated in the subsequent measure.

MEASURES 5–8: In measure 5, the opening lick is transposed to the key of D to outline the new harmony. However, since the D9 harmony is maintained for an additional measure, the lick is adjusted on beat 4, continuing down the D composite blues scale in measure 6. Like the end of measure 2, beat 4 of measure 6 features a C-to-C♯ hammer-on to resolve to the I (A9) chord in measure 7, where two measures of the sliding-9ths riff commence.

MEASURES 9–12: A descending lick derived from the E composite blues scale is employed in measure 9 to outline the V (E9) chord. This lick is then transposed down one step to the key of D to handle the new D9 harmony (measure 10). Finally, the Jam wraps up with a restatement of the A9 chordal slides and a chromatic walk-up (D–D♯–E) to the turnaround chord, E9.

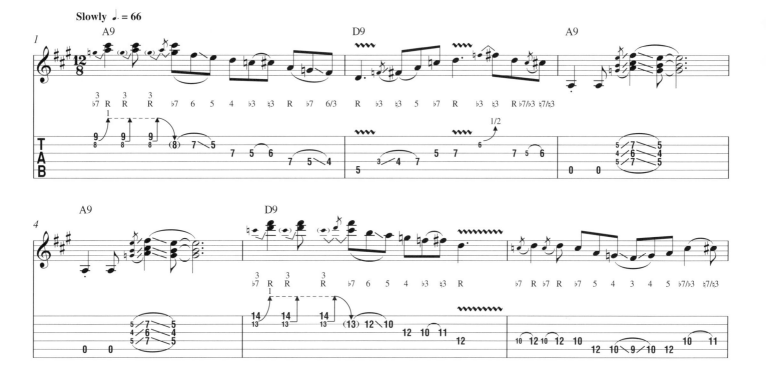

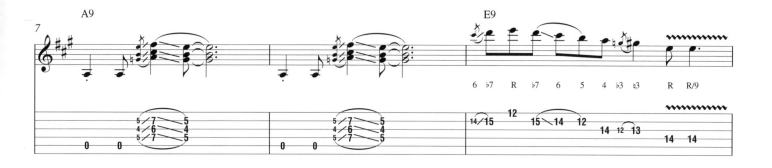

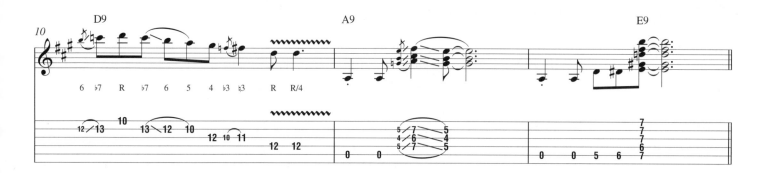

🔊 JAM #22: ONE-BAR RHYTHM/LEAD ALTERNATIONS

In this example, the sequence of the lead/rhythm alternations from Jams 20–21 is reversed. Here, one bar of rhythm is alternated with one bar of lead throughout the Jam's 12 measures. The lead lines are derived from the A composite (A–B–C–C♯–D–E♭–E–F♯–G) and D composite (D–E–F–F♯–G–A♭–A–B–C) blues scales for the A9 and D9 changes, respectively (no lead is played over E9), and feature a six-note motif that makes no less than four appearances.

MEASURES 1–4: Sliding 9ths kick off the Jam to handle the A9 harmony before segueing to the first occurrence of the six-note motif, played here (measure 2) over the IV (D9) chord. The motif is comprised of a slide, hammer-on, half-step bend, and a pull-off, and the measure concludes with stepwise movement down the sixth string (D–C–B), leading to the root of the A9 chordal slides (measure 3). In measure 4, the opening lick has been transposed to the key of A to outline the I (A9) chord. On beat 4, however, the phrase has been altered to create a chromatic line (C–C♯–D) to smoothly transition from the I chord to the root of the IV chord.

MEASURES 5–8: In measure 5, sliding 9ths are used over the IV (D9) chord for the first time and quickly transition to another statement of the motif (measure 6). In the second half of the measure, the lick ascends (rather than descends) the strings, ending on the A note at fret 10 of the second string, which subtly implies a return to the I (A9) chord in measure 7. After another measure of sliding 9ths, the lick from measure 6 is restated, in the key of A, in measure 8. Again, notice that the last note of the phrase, E, is the root of the forthcoming chord, E9.

MEASURES 9–12: After sliding 9ths handle the E9 harmony in measure 9, a descending lick derived from the D composite blues scale moves across strings 2–4, following repetitions of the open D string. Notice that the final three notes (D, C, and B) are the same three notes that concluded measure 2's lick (only an octave higher), and, like that lick, lead stepwise to the I (A9) chord. The Jam comes to an end in measures 11–12 with a bar of sliding 9ths (A9) and a chromatic (D–D♯–E) walk-up to the turnaround chord, E9.

JAM #23: TWO-BAR RHYTHM/LEAD ALTERNATIONS

In this Jam, the rhythm/lead alternations from Jam #22 have been extended from one measure to two. The sliding 9ths for each chord change are holdovers from Jams 19–22, while the lead phrases, all of which are played over the I (A9) chord, are rooted in the A composite blues scale (A–B–C–C♯–D–E♭–E–F♯–G).

MEASURES 1–4: After two bars of sliding 9ths—one for the opening A9 change and one for D9—a two-bar, fifth-position A composite blues scale lick outlines the second occurrence of the A9 chord (measures 3–4). Notice that the lick opens with repetitions of the open A string to signal a return to the A9 harmony and ends on an F♯ note (fret 4, fourth string), which is the major 3rd of the forthcoming D9 chord.

MEASURES 5–8: Sliding 9ths handle the two bars of D9 harmony (measures 5–6) before giving way to a descending lick that flows down strings 1–4, moving from eighth position to fifth position. Again, notice the open A string at the beginning of the phrase, which alerts the listener to the new A9 harmony, and the G-to-G♯ (minor-to-major) hammer-on that resolves to the root of the E9 change (measure 9).

MEASURES 9–12: The V-chord (E9) and IV-chord (D9) changes are played with sliding 9ths (measures 9–10) and are followed by a pedal-tone turnaround phrase that's performed with hybrid picking (a combination of pick and fingers). Keep your pinky planted on fret 5 of the first string as you descend strings 4 and 2 with your middle and ring fingers, respectively, switching to an index-finger barre on beat 4. In measure 12, use your middle finger for the hammer-and-slide passage on string 4, which will put it into position to voice the E7 chord.

 # JAM #24: RANDOM RHYTHM/LEAD ALTERNATIONS

In this example, the rhythm/lead alternations are arranged in random fashion, giving the Jam a more spontaneous feel. Rather than a predictable structure, in which all the alternations occur in one- or two-bar intervals, the rhythm/lead tradeoffs in this Jam are arranged in an asymmetrical, 2–2–2–1–3–2 pattern. Meanwhile, the lead phrases have a distinct country feel—particularly the oblique bending in measures 5, 9, and 10.

MEASURES 1–4: The Jam kicks off with a pick up note that commences a two-bar lick that effectively outlines the opening I–IV (A9–D9) chord change. At the end of both measure 1 and measure 2, a half-step, minor-to-major bend signals an impending chord change. In measures 3–4, sliding 9ths are employed to handle the return to the I (A9) chord.

MEASURES 5–8: A two-bar D composite blues scale lick outlines the D9 chord in measures 5–6. While an oblique bend imparts a subtle country sound, the chord's harmony is hammered home via multiple statements of its root, D (fret 7, third string), among other chord tones. Sliding 9ths handle the first bar (measure 7) of the two-bar A9 passage before giving way to a bluesy phrase that seamlessly segues to the V (E9) chord change in measure 9.

MEASURES 9–12: An oblique-bend figure, derived from the E major pentatonic scale (E–F♯–G♯–B–C♯), targets chord tones to outline the E9 chord in measure 9. The passage is then moved down two frets (to the key of D) to handle measure 10's D9 harmony. At the tail end of the phrase, a half-step, C-to-C♯ bend signals a return to the I (A9) chord in measure 11. After a measure of A9 chordal slides, the Jam concludes with a chromatic (D–D♯–E) walk-up to the E9 chord, which signals a return to measure 1.

CHAPTER 5: MINOR-BLUES RIFF
THE RESOURCES

CHORDS

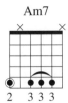
Am7

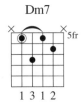
Dm7

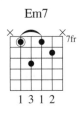
Em7

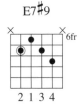
E7#9

SCALES

A Blues Scale (Extended Form):
A–C–D–E♭–E–G
(1–♭3–4–♭5–♮5–♭7)

A Blues Scale (Open Position)

A Blues Scale (2nd Position)

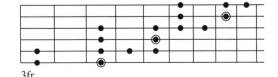

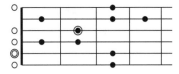

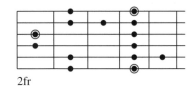

A Blues Scale (5th Position)

D Blues Scale:
D–F–G–A♭–A–C
(1–♭3–4–♭5–♮5–♭7)

D Dorian:
D–E–F–G–A–B–C
(1–2–♭3–4–5–6–♭7)

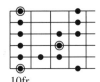

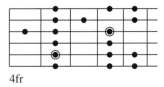

D Minor Pentatonic (Extended Form):
D–F–G–A–C
(1–♭3–4–5–♭7)

E Blues Scale:
E–G–A–B♭–B–D
(1–♭3–4–♭5–♮5–♭7)

E Minor Pentatonic (Extended Form):
E–G–A–B–D
(1–♭3–4–5–♭7)

 JAM #25: THE 12-BAR FORM

Unlike all of the previous Jams, which were written in major keys, this example is rooted in A minor. Like the other Jams, though, the song form here is a 12-bar blues, with the "quick change" (the IV chord) occurring in measure 2. In addition to the single-note riffs that approach each chord change, three-note voicings are slid up and down one whole step, much like the "sliding 9ths" from Jams 19–24. After a standard arrangement of the i (Am7) iv (Dm7), and v (Em7) chords in measures 1–11, an E7#9 chord is substituted for a minor seventh voicing in the turnaround (measure 12).

MEASURES 1–4: The opening four measures feature the quick change, resulting in an Am7–Dm7–Am7–Am7 progression. The pickup notes that precede measure 1 comprise much of the Jam's riff, which is reminiscent of the guitar work of Chicago blues icon Muddy Waters. The notes are derived from the A minor pentatonic scale (A–C–D–E–G) and lead to repetitions of each chord's root note and chordal slide.

MEASURES 5–8: In measures 5–6, the Dm7 riff is played two times before segueing to two measures of the Am7 riff. Notice that, although the chord voicings differ, the single-note riff remains constant. At the end of measure 8, the riff is adjusted to anticipate the v (Em7) chord change, resulting in a three-note chromatic line (D–D♯–E) along string 4.

MEASURES 9–12: Following a measure of the Em7 riff, the Dm7 and Am7 riffs make another appearance, respectively, leading to the turnaround chord, E7♯9, at the midpoint of measure 12. However, due to the presence of the single-note riff at the end of the measure (signaling a return to the top of the form), the chord is held for only the duration of a quarter note (here, played as tied eighth notes).

57

JAM #26: ONE-BAR LEAD/RHYTHM ALTERNATIONS

The lead/rhythm alternations in this Jam are alternated in one-bar intervals throughout the form's 12 bars. The rhythm parts employ the riffs that were introduced Jam #25, while the lead lines are derived from the A blues (A–C–D–E♭–E–G), D blues (D–F–G–A♭–A–C), and E blues (E–G–A–B♭–B–D) scales for the Am7, Dm7, and Em7 chord changes, respectively.

MEASURES 1–4: Measure 1 launches a repetitive three-note motif that is carried throughout much of the Jam. Rooted in fifth position and derived from the A blues (or A minor pentatonic) scale, the motif consists of a fourth-string slide to the root (A) followed by two quarter-step bends of the ♭3rd (C), which, combined, are played three times. In measure 2, a truncated version of the Dm7 riff is played before the motif is restated two times in measure 3, followed by a descending line that segues to a measure of the Am7 riff (measure 4).

MEASURES 5–8: In measure 5, the Jam's opening lick has been transposed to the key of D for the new (Dm7) harmony. After a measure of the Dm7 riff (measure 6), the motif is restated at the onset of measure 7, leading to an ascending lick that ends on the note C, the ♭3rd of Am7, creating a strong pull towards the root of the forthcoming Am7 riff (measure 8).

MEASURES 9–12: The open low E string marks the arrival of the v (Em7) chord and is followed by a Chuck Berry–style lick. Following a measure of the Dm7 riff (measure 10), a variation of the motif, featuring double-stop bends in place of single notes, is played in measure 11. This phrase leads to more quarter-step bends and resolution to the root of the E7♯9 chord for the turnaround (measure 12).

58

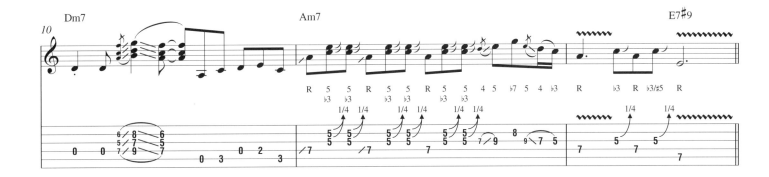

JAM #27: TWO-BAR LEAD/RHYTHM ALTERNATIONS

The alternations in this Jam fluctuate between two bars of lead playing and two bars of the minor-key riff. These two-bar lead/rhythm tradeoffs are maintained throughout the Jam's 12 bars, resulting in some of the lead lines being played over multiple chords. The scales used in the leads include the A blues scale (A–C–D–Eb–E–G), D blues scale (D–F–G–Ab–A–C), D Dorian mode (D–E–F–G–A–B–C), and E blues scale (E–G–A–Bb–B–D).

MEASURES 1–4: The Jam kicks off with a lick that is played in the "root pattern" of the A blues scale, flowing seamlessly to a D minor lick that is derived from the D Dorian mode (measure 2). Notice the recurring rhythmic motif (16th-note triplet plus two eighth notes) located on beats 2 and 4 of each measure, lending some continuity to the phrase. This lead passage is followed by two measures of the Am7 riff (measures 3–4).

MEASURES 5–8: The lick in measure 5 is a note-for-note reproduction of the Jam's opening lick, only it's played here in the key of D minor. This phrase is followed by a bluesy lick (measure 6) that begins with a whole-step bend and ends on the note A, which happens to be the root of the forthcoming Am7 chord change. The Am7 riff is played for two measures (7–8) and adjusted in the latter to anticipate the v (Em7) chord's arrival in measure 9.

MEASURES 9–12: The Em7 harmony is driven home at the onset of measure 9 via repetitions of the open low E string, followed by a bluesy phrase that is reminiscent of the one found in measure 6. Measure 9's phrase is recreated in measure 10, only it has been transposed to the key of D minor for the new (Dm7) harmony and adjusted so that the lick ends on the note A, which anticipates the Am7 harmony in measure 11. Here, the Am7 riff is played for the entire measure, leading to a chromatic (D–D♯–E) walk-up to the turnaround chord, E7♯9.

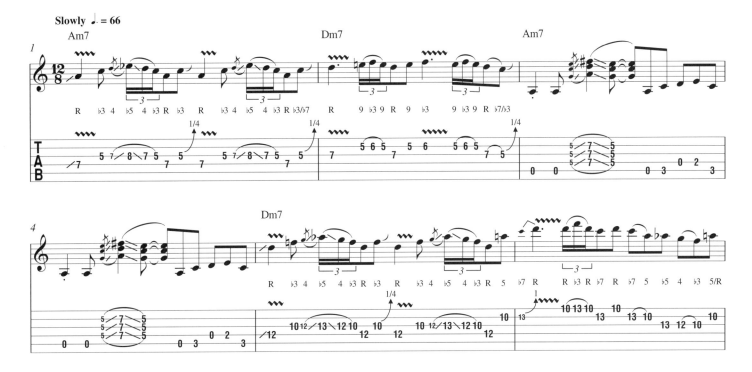

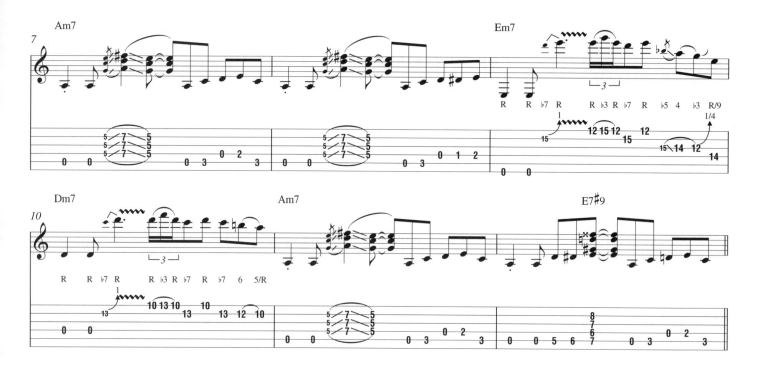

🔊 JAM #28: ONE-BAR RHYTHM/LEAD ALTERNATIONS

In this version of the minor-key Jam, the lead and rhythm parts are reversed and played for one measure apiece. The Jam commences with a bar of the Am7 riff and is followed by a measure of lead, a sequence that is maintained throughout the form's 12 bars. The lead phrases for the Am7 changes are derived from the extended form of the A blues scale (A–C–D–E♭–E–G), while the D blues scale (D–F–G–A♭–A–C) and extended form of the D minor pentatonic scale (D–F–G–A–C) are used for the Dm7 changes.

MEASURES 1–4: After the Am7 riff covers the initial Am7 change, the extended form of the D minor pentatonic scale provides the notes for a lick that handles the arrival of the iv (Dm7) chord. This phrase creates a motif—both melodic and rhythmic in nature—that is restated several times throughout the form's 12 bars. In measure 3, the Am7 riff marks the return of the i chord before segueing to a restatement of the lick from measure 2, only it's played here in the key of A minor.

MEASURES 5–8: The two measures of the iv chord (measures 5–6) are handled by the Dm7 riff and a bluesy lick that is derived from the D blues scale, respectively. The final note of the lick, C, is the minor 3rd of the forthcoming Am7 harmony and, therefore, creates a strong urge to resolve to that chord. Following a measure of the Am7 riff (measures 7), a variation of the original motif is played. The lick is an octave higher than the one from measure 4 and ends with a chromatic (E♭–E) hammer-on that signals the arrival of the v (Em7) chord.

MEASURES 9–12: To outline the v–iv change in measures 9–10, the Em7 riff is employed for the former, while the latter is handled by a bluesy lick whose notes are borrowed from the D blues scale. Notice that the last note of the phrase, A, signals the return of the i (Am7) chord in measure 11, which consists of a bar of the Am7 riff, followed by a chromatic (D–D♯–E) walk-up to the E7♯9 chord.

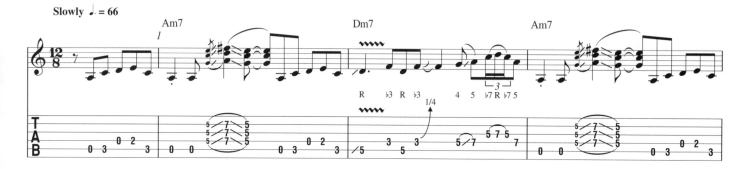

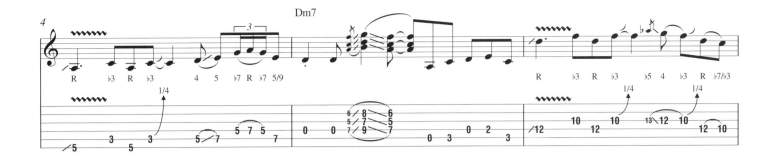

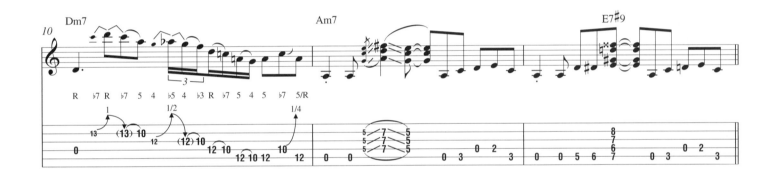

🔊 JAM #29: TWO-BAR RHYTHM/LEAD ALTERNATIONS

For this example, the rhythm/lead alternations from Jam #28 have been extended to two bars. While the minor-key riff remains the same, the soloing has been relocated to (mostly) open position, culling notes exclusively from for the A blues scale (A–C–D–Eb–E–G).

MEASURES 1–4: After the minor-key riff implies the i (Am7) and iv (Dm7) chord changes in measures 1–2, an open-position A blues scale lick flows up and down the strings before arriving on the note D (fret 3, second string) to anticipate the return of the iv chord in measure 5. Notice the chromaticism (E–Eb–D) that leads to the target note, D.

MEASURES 5–8: The Dm7 riff handles the return of the iv chord in measures 5–6, leading to another A blues scale lick. This time, however, the lick ventures up the fretboard a bit, pulling notes from the second-position pattern of the scale. To set up resolution to the v (Em7) chord, the G note (the b3rd of Em7) at fret 3 of the first string is nudged upward a quarter step.

MEASURES 9–12: The v–iv change in measures 9–10 is implied by a return to the main riff, which is followed in measures 11–12 by a descending lick that is derived from the A blues scale and quickly shifts from second position to open position. For the turnaround, fret the fourth-string chromatic (D–D♯–E) line with your middle finger, which is the finger that will be used to voice that string in the forthcoming E7♯9 chord.

🔊 JAM #30: RANDOM RHYTHM/LEAD ALTERNATIONS

The word "random" certainly applies to this Jam. Rather than follow strict, measure-by-measure alternations, this Jam shifts between rhythm and lead "on the fly"—twice changing from one to the other within the same measure! Keeping proper time is a challenge while performing this Jam, so take it slowly at first. The note sources for the lead phrases are the extended form of the A blues scale (A–C–D–E♭–E–G), the D Dorian mode (D–E–F–G–A–B–C), and the extended form of the E minor pentatonic scale (E–G–A–B–D).

MEASURES 1–4: The Jam kicks off with a bluesy lick that outlines the Am7 chord (measure 1) and leads seamlessly to a D Dorian phrase for the Dm7 change (measure 2). In measures 3–4, the minor-key riff makes its first appearance, outlining the return of the i (Am7) chord. At the end of measure 4, however, a lead phrase is played in lieu of the single-note riff, smoothly segueing to another D Dorian lick, this time for the Dm7 harmony in measure 5.

MEASURES 5–8: The D Dorian lick in measure 5 spills over to measure 6, where a third-string D note (fret 7) is played in lieu of the open D string to commence the Dm7 riff. The riff also handles the Am7 change in measure 7 before transitioning to a run up the extended A blues (or minor pentatonic) scale, creating anticipation for the v chord in measure 9.

MEASURES 9–12: The lick from measure 8 is carried over to measure 9, where the scale of choice switches seamlessly from A blues (or minor pentatonic) to the extended form of E minor pentatonic. Notice how repetitions of the root (E) on beat 1 and the ♭3rd (G) on beat 2 hammer home the new (Em7) harmony. The riff reappears for the iv-chord change in measure 10, where, once again, the single-note riff is replaced with a lead phrase. In measures 11–12, the Jam concludes with a return to the Am7 riff and a chromatic walk-up (D–D♯–E) to the turnaround chord, E7♯9.

CHAPTER 6: DELTA BLUES FINGERPICKING PATTERN
THE RESOURCES

CHORDS

SCALES

E Composite Blues Scale:
E–F♯–G–G♯–A–B♭–B–C♯–D
(1–2–♭3–♮3–4–♭5–♮5–6–♭7)

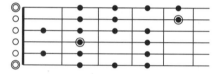

A Composite Blues Scale:
A–B–C–C♯–D–E♭–E–F♯–G
(1–2–♭3–♮3–4–♭5–♮5–6–♭7)

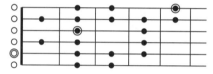

A Mixolydian Mode:
A–B–C♯–D–E–F♯–G
(1–2–3–4–5–6–♭7)

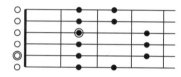

B Composite Blues Scale:
B–C♯–D–D♯–E–F–F♯–G♯–A
(1–2–♭3–♮3–4–♭5–♮5–6–♭7)

B Major Pentatonic (Extended Form):
B–C♯–D♯–F♯–G♯
(1–2–3–5–6)

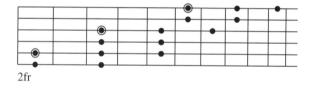

2fr

JAM #31: THE 12-BAR FORM

This fingerpicking pattern is styled after the acoustic blues that originated in the Mississippi Delta in the early 20th century, played by guitarists such as Son House, Charlie Patton, and, of course, Robert Johnson. The pattern is performed with open-position E7, A7, and B7 voicings (I, IV, and V chords, respectively). While bass notes are plucked in a quarter-note rhythm with the thumb (or pick), the treble strings are articulated with the remaining fret-hand fingers. Short melodies are created on the treble strings, so some fret-hand finger movement is required, as well.

MEASURES 1–4: While the thumb alternates between E and B notes on the sixth and fifth strings, respectively, the index finger hammers from the minor 3rd (G) to the major 3rd (G♯) of the E7 harmony, followed by application of the pinky finger to fret 3 of the second string, which turns the E major triad into a dominant seventh chord. This two-bar pattern is repeated in measures 3–4.

MEASURES 5–8: Although the harmony (and chord voicing) is different in measures 5–6, the approach is the same. Here, the index and middle fingers handle the minor-to-major (C-to-C♯) hammer-on, while the pinky frets the ♭7th (G) at the onset of measure 6. At measure 7, the E7 pattern returns to handle the I chord.

MEASURES 9–12: An open-position B7 chord voicing is implemented for the V-chord change, where an alternating root–3rd bass line is substituted for the root–5th pattern that was utilized for the I and IV chords. A truncated version of the IV-chord pattern is played in measure 10 to handle the A7 harmony, leading to a cool turnaround pattern that is comprised of chromatically descending 6ths played along strings 3 and 5 and bookended by the low E and high E strings. These 6ths lead to another chromatic passage—an ascending fifth-string line (A–A♯–B)—that leads to the turnaround chord, B7.

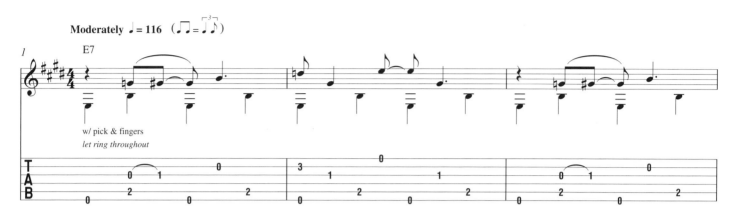

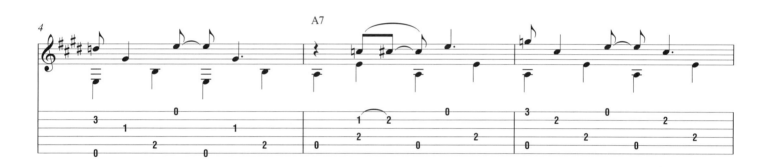

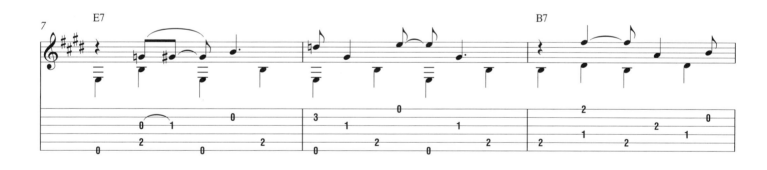

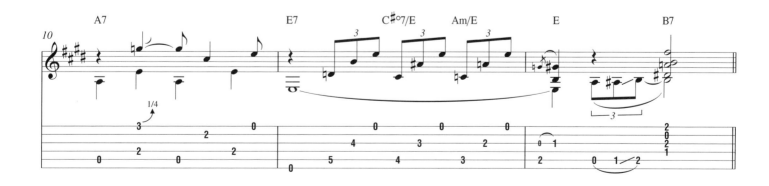

JAM #32: ONE-BAR LEAD/RHYTHM ALTERNATIONS

For this Jam, one-bar lead phrases are continuously alternated with one measure of the Delta blues fingerpicking pattern throughout the 12-bar form. The entire Jam is played in open position, including the lead licks, which are derived from the E composite (E–F#–G–G#–A–Bb–B–C#–D), A composite (A–B–C–C#–D–Eb–E–F#–G), and B composite (B–C#–D–D#–E–F–F#–G#–A) blues scales.

MEASURES 1–4: The opening E7 harmony is hammered home via the open low E string on beat 1 of measure 1, as well as the notes D (b7th) and G# (major 3rd), which are played on the downbeats of beats 2–3. Measure 2 features a one-bar version of the E7 pattern which leads to a variation of the opening lick (measure 3) and another bar of the fingerpicking pattern (measure 4).

MEASURES 5–8: In measure 5, a variation of the opening lick is used to outline the A7 harmony. While the rhythm and articulation are the same, the notes, relative to their respective harmony, differ. Measure 6 features a bar of the A7 fingerpicking pattern, followed by yet another variation of the opening lick (measure 7). The E7 pattern is reprised for measure 8 before giving way to the V-chord lick in measure 9.

MEASURES 9–12: Measure 9's lick is derived from the B composite blues scale and features the ubiquitous minor-to-major 3rd (D-to-D#) "rub" in two octaves (see string 4 and the slide on string 2). Following another bar of the A7 pattern (measure 10), the turnaround, borrowed from Jam #31, ensues, resolving to the open-position B7 voicing.

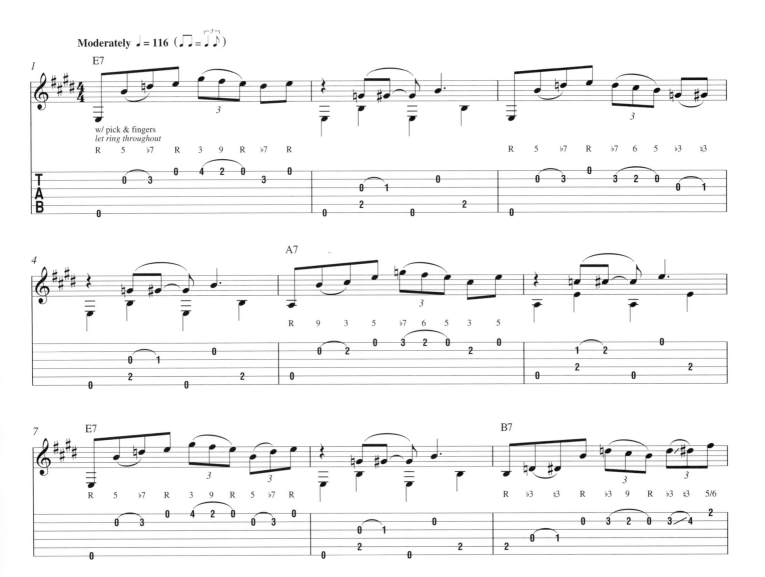

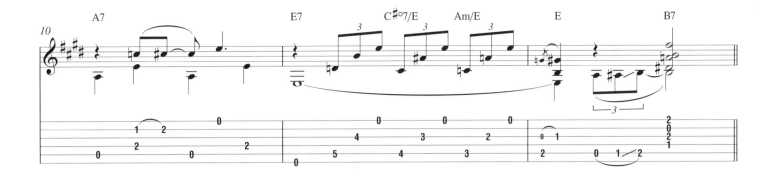

JAM #33: TWO-BAR LEAD/RHYTHM ALTERNATIONS

The one-bar alternations from Jam #32 have been extended to two-bar intervals in this example; that is, two bars of lead are continuously offset by two bars of the fingerpicking pattern throughout the form's 12 bars. As was the case in the previous Jam, the lead lines are crafted from the E composite (E–F#–G–G#–A–B♭–B–C#–D), A composite (A–B–C–C#–D–E♭–E–F#–G), and B composite (B–C#–D–D#–E–F–F#–G#–A) blues scales to outline the E7, A7, and B7 changes, respectively.

MEASURES 1–4: The Jam's opening phrase is played exclusively in open position and features all but two notes (F# and C#) of the E composite blues scale. In measures 3–4, the two-bar E7 pattern that was introduced in Jam #31 is employed to bridge the opening lick and the phrase that outlines the A7 (IV chord) harmony in measure 5.

MEASURES 5–8: In measures 5–6, a slippery, two-bar A composite blues scale phrase handles the IV chord. The phrase commences with a lick that is somewhat reminiscent of Freddie King's "Hideaway" and ends on the open high E string, signaling the arrival of the E7 chord (measure 7). The E7 fingerpicking pattern is played for two bars and keeps the momentum moving until the arrival of the V (B7) chord in measure 9.

MEASURES 9–12: The B7 lick (measure 9) is a bass-string-laden passage that shifts seamlessly to a one-bar A7 phrase (measure 10). Notice that the open B string at the end of the former produces stepwise (whole step) movement to the root of the A7 change, contributing greatly to the seamless nature of the passage. Likewise, the final note of the A7 phrase, G, is the minor 3rd of the forthcoming E7 harmony and has a strong urge to resolve to that chord's tonic. The Jam concludes with two bars of the E7 fingerpicking pattern (no turnaround phrase in this example).

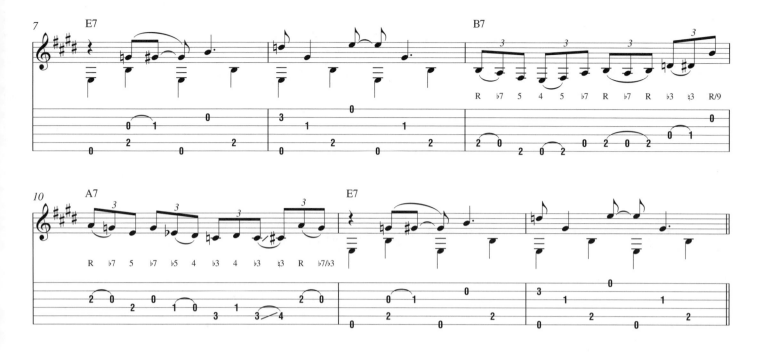

JAM #34: ONE-BAR RHYTHM/LEAD ALTERNATIONS

The lead/rhythm alternations from Jams 32–33 are flipped in this example. Here, one bar of the fingerpicking pattern is continuously alternated with one bar of lead playing. The E7 chord changes are implied via passages derived from the E composite blues scale (E–F#–G–G#–A–Bb–B–C#–D), while the A7 changes are handled by the A Mixolydian mode (A–B–C#–D–E–F#–G).

MEASURES 1–4: Following a measure of the E7 fingerpicking pattern, an open-position legato phrase travels across strings 6–4, incorporating the open B string at the end of the passage to help transition back to the fingerpicking pattern in measure 3. A variation of measure 2's lick is played in measure 4; in this instance, however, the lick descends the strings and moves to the IV (A7) chord in scalar fashion (F#–E–D–C#–B–A), starting on beat 3.

MEASURES 5–8: In measure 5, the fingerpicking pattern handles the first of two bars of the IV (A7) chord, followed by a restatement of the lick from measure 2, only it's played here in the key of A. The open high E string at the end of the phase serves two purposes: first, it helps with the transition back to the fingerpicking pattern; second, it signals a return to the I (E7) chord in measure 7. Following one measure of the E7 pattern, a triplet-based legato passage swiftly descends strings 2–5, moving seamlessly to the root of the B7 chord in measure 9.

MEASURES 9–12: In measures 9–10, the V–IV (B7–A7) chord change is handled by one measure of the fingerpicking pattern and a variation of the legato passage from measure 8, respectively. In its entirety, the passage spells out the A Mixolydian mode (with one repeated note, B). The Jam concludes with the two-measure version of the E7 fingerpicking pattern.

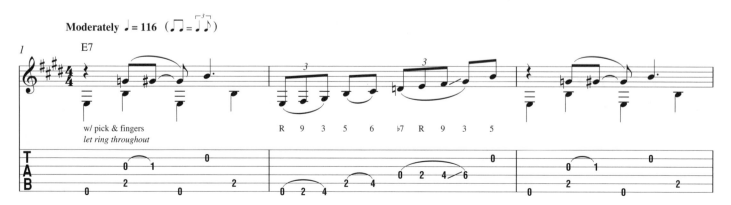

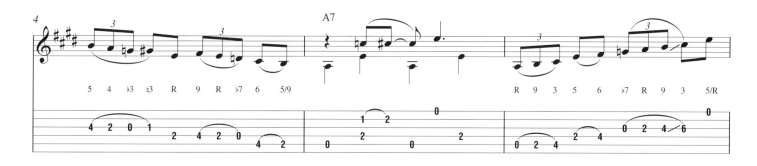

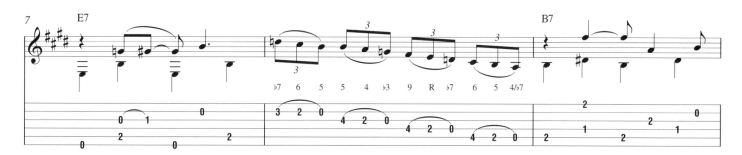

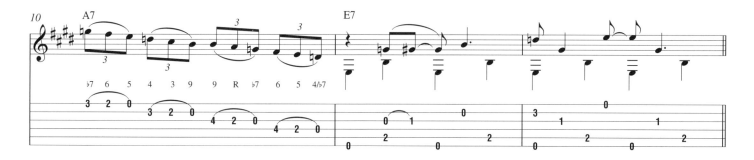

🔊 JAM #35: TWO-BAR RHYTHM/LEAD ALTERNATIONS

The alternations in this Jam are two measures long, played in the same rhythm/lead sequence that was used in Jam #34. The fingerpicking patterns are the two-measure versions that were introduced in Jam #31 (and used in Jam #33). Meanwhile, the lead phrases are derived from the open-position pattern of the E composite blues scale (E–F♯–G–G♯–A–B♭–B–C♯–D).

MEASURES 1–4: The Jam commences with two bars of the E7 fingerpicking pattern, followed by a lead phrase that is reminiscent of the riff that Robert Johnson played in his epochal tune "I Believe I'll Dust My Broom." The two-bar phrase incorporates slides, bends, hammer-ons, and pull-offs and strategically concludes with the note A, which anticipates the arrival of the IV (A7) chord in measure 5.

MEASURES 5–8: The IV chord is handled in measures 5–6 by the A7 fingerpicking pattern before segueing to a restatement of the lick from measure 3. In measure 8, the phrase deviates from the original two-bar phrase, however, favoring a bass-string run to set up the arrival of the V (B7) chord in measure 9.

MEASURES 9–12: The final four measures are a duplication of the final four bars of Jam #31: one bar of the B7 pattern, one bar of the A7 pattern, and the chromatic-6ths turnaround figure. Additionally, the V (B7) chord is voiced in open position and preceded by a fifth-string chromatic line (A–A♯–B).

🔊 JAM #36: RANDOM RHYTHM/LEAD ALTERNATIONS

This Jam arranges the rhythm/lead alternations in random fashion, with heavy emphasis on lead playing. In fact, just four of the Jam's 12 bars are allocated to rhythm. Nevertheless, because the lead phrases are laden with chord tones, the harmonies in these measures are implied nearly as effectively as the chord changes implied by the fingerpicking patterns. For the E7, A7, and B7 changes, the lead phrases are culled from the E composite blues scale (E–F♯–G–G♯–A–B♭–B–C♯–D), A composite blues scale (A–B–C–C♯–D–E♭–E–F♯–G), and the extended form of the B major pentatonic scale (B–C♯–D♯–F♯–G♯), respectively.

MEASURES 1–4: The Jam is launched with a double-stop figure that pairs D/G♯ and B/E dyads with a single-note hammer-on phrase. Nearly every note of this two-bar phrase is an E7 (E–G♯–B–D) chord tone. The four measures of E7 harmony (measures 1–4) conclude with two bars of the fingerpicking pattern.

MEASURES 5–8: In measures 5–6, a variation of the double-stop phrase from measures 1–2 is employed to outline the IV-chord (A7) harmony. Like its predecessor, this lick contains a heavy dose of A7 (A–C♯–E–G) chord tones. In fact, collectively, the phrase's notes imply an A9 harmony (A–C♯–E–G–B), even though the root (A) is not present. The E7 fingerpicking pattern makes another appearance in measure 7 before giving way to a bass-string lick that leads to the V (B7) chord. The hammer-on at the end of the phrase consists of the B7 chord's minor 3rd (D) and major 3rd (D♯), urging the phrase to resolve to the root of the new chord.

MEASURES 9–12: The extended form of the B major pentatonic scale provides the notes for the ascending/descending lick that outlines the V (B7) chord. This lick leads to a phrase that mimics the rhythm of its predecessor, although the notes here (measure 10) are derived from the A composite blues scale and played in open position. The E7 fingerpicking pattern is restated in measure 11, followed by a short lick that moves seamlessly from the E composite blues scale to repetitions of the B7 chord's root (B) and ♭7th (A).

SECTION II: ROCK

CHAPTER 7: ROCK 'N' ROLL WALKING BASS LINE
THE RESOURCES

CHORDS

B7

SCALES

E Composite Blues Scale (Open Position):
E–F♯–G–G♯–A–B♭–B–C♯–D
(1–2–♭3–♮3–4–♭5–♮5–6–♭7)

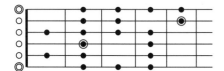

E Composite Blues Scale (6th Position)

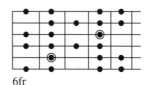

6fr

E Blues Scale (12th Position):
E–G–A–B♭–B–D
(1–♭3–4–♭5–♮5–♭7)

12fr

E Blues Scale (Extended Form)

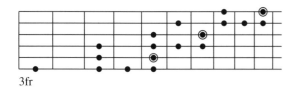

3fr

A Composite Blues Scale (Open Position):
A–B–C–C♯–D–E♭–E–F♯–G
(1–2–♭3–♮3–4–♭5–♮5–6–♭7)

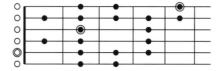

A Composite Blues Scale (4th Position)

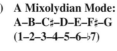

A Mixolydian Mode:
A–B–C♯–D–E–F♯–G
(1–2–3–4–5–6–♭7)

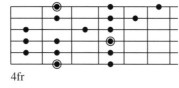

4fr   4fr

B Composite Blues Scale:
B–C♯–D–D♯–E–F–F♯–G♯–A
(1–2–♭3–♮3–4–♭5–♮5–6–♭7)

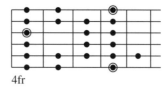

4fr

B Mixolydian Mode:
B–C♯–D♯–E–F♯–G♯–A
(1–2–3–4–5–6–♭7)

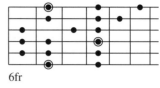

6fr

JAM #37: THE 12-BAR FORM

Like Jams 7–12, the next six examples utilize a bass line for the rhythm parts. The bass line introduced here, however, is a "walking" bass line played in scalar fashion with steady quarter notes, whereas the Chicago blues bass line was a riff-based line that was shuffled in an eighth-note rhythm.

The progression here is a standard set of blues changes played in the key of E: E (I chord), A (IV chord), and B (V chord). The notes themselves are derived from the Mixolydian mode relative to each change: E Mixolydian (E–F♯–G♯–A–B–C♯–D), A Mixolydian (A–B–C♯–D–E–F♯–G), and B Mixolydian (B–C♯–D♯–E–F♯–G♯–A). (*Note:* Since the ♭7th, A, is not played over the B7 change, the scale could be perceived as B major, rather than B Mixolydian).

MEASURES 1–4: The first four measures of the 12-bar form contain two repetitions of the two-bar pattern. To imply the E major harmony, the quarter-note bass line emphasizes, in order, the chord's root (E), 3rd (G♯), 5th (B), 6th (C♯), and ♭7th (D) before reversing course on beat 2 of the second measure and walking back down the scale.

MEASURES 5–8: Measures 5–6 mimic the E chord's bass line, only it's been transposed to the key of A. The resultant tones are: A (root), C♯ (3rd), E (5th), F♯ (6th), and G (♭7th). After one repetition of the A major/dominant bass line, the E major line is restated in measure 7–8.

MEASURES 9–12: For the V (B) chord, the pattern is transposed to the key of B and truncated to one measure, resulting in the notes B (root), D♯ (3rd), F♯ (5th), and G♯ (6th). Measures 10–11 feature the first bars of their respective two-bar patterns, followed by the turnaround chord, B7, which is strummed on the "and" of beat 2 of measure 12.

JAM #38: ONE-BAR LEAD/RHYTHM ALTERNATIONS

In this Jam, lead phrases are alternated with the walking bass line in one-bar intervals throughout the 12-bar form. The two-bar bass lines from Jam #37 have been truncated to one bar here, and the lead phrases are derived from the E composite (E–F♯–G–G♯–A–B♭–B–C♯–D), A composite (A–B–C–C♯–D–E♭–E–F♯–G), and B composite (B–C♯–D–D♯–E–F–F♯–G♯–A) blues scales. (*Note:* The phrase in measure 5 only contains the notes B, C♯, and E, so the scale source for the A major change could also be perceived as A major pentatonic [A–B–C♯–E–F♯].)

MEASURES 1–4: This Jam kicks off with a "Pride and Joy"–style lick that pairs fretted E notes with the open high E string. In measure 2, the walking bass line is employed to link the opening lick to a phrase that involves first-string chromaticism (beats 1–2) and pull-offs (beats 3–4). The walking bass line is reprised in measure 4, where it facilitates transition to the IV (A) chord, as the last note of the bass line, C♯, also functions as the major 3rd of the forthcoming A major harmony (measure 5).

MEASURES 5–8: Measure 5 features a lick that would feel right at home in Freddie King's "Hideaway." The open-position hammer-on lick is followed by a measure of the A major bass line and a one-bar E composite blues scale lick that ends with a half-step, G-to-G♯ slide that provides strong resolution to the E major bass line (measure 8).

MEASURES 9–12: A fourth-position B composite blues scale lick outlines the B major harmony in measure 9, followed by another bar of the A major bass line (measure 10). The turnaround (measures 11–12) is handled by a triplet-fueled lick that features repetitions of the notes B, D, and E, implying a dominant seventh (E7) tonality. This phrase leads to a chromatic passage (A–A♯–B) that ends on the root of the V (B7) chord.

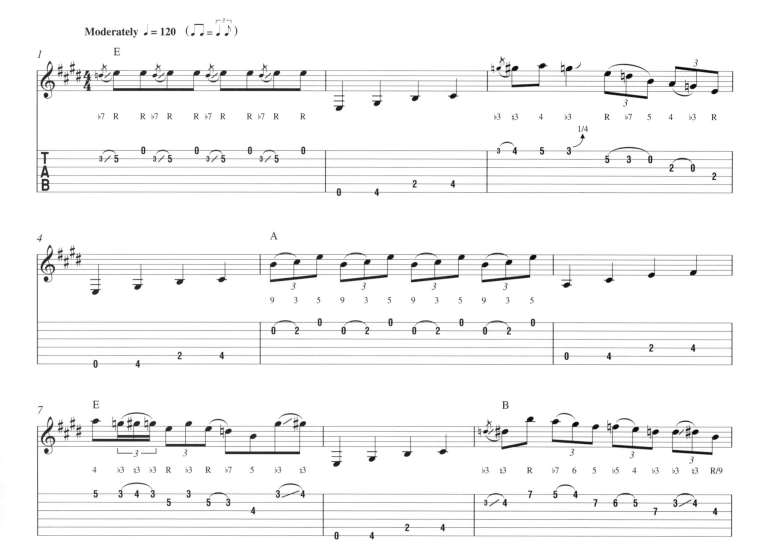

74

JAM #39: TWO-BAR LEAD/RHYTHM ALTERNATIONS

In this Jam, the lead/rhythm alternations from Jam #38 have been extended to two bars. Consequently, the bass lines are now played in their entirety, rather than as truncated one-bar patterns. The lead phrases for the E, A, and B chord changes are culled from the E blues scale (E–G–A–Bb–B–D), A Mixolydian mode (A–B–C#–D–E–F#–G), and B Mixolydian mode (B–C#–D#–E–F#–G#–A), respectively.

MEASURES 1–4: The Jam commences with a Chuck Berry–style lick that pairs whole-step bends with fretted notes on strings 1–2. This phrase concludes with a one-bar passage (measure 2) that descends the E blues scale, ending with a quarter-step bend of the scale's b3rd tone (G). The second half of the four-measure I-chord harmony is handled by the walking bass line.

MEASURES 5–8: At measure 5, a two-bar phrase opens with a wide interval (minor 6th) that jumps from C# (3rd of A) on string 3 to A (root) on string 1. On beat 4, a whole-step bend-and-release kick off a more active line that resolves to the E note at fret 5 of the second string, signaling a return to the I (E) chord. In measures 7–8, the E bass line is restated and carries the progression to the V (B) chord (measure 9).

MEASURES 9–12: In measure 9, the V chord is outlined with a phrase that mimics the lick from measure 5. The wide-interval phrase—again, built from chord tones (D#, the 3rd, and B, the root)—is moved down one whole step and repeated to imply the IV (A) chord change. On beat 4 of measure 10, a slick legato passage moves from the root of the A chord to the minor 3rd (G) and major 3rd (G#) of the forthcoming E chord. The Jam concludes with one measure of the E bass line and an open-position B7 chord to signal a return to the top of the form.

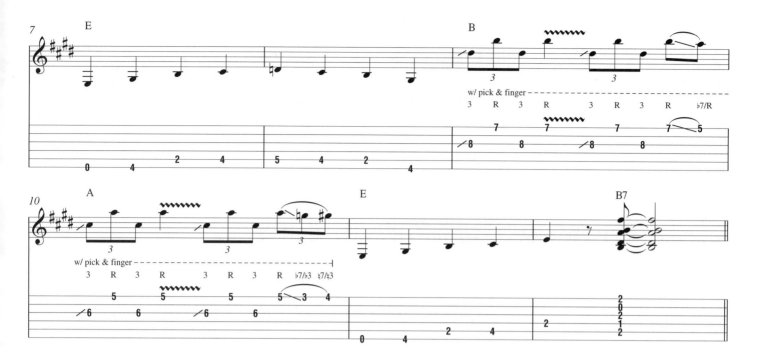

JAM #40: ONE-BAR RHYTHM/LEAD ALTERNATIONS

The alternations in this Jam consist of one bar of the bass line and one bar of lead playing, which are continuously alternated throughout the 12-bar form. The bass lines are truncated versions of the two-bar patterns that were introduced in Jam #37, while the lead playing is comprised of open-position licks derived from the E composite (E–F♯–G–G♯–A–B♭–B–C♯–D) and A composite (A–B–C–C♯–D–E♭–E–F♯–G) blues scales, with emphasis on the guitar's bass strings.

MEASURES 1–4: Following one bar of the E-major bass line, a triplet-fueled E composite blues scale lick is introduced in measure 2. The sixth-string, G-to-G♯ bend on beat 4 creates a strong urge to resolve to the open low E string, which happens to be the first note of the E bass line in measure 3. In measure 4, the first half of the lick from measure 2 is restated before ascending to the open E and open B strings.

MEASURES 5–8: The one-bar version of the A bass line is played in measure 5 before segueing to the A-major version (with slight variations) of the lick from measure 2. At measure 7, the E bass line makes another appearance, followed by a bass-string-laden E composite blues scale lick that incorporates seven of the scale's nine notes. Notice that the hammer-on at the end of the phrase creates a chromatic walk-up (G–G♯–A–A♯–B) to the root of the V (B) chord.

MEASURES 9–12: The V–IV (B–A) change in measures 9–10 is handled by one measure of the B bass line and an A composite blues lick, respectively. Similar to the sixth-string bends in measures 2 and 6, the hammer-on figure on beat 4 of measure 10 moves from G to G♯ before resolving to the root of the forthcoming E chord on the last note of the phrase. In measures 11–12, the Jam comes to a conclusion with a measure of the E bass line and an open-position B7 chord, which signals a return to the top of the form.

JAM #41: TWO-BAR RHYTHM/LEAD ALTERNATIONS

The full, two-bar bass lines return for this Jam. Here, they continuously alternate with two-bar lead phrases that are derived from the E blues (E–G–A–Bb–B–D) and E composite blues (E–F#–G–G#–A–Bb–B–C#–D) scales.

MEASURES 1–4: Two bars of the E-major bass line set up the Jam before giving way to a two-bar phrase that is carved from the extended form of the E blues scale. (*Note:* Since Bb is not present in this phrase, E minor pentatonic [E–G–A–B–D] could also be considered the scale source.) Notice that the phrase begins with the open low E string, which helps to reinforce the E major harmony as the Jam moves from bass line to lead phrase.

MEASURES 5–8: In measures 5–6, the two-bar A-major bass line handles the IV (A) chord, which is followed by a two-bar phrase that begins with a restatement of the lick from measure 3 before meandering down the extended E blues scale. Note the inclusion of A and Bb notes on beat 4 of measure 8, creating chromaticism that leads to the root of the B chord change (measure 9).

MEASURES 9–12: One-bar versions of the B and A bass lines are employed to imply the V–IV (B–A) chord change in measures 9–10. The bass lines are followed by an E composite blues scale lick that is (mostly) played in open position and commences with the open low E string—again, used to reinforce the E major harmony. On beat 2 of measure 12, the dominant (B7) harmony is outlined via open and fretted pitches of the root (B), as well as a fretted pitch of the b7th (A), the last note of the phrase.

🔊 JAM #42: RANDOM RHYTHM/LEAD ALTERNATIONS

The alternations in this Jam occur randomly, giving the example a spontaneous feel. Instead of predetermined one- or two-bar intervals, the Jam commences with multiple two-bar tradeoffs before yielding to one bar of bass line (measure 7) and three bars of lead playing (measures 8–10). Finally, the Jam wraps up with one bar of the E-major bass line and the turnaround chord, B7. Meanwhile, the lead phrases feature a double-stop motif that is similar to the one introduced in Jam #36, particularly the C#/G dyads in measures 5–6.

MEASURES 1–4: The opening I-chord harmony (measures 1–4) is handled by two measures of lead and two measure of the E-major bass line. The initial double stops involve pushing fret 8 of the second string up a quarter step with the middle finger, keeping fret 7 of the first string stationary with the index finger. Notice how the open low E string is articulated at the beginning of each one-bar phrase to emphasize the E major harmony.

MEASURES 5–8: Measures 5–6 feature a repetitive lick that is the A-major version (with slight alterations) of the phrase from measures 1–2. Similarly, notice how the open A string signals a change in harmony (from E to A). Following another bar of the E bass line (measure 7), an open-position E composite blues scale (E–F#–G–G#–A–Bb–B–C#–D) lick is employed to segue to the V (B) chord (measure 9).

MEASURES 9–12: The composite blues scale phrase that began in measure 8 flows seamlessly over the V (B) and IV (A) chords in measures 9–10, culling its notes from the composite blues scale respective to each chord change. In measure 11, the E bass line is restated for the turnaround, leading to an open-position B7 chord, which signals a return to the top of the form.

CHAPTER 8: BLUES-ROCK BOOGIE BASS LINE
THE RESOURCES

CHORDS

E5

1 1

A5

1 1

B5

1 3 3

SCALES

E Blues Scale:
E–G–A–B♭–B–D
(1–♭3–4–♭5–5–♭7)

12fr

E Composite Blues Scale (Open Position):
E–F♯–G–G♯–A–B♭–B–C♯–D
(1–2–♭3–♮3–4–♭5–5–6–♭7)

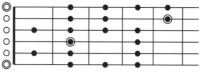

E Composite Blues Scale (4th Position)

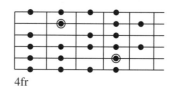

4fr

E Composite Blues Scale (6th Position)

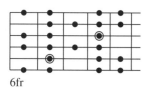

6fr

E Composite Blues Scale (Extended Form)

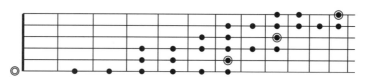

E Minor Pentatonic (12th Position):
E–G–A–B–D
(1–♭3–4–5–♭7)

12fr

E Minor Pentatonic (4th Position)

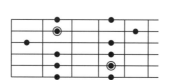

4fr

A Composite Blues Scale (Open Position):
A–B–C–C♯–D–E♭–E–F♯–G
(1–2–♭3–♮3–4–♭5–♮5–6–♭7)

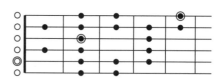

A Composite Blues Scale (4th Position)

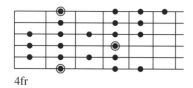

4fr

A Mixolydian Mode:
A–B–C♯–D–E–F♯–G
(1–2–3–4–5–6–♭7)

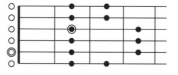

B Composite Blues Scale (Open Position):
B–C♯–D–D♯–E–F–F♯–G♯–A
(1–2–♭3–♮3–4–♭5–♮5–6–♭7)

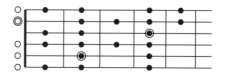

B Composite Blues Scale (4th Position)

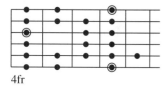

4fr

B Composite Blues Scale (6th Position)

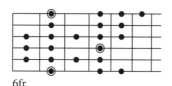

6fr

JAM #43: THE 12-BAR FORM

The bass line used in the next six Jams is a hybrid of the bass lines from Jams #13 and #37. Like the Texas blues riff (Jam #13), this example is played in an eighth-note rhythm and features hammer-ons that move from the minor 3rd to the major 3rd of each chord change. What makes this bass line similar to the rock 'n' roll walking bass line (Jam #37) is the inclusion of the ♭7th in the second measure (beat 2) of the two-bar patterns. What gives this boogie bass line its unique vibe, however, is the tie that connects that last eighth note of measure 1 to the first eighth note of measure 2, creating a touch of syncopation in an otherwise rhythmically straightforward pattern.

MEASURES 1–4: The E-major pattern in measures 1–2 can be perceived as being derived from either the E composite blues scale (E–F♯–G–G♯–A–B♭–B–C♯–D) or a combination of the E Mixolydian mode (E–F♯–G♯–A–B–C♯–D) and the E minor pentatonic scale (E–G–A–B–D), from which the minor 3rd (G) is borrowed. The pattern is then repeated in measures 3–4.

MEASURES 5–8: The bass line in measures 5–6 is a note-for-note reproduction of the E-major pattern, only it's played here in the key of A. To transpose the pattern from E major to A major, the bass line is shift up one string set, to strings 3–5, with the open A string acting as the tonic. The E-major pattern is reprised in measure 7–8 to handle the return to the I chord.

MEASURES 9–12: A truncated bass pattern is played over the V (B) chord in measure 9, with the same approach applied to the IV (A) chord in measure 10. In measures 11–12, the Jam concludes with one last repetition of the E-major bass line.

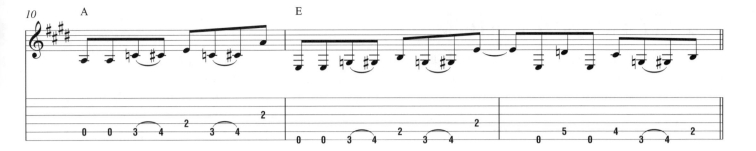

🔊 JAM #44: ONE-BAR LEAD/RHYTHM ALTERNATIONS

In this first Jam involving the blues-rock boogie bass line, one bar of lead and one bar of the bass line are continuously alternated throughout the 12-bar form. Due to the one-bar intervals, the two-bar bass patterns from Jam #43 have been shortened to one bar.

The lead lines for the I (E) chord are derived from the E blues (E–G–A–B♭–B–D) and E composite blues (E–F♯–G–G♯–A–B♭–B–C♯–D) scales, while the IV (A) and V (B) chords are handled by the A composite (A–B–C–C♯–D–E♭–E–F♯–G) and B composite (B–C♯–D–D♯–E–F–F♯–G♯–A) blues scales, respectively.

MEASURES 1–4: A 12th-position blues-scale lick kicks off the Jam and is followed by a measure of the I-chord bass line. In measure 3, a variation of the lick from measure 1 is played an octave lower, in open position, before giving way to another bar of the E boogie pattern.

MEASURES 5–8: For the arrival of the IV chord, an A composite blues scale lick mimics the opening lick, lending continuity to the Jam. In measure 6, the one-bar version of the A bass line in is played, leading to the I (E) chord in measure 7. Here, a variation of the lick from measure 3 is employed to outline the new (E) harmony. This one-bar phrase is followed by another measure of the E boogie bass line (measure 8).

MEASURES 9–12: To signal the arrival of the V (B) chord, a repetitive hammer-on passage featuring the chord's minor 3rd (D), major 3rd (D♯), and root (B) is performed. After one bar of the A bass line (measure 10), an ascending E composite blues scale phrase leads to a B/F♯ dyad that implies a return to the V chord for the turnaround. Similar to the bass lines, the D-to-D♯ (minor-to-major) hammer-on that precedes the dyad creates a strong urge to resolve to the root of the V chord.

JAM #45: TWO-BAR LEAD/RHYTHM ALTERNATIONS

In this Jam, the alternations have been extended to two-bar intervals, starting with two measures of lead. Unlike the one-bar intervals of Jam #44, the extended intervals enable the bass-line patterns to be played in their entirety.

All of the lead phrases are derived from the composite blues scales respective to the chord changes: the E composite blues scale (E–F♯–G–G♯–A–B♭–B–C♯–D) handles the E-chord harmonies, the A composite blues scale (A–B–C–C♯–D–E♭–E–F♯–G) handles the A-chord harmonies, and the B composite blues scale (B–C♯–D–D♯–E–F–F♯–G♯–A) covers the B-chord harmony in measure 9.

MEASURES 1–4: The Jam launches with a two-measure excursion down the extended form of the E composite blues scale. Two notable components of this lick are the opening double stop and the sixth-string quarter-step bends. The former acknowledges the harmony from the get-go via the E chord's 3rd (G♯) and 5th (B), while the latter produce a strong pull toward the open low E string, the root of the forthcoming bass line (measures 3–4).

MEASURES 5–8: The lick in measures 5–6 loosely mimics the opening lick, although it's played here in the key of A. The new harmony is defined upfront via the open A string and the G/C♯ (♭7th/5th) double stop (bent a quarter step). The inclusion of the ♭7th gives the passage a dominant (A7) flavor, and the G-to-G♯ hammer-on at the tail end of the phrase directs the line back to the E boogie pattern, which covers measures 7–8.

MEASURES 9–12: The V (B) chord change in measure 9 is implied via a phrase that ascends the B composite blues scale. This lick is then recreated (though note identically) a whole-step lower for the IV (A) chord. The third-string pull-off at the end of measure 10 concludes with the note G, which, like the sixth-string bends in measure 2, pulls the passage toward the root of the E boogie bass line (measures 11–12).

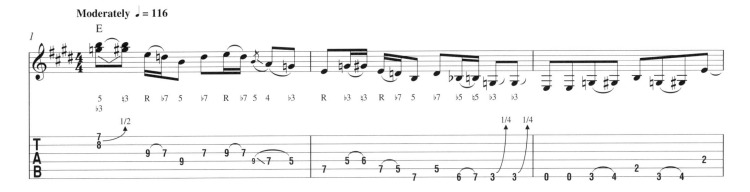

🔊 JAM #46: ONE-BAR RHYTHM/LEAD ALTERNATIONS

The sequence of the alternations in this example is reversed from the previous two Jams (44–45). Here, the boogie bass line commences the Jam, followed by continuous one-bar alternations. For the lead phrases, a rhythmic and melodic motif is introduced in measure 1 and carried throughout the Jam's 12 measures, borrowing notes from three primary sources: the E composite blues scale (E–F#–G–G#–A–Bb–B–C#–D), the A composite blues scale (A–B–C–C#–D–Eb–E–F#–G), and the A Mixolydian mode (A–B–C#–D–E–F#–G).

MEASURES 1–4: Following a measure of the E bass line, a rhythmic grouping consisting of a 16th-note triplet and an eighth note fuels a rapid-fire legato phrase that pairs repetitive second-string hammer-ons with a descending melody (G#–F#–E–B). The bass line returns in measure 3 before segueing to a variation of measure 2's phrase. This time, first-string pull-offs are paired with the melody. On the "and" of beat 4 of measure 4, a B-to-C# hammer-on pulls the phrase toward the root of the A bass line (measure 5).

MEASURES 5–8: The A boogie pattern is used to acknowledge the change in harmony (to A major) in measure 5, which is followed by yet another variation of the motif from measure 2. Here, second-string hammer-ons are paired with a G–F#–E–B melody. Following the return of the E boogie pattern (measure 7), a descending legato phrase leads the Jam to the V (B) chord. Although most of the notes are derived from the E composite blues scale, a touch of chromaticism is incorporated (see string 4), as well.

MEASURES 9–12: The one-bar version of the B boogie bass line is used to imply the V (B) chord in measure 9, which is followed by an A Mixolydian lick that "answers" the lick from measure 8 by ascending the strings. The open high E string at the end of the phrase implies a return to the I chord (measures 11–12), which is handled by the E bass line.

🔊 JAM #47: TWO-BAR RHYTHM/LEAD ALTERNATIONS

In this example, the one-bar rhythm/lead alternations from Jam #46 have been extended to two bars. After commencing with two bars of the E boogie bass line, the Jam unfolds with continuous two-bar tradeoffs. With the exception of the closing passage, all of the lead phrases are derivatives of the motif that is introduced in measure 3.

MEASURES 1–4: Following two measures of the E boogie bass line, an E minor pentatonic lick is played in fifth position, creating a motif that is carried throughout the Jam. In fact, the phrase is duplicated one octave higher in the next bar (measure 4), where it's played in the "root position" of the E minor pentatonic scale.

MEASURES 5–8: After the A boogie line covers the IV-chord change (measures 5–6), the E composite blues scale, played in open position, is used to perform variations of the motif in two separate octaves. To signal the arrival of the B (V) chord in measure 9, a half-step, D-to-D♯ bend (the minor 3rd and major 3rd of B, respectively) is employed at the end of the two-measure phrase.

MEASURES 9–12: One-bar versions of the B and A bass lines cover the V–IV chord change, respectively, followed by an open-position lick that flows down strings 1–4 before reversing course and resolving to the root of the I (E) chord via a unison slide. An alternative way to end this phrase is to resolve to the E chord's 5th, B, which would imply the V (B) chord for the turnaround—a common harmonic approach to 12-bar blues (and one that is used throughout this book).

🔊 JAM #48: RANDOM RHYTHM/LEAD ALTERNATIONS

The rhythm/lead alternations are arranged randomly in this example, starting with a two-measure lead phrase. After the two bars of lead, the Jam unfolds as follows: one bar of bass line, two bars of lead, three bars of bass line, two bars of lead, and two bars of bass line. The randomness of the rhythm and lead parts lends a more practical (and less predictable) approach to the I–IV–V (E–A–B) chord changes. For the lead lines, the scales of choice are the composite blues scales respective to the chord changes: E composite (E–F♯–G–G♯–A–B♭–B–C♯–D), A composite (A–B–C–C♯–D–E♭–E–F♯–G), and B composite (B–C♯–D–D♯–E–F–F♯–G♯–A).

MEASURES 1–4: The Jam kicks off with a chromatic-laden passage derived from the E composite blues scale, which consists of an eight-note phrase that is established in measure 1 and repeated, an octave lower, in measure 2. Following a bar of the E bass line (measure 3), a one-bar E composite blues scale phrase sets up the forthcoming A-major harmony (measure 5) via a hammer-on from C to C♯ (the minor 3rd and major 3rd of A, respectively).

MEASURES 5–8: The phrase that started in measure 4 flows seamless to the A composite blues scale lick that is employed for the first bar of the A-major harmony (measure 5). The lick is followed by the one-measure version of the A bass line (measure 6) and the full, two-measure version of the E bass line (measures 7–8).

MEASURES 9–12: In measure 9, the V-chord harmony is handled by a B composite blues lick, which is shifted down a whole step, to the key of A, for the IV-chord harmony (measure 10). Although beats 1–2 are identical, the second half of the phrase has been altered, particularly beat 4, which features a G-to-G♯ (minor-to-major) hammer-on to set up resolution to the I chord (measures 11–12). To wrap up the Jam, the two-measure E boogie pattern is restated.

CHAPTER 9: BLUES-ROCK RIFF
THE RESOURCES

CHORDS

E7

2 1 4

A7
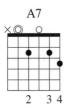
2 3 4

B7

1 3 1 4

B7
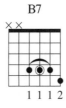
1 1 1 2

SCALES

E Major Pentatonic:
E–F♯–G♯–B–C♯
(1–2–3–5–6)

9fr

E Composite Blues Scale (Open Position):
E–F♯–G–G♯–A–B♭–B–C♯–D
(1–2–♭3–♮3–4–♭5–♮5–6–♭7)

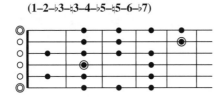

E Composite Blues Scale (8th Position)

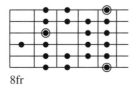
8fr

E Composite Blues Scale (11th Position)

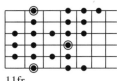

11fr

E Composite Blues Scale (Extended Form)

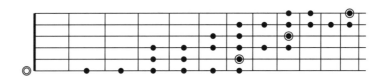

E Minor Pentatonic (Extended Form):
E–G–A–B–D
(1–♭3–4–5–♭7)

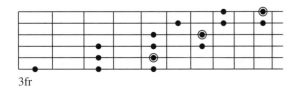
3fr

E Blues Scale:
E–G–A–B♭–B–D
(1–♭3–4–♭5–5–♭7)

12fr

A Major Pentatonic:
A–B–C♯–E–F♯
(1–2–3–5–6)

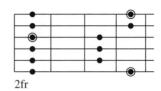
2fr

A Composite Blues Scale:
A–B–C–C♯–D–E♭–E–F♯–G
(1–2–♭3–♮3–4–♭5–♮5–6–♭7)

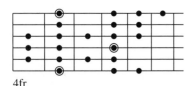
4fr

B Major Pentatonic (Extended Form):
B–C♯–D♯–F♯–G♯
(1–2–3–5–6)

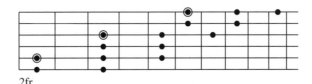
2fr

JAM #49: THE 12-BAR FORM

This Jam features a standard set of I (E7), IV (A7), and V (B7) chord changes, played here as a blues-rock riff à la Eric Clapton's work in '60s power-trio Cream. The open-position riff incorporates everything from hammer-ons and pull-offs to slides and quarter-step bends. While the E7 and A7 riffs utilize open strings for their roots, the B7 riff is played in second position, with the fifth-string B note (fret 2) serving as home base.

MEASURES 1–4: No "quick change" is used here; instead, the I (E7) chord is sustained for four measures. Since the riff is two measures long, the pattern is played twice for this initial appearance of the I chord.

MEASURES 5–8: For the A7 harmony in measures 5–6, the riff is shifted from strings 6–2 to strings 5–1, with the open A string now serving as the riff's tonic. After two measures of A7, the E7 riff returns for the second appearance of the I chord (measures 7–8).

MEASURES 9–12: The riff must be relocated to second position for the V (B7) chord. Also, because the V and IV chords in measures 9–10 appear for only one measure apiece, the riffs for the changes are likewise shortened to one bar each. For the turnaround (measures 11–12), the E7 riff covers the first one-and-a-half bars, with the V chord arriving on beat 3 of the final measure.

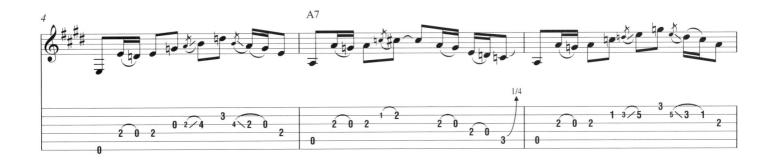

JAM #50: ONE-BAR LEAD/RHYTHM ALTERNATIONS

This Jam involves continuously alternating one bar of lead playing with one bar of the blues-rock riff. The one-bar intervals are maintained until measure 11, where a two-measure run up the E composite blues scale (E–F#–G–G#–A–B♭–B–C#–D) caps the 12-bar progression. The lead playing in this example is very active, with 16th notes providing a majority of the rhythms.

MEASURES 1–4: In measure 1, a 16th-note sequence (played twice) is used to descend the ninth-position pattern of the E major pentatonic scale. Following a truncated (one-bar) version of the E7 riff (measure 2), a variation of the opening lick is constructed from the E composite blues scale. This phrase is punctuated by another bar of the E7 riff (measure 4).

MEASURES 5–8: The lead phrase in measure 5 is the A major version of the opening lick, only it has been displaced (by half a beat) by the open A string. Following a one-bar version of the A7 riff (measure 6), a repetitive four-note sequence ascends the E major pentatonic scale, followed by another bar of the E7 riff (measure 8).

MEASURES 9–12: The V–IV change in measures 9–10 is implied by a run up the extended form of the B major pentatonic scale and the truncated A7 riff, respectively. Then, the Jam climaxes with a repetitive four-note sequence that gradually makes its way up to the B note at fret 7 of the first string, signaling the arrival of the V (B7) chord.

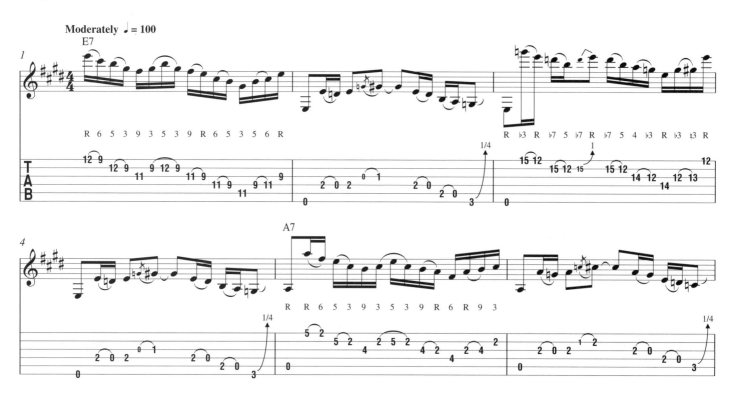

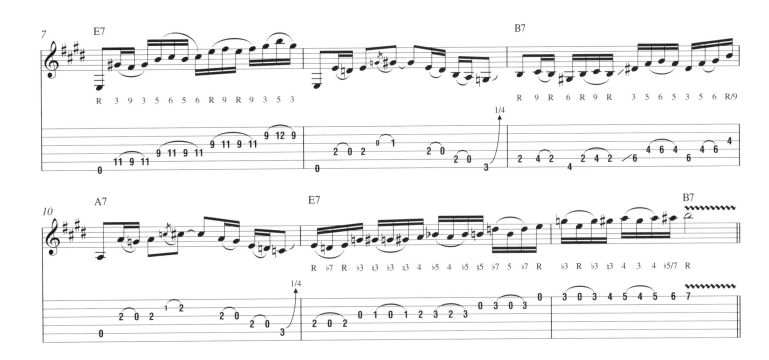

JAM #51: TWO-BAR LEAD/RHYTHM ALTERNATIONS

In this Jam, the lead/rhythm alternations are played in two-measure intervals. As a result, the leads are offset by the full, two-measure versions of the blues-rock riff throughout the 12-bar form. The lead lines that are played over the I (E7) and IV (A7) chords are derived from the E blues (E–G–A–Bb–B–D) and A composite blues (A–B–C–C#–D–Eb–E–F#–G) scales, respectively.

MEASURES 1–4: The bluesy phrase in measure 1 features a one-octave interval jump on beat 2, followed by sequenced decent of the E blues scale. Another notable moment within this lick is the quarter-step bend of the b3rd (G) at the end of the phrase, which creates strong resolution to the tonic note (open low E string) of the E7 riff (measures 3–4).

MEASURES 5–8: The one-octave jump that was introduced in measure 1 makes an appearance on beat 1 of measure 5, as well, played here in the key of A. The wide leap is followed by gradual descent of the A composite blues scale. To reinforce the A7 harmony, the chord's 3rd (C#) is held for the duration of a quarter note on beat 1 of measure 6. Notice, too, the quarter-step bend of the sixth-string G note to facilitate the return to the E7 riff in measure 7.

MEASURES 9–12: Following the two-bar E7 riff, measure 9 features a riff-like phrase that features sliding minor-6th intervals that are derived from the B Mixolydian mode (B–C#–D#–E–F#–G#–A). A variation of the phrase is played in measure 10, for the IV (A) chord, and features a slow-moving half-step bend that travels from the b7th of the A7 chord (G) to the major 3rd of the E7 chord (G#), setting up the E7 riff for the turnaround (measures 11–12).

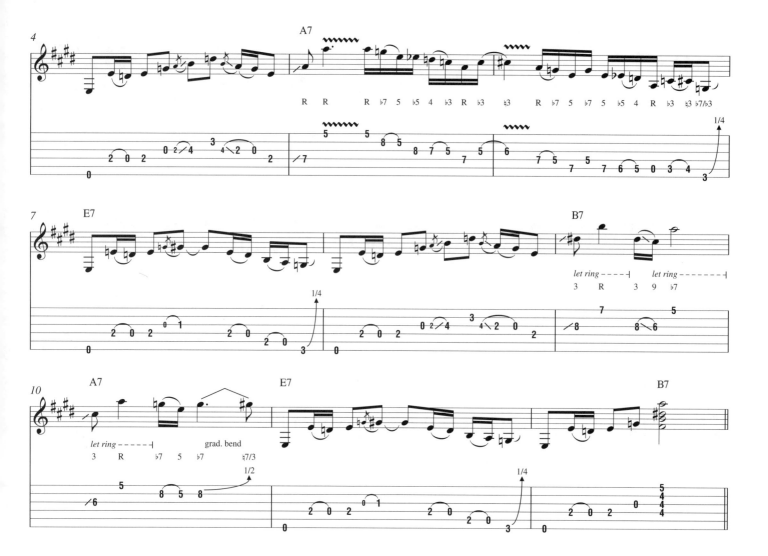

JAM #52: ONE-BAR RHYTHM/LEAD ALTERNATIONS

The rhythm and lead parts in this Jam are alternated in one-bar intervals, starting with one measure of the E7 riff. The rhythm/lead tradeoffs continue until measures 11–12, where the E7 riff is reprised and punctuated with a close-voiced B7 (V) chord. Several scales serve as note sources for the lead phrases, including the extended form of the E minor pentatonic scale (E–G–A–B–D), the E Mixolydian mode (E–F♯–G♯–A–B–C♯–D), the A Mixolydian mode (A–B–C♯–D–E–F♯–G), and the A major pentatonic scale (A–B–C♯–E–F♯).

MEASURES 1–4: One measure of the E7 riff is used to open the Jam and is followed by an E minor pentatonic lick that consists of a five-note motif that is established on beats 1–2 and then repeated (with different notes) on beats 3–4. After another bar of the E7 riff (measure 3), the motif is restated in measure 4. However, in an effort to anticipate the arrival of the IV (A7) chord in measure 5, the lick is altered on beat 4, ending with the A note at fret 10 of the second string.

MEASURES 5–8: The next four measures of the Jam consist of a measure of the A7 riff (measure 5), a third-string pull-off lick (measure 6), one bar of the E7 riff (measure 7), and a fourth-string pull-off lick (measure 8). The lick in measure 6 is derived from the A Mixolydian mode, and then transposed (to the key of E) and restated in measure 8. The open B string that concludes the latter serves a couple of purposes: first, it facilitates the transition back to second position (for the B7 riff); second, it anticipates the V (B7) chord change in measure 9.

MEASURES 9–12: Following one measure of the B7 riff, the open A string announces the arrival of the IV (A7) chord (measure 10), which is followed by a countrified lick that derives its notes from the A major pentatonic scale and features a third-string oblique bend. The turnaround (measures 11–12) is comprised of the E7 riff, which is cut off abruptly on beat 3 of measure 12 by the V (B7) chord, signaling a return to the top of the Jam.

JAM #53: TWO-BAR RHYTHM/LEAD ALTERNATIONS

While the rhythm/lead sequence from Jam #52 is retained in this example, the length of the intervals has been extended from one bar to two. Here, the riffs are played as full, two-bar patterns and paired with lead lines that are performed in an active, 16th-note rhythm. All of the phrases are played over the I (E7) chord and are derived from a multitude of E-based scales, including E major pentatonic (E–F♯–G♯–B–C♯), E blues (E–G–A–B♭–B–D), E composite blues (E–F♯–G–G♯–A–B♭–B–C♯–D), and E Dorian (E–F♯–G–A–B–C♯–D).

MEASURES 1–4: After the E7 riff introduces the Jam (measures 1–2), an active, two-bar lick is launched in measure 3. This phrase commences in the ninth-position pattern of the E major pentatonic scale before moving up the fretboard, to the E composite blues scale, for a phrase that features half- and whole-step bends performed on string 2. The final bend of the phrase (C to C♯, the minor 3rd and major 3rd of A7, respectively) sets up resolution to the IV chord (measure 5).

MEASURES 5–8: The two-bar version of the A7 riff handles the IV chord (measures 5–6) and is followed by another note-heavy phrase (measures 7–8). This two-bar passage moves from relatively common blues-scale playing to a rock-inspired (think George Lynch) intervallic phrase that pairs major and minor 3rds to travel down strings 3–4.

MEASURES 9–12: One-bar versions of the B7 and A7 riffs outline the V and IV chords, respectively, leading to a longer version of the intervallic lick that was introduced in measure 8. Like its predecessor, this lick employs minor and major 3rds, derived from the D Dorian mode, to move seamlessly down the third and fourth strings. To signal the arrival of the V chord, the phrase ends on the B note at fret 4 of the third string.

🔊 JAM #54: RANDOM RHYTHM/LEAD ALTERNATIONS

In this example, the alternations from Jams 49–53 have been arranged in random fashion. Instead of predetermined one- or two-bar tradeoffs, the Jam unfolds with seemingly spontaneous lead and rhythm parts. Overall, the lead phrases have a distinct country flavor, while the riffs maintain their blues-rock vibe. Despite the disparate sounds, the pairing actually works out nicely!

MEASURES 1–4: The Jam commences with a long, two-bar descent of the extended form of the E composite blues scale, moving from ninth position to fifth position, where the G note at fret 5 of the fourth string is bumped up a quarter step to initiate resolution to the open low E string (measure 3). The E7 riff handles measure 3 and most of measure 4; however, on beats 3–4 of the latter, an ascending phrase is substituted to create a chromatic line (G–G♯–A) that moves from the minor 3rd and major 3rd of E7 to the root of A7 (the IV chord).

MEASURES 5–8: In measure 5, an A composite blues scale (A–B–C–C♯–D–E♭–E–F♯–G) lick mimics the opening phrase before transitioning to the A7 riff in measure 6. For the return of the I chord, the E7 riff is played in measure 7, followed by a bass-string lick derived from the E composite blues scale (E–F♯–G–G♯–A–B♭–B–C♯–D), which smoothly transitions to the V (B7) chord in measure 9.

MEASURES 9–12: The extended form of the B major pentatonic scale supplies the notes for the lick in measure 9, which seamlessly transitions to a one-bar A composite blues scale lick via a half-step, G♯-to-A slide. To signal the beginning of the turnaround (measures 11–12), a half-step, G-to-G♯ bend is performed on beat 4 of measure 10. This bend creates a strong urge to resolve to the note E, which happens to be the first note of the E7 riff!

95

CHAPTER 10: RHYTHM & BLUES (R&B) RIFF
THE RESOURCES

CHORDS

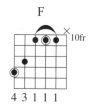

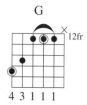

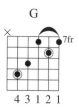

SCALES

C Major Pentatonic:
C–D–E–G–A
(1–2–3–5–6)

C Major Pentatonic (6th-string Root Extended Form)

C Major Pentatonic (5th-string Root Extended Form)

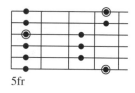

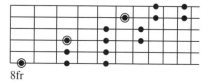

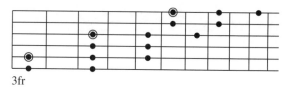

C Composite Blues Scale (Open Position):
C–D–E♭–E–F–G♭–G–A–B♭
(1–2–♭3–♮3–4–♭5–♮5–6–♭7)

C Composite Blues Scale (7th Position)

F Major Pentatonic (6th-string Root Extended Form):
F–G–A–C–D
(1–2–3–5–6)

F Major Pentatonic (5th-string Root Extended Form)

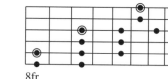

F Major Pentatonic (10th Position)

F Major:
F–G–A–B♭–C–D–E
(1–2–3–4–5–6–7)

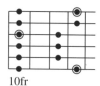

G Major Pentatonic (6th-string Root Extended Form):
G–A–B–D–E
(1–2–3–5–6)

G Major Pentatonic/Aeolian Hybrid Scale:
G–A–B♭–B–C–D–E♭–E–F
(1–2–♭3–♮3–4–5–♭6–♮6–♭7)

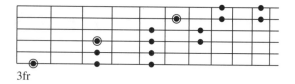

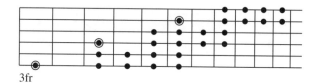

JAM #55: THE 12-BAR FORM

If Jimi Hendrix or Curtis Mayfield had played the main guitar riff to the Temptations' classic "My Girl," this R&B-style Jam might've been the result. Featuring single-note lines and double stops, the riff ascends the major pentatonic scale relative to the harmony being implied at the time, adding a touch of syncopation (see the tie that connects beats 2 and 3) along the way. The song form is a standard set of blues changes (I–IV–V), played here in the key of C (C–F–G), with the "quick change" occurring in measure 2.

MEASURES 1–4: After the main riff is established in the Jam's key, C, in measure 1, it's quickly transposed up a perfect 4th, to the key of F, to cover the IV chord. At measure 3, the C-major riff returns for two repetitions.

MEASURES 5–8: In measures 5–6, the F-major version of the riff is played twice, followed by two repetitions of the C-major riff (measures 7–8). The only differences between the two versions of the riff are their keys and, therefore, their locations

MEASURES 9–12: The C-major riff is transposed up a perfect 5th, to the key of G, for the V chord (measure 9), which is followed by the F-major and C-major riffs in measures 10 and 11, respectively. To imply the V (G) chord during the turnaround (measure 12), a B/D double stop (the 3rd and 5th of G major, respectively) is played after a truncated version of the C-major riff.

JAM #56: ONE-BAR LEAD/RHYTHM ALTERNATIONS

This Jam continuously alternates one bar of lead playing and one bar of the R&B riff. The lead phrases are derived from the C major pentatonic (C–D–E–G–A), F major pentatonic (F–G–A–C–D), and G major pentatonic (G–A–B–D–E) scales and feature several techniques that are a staple of lead-guitar playing, including oblique bends, unison bends, and double-stop slides, among others.

MEASURES 1–4: The Jam kicks off with a pedal-steel-style lick that features a whole-step pre-bend that resolves to the root of the I (C) chord and commences a major pentatonic lick that mimics that C-major riff. In measure 2, the F-major version of the riff is played once before a double-stop passage, derived from the C major pentatonic scale, descends strings 1–5. This phrase is followed by a return to the I-chord riff.

MEASURES 5–8: The double-stop lick from measure 3 is restated, in the key of F, in measure 5, followed in measure 6 by another bar of the F-major riff. In measure 7, unison bends are used to create a line that walks down four notes of the C major pentatonic scale (in order: C–A–G–E), leading to another bar of the I-chord riff (measure 8).

MEASURES 9–12: In measure 9, a G major pentatonic lick loosely mimics the G-major riff before segueing to another bar of the IV-chord rhythm pattern. The Jam's turnaround (measures 11–12) features a syncopated line, played with octave shapes, that recalls the unison bends from measure 7. This phrase concludes with an oblique bend/release that segues to a truncated version of the C-major riff and a B/D double stop, which implies the V (G) chord.

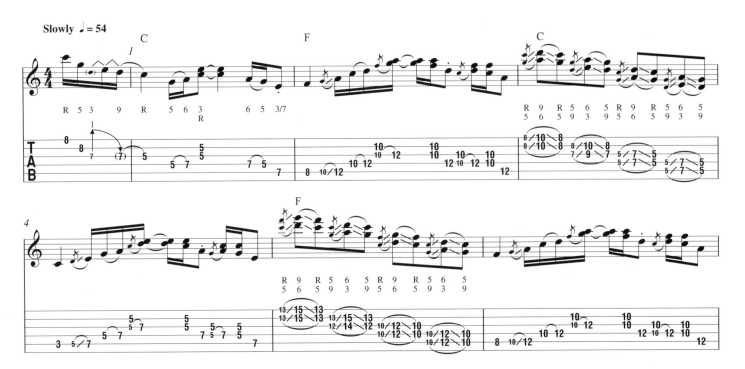

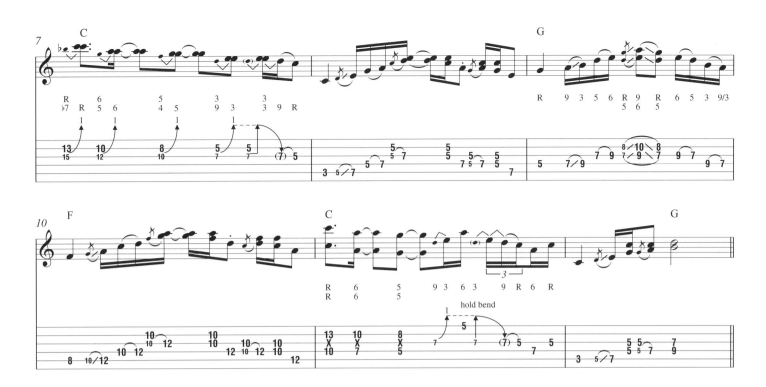

JAM #57: TWO-BAR LEAD/RHYTHM ALTERNATIONS

This example expands on Jam #56's one-bar alternations, juggling two bars of lead playing with two bars of C-major riffing throughout the Jam's 12 bars. The lead playing consists of single-note lines derived from the C major pentatonic (C–D–E–G–A), F major (F–G–A–B♭–C–D–E), and F major pentatonic (F–G–A–C–D) scales, as well as "sliding 6ths" that target G major and F major chord tones (measures 9–10).

MEASURES 1–4: The Jam commences with a slippery C major pentatonic line that works its way down the scale, targeting the root of the IV (F) chord on beat 1 of measure 2. Here, the passage mimics the Jam's main riff via notes from the F major pentatonic scale. After two bars of lead playing, the C major riff is introduced and played twice (measures 3–4).

MEASURES 5–8: Measure 5 begins with a phrase that recalls the opening phrase of the Jam, transitioning to a quick double-stop passage on the "and" of beat 3. The lick re-emphasizes the F major harmony on beat 1 of measure 6 via the fourth-string root note, which is followed by a bass-string passage that is derived from the F major scale. Notice that the last note of the phrase, C, anticipates the return of the C-major riff (measures 7–8).

MEASURES 9–12: Sliding minor- and major-6th intervals are employed in measures 9–10, where they target G (G–B–D) and F (F–A–C) chord tones, respectively. Meanwhile, the Jam's turnaround (measures 11–12) is handled by the C-major riff (for the I chord) and a B/D dyad (the 3rd and 5th of G [the V chord], respectively).

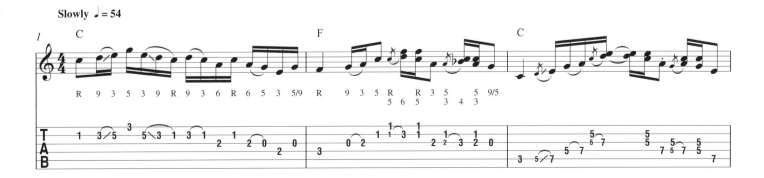

99

 # JAM #58: ONE-BAR RHYTHM/LEAD ALTERNATIONS

The sequence of the lead/rhythm alternations from Jams 56–57 is reversed in this example. Here, one bar of riffing is continuously alternated with one bar of lead playing. The lead lines are a case study in major-pentatonic soloing and have a distinct country flavor, although the Jam still retains much of its R&B sound. The I and IV chords are outlined with the C major pentatonic (C–D–E–G–A) and F major pentatonic (F–G–A–C–D) scales, respectively, played in various positions of the fretboard.

MEASURES 1–4: Following one bar of the C-major riff, the IV chord is implied via a run up the F major pentatonic scale. The target note, C, played on beat 4, anticipates the return of the I chord by one beat. The C-major riff is restated in measure 3, followed by a run up the C major pentatonic, which is a variation of the line played in measure 2, lending continuity to the Jam.

MEASURES 5–8: The F-major riff is played in measure 5 and is followed by a country-style passage that features an oblique bend and heavily targets F major chord tones. The I-chord change in measures 7–8 follows a similar riff-lead sequence; however, this lead passage (measure 8) moves up the scale following the oblique bend, finishing on the root of the impending V chord—the G note at fret 8 of the second string.

MEASURES 9–12: In measures 9–10, the G and F (V and IV) chord changes are handled by the G-major riff and a 10th-position run up the F major pentatonic scale, respectively. This passage leads to the turnaround (measures 11–12), which features another repetition of the C-major riff and a B/D dyad—the 3rd and 5th of the G (V) chord, respectively.

JAM #59: TWO-BAR RHYTHM/LEAD ALTERNATIONS

In this Jam, two bars of riffing alternate with two bars of soloing throughout the 12-bar form. All of the lead playing occurs over the I (C) chord, with notes predominantly supplied by the C major pentatonic scale (C–D–E–G–A). Although the tempo is slow (54 bpm), the notes come at you relatively fast due to the 16th-note rhythms.

MEASURES 1–4: The main riff covers the I (C) and IV (F) chords in measures 1–2. At measure 3, however, the playing segues to a swift C major pentatonic line that moves from 10th position to 13th position over the course of the measure. In measure 4, an oblique bend emphasizes C major chord tones (E and G) before flowing smoothly down the scale. The passage's final note, E, creates an efficient, half-step transition to the root of the F-major riff in measure 5.

MEASURES 5–8: Following two bars of the F-major riff (measures 5–6), a two-notes-per-string C6 arpeggio outlines the I-chord harmony. Once the line arrives at string 1, notes are borrowed from the C major scale (C–D–E–F–G–A–B) to shift the pattern down to eight-position, where a descending version of the arpeggio is played.

MEASURES 9–12: In measures 9–10, the G- and F-major riffs handle the V and IV chord changes, respectively. For the turnaround (measures 11–12), a lead line is carved from the C major pentatonic scale, featuring a repetitive double-stop passage that mimics the main riff. On beat 3 of measure 12, a G major triad shape handles the V chord, signaling a return to the top of the form.

🔊 JAM #60: RANDOM RHYTHM/LEAD ALTERNATIONS

The alternations in this Jam are arranged randomly, resulting in the following intervals: one bar of rhythm, three bars of lead, one bar of rhythm, two bars of lead, one bar of rhythm, two bars of lead, and two bars of rhythm. As you can see, the arrangement skews heavily toward lead playing. The note sources for the lead phrases include the C major pentatonic (C–D–E–G–A), C composite blues (C–D–Eb–E–F–Gb–G–A–Bb), F major pentatonic (F–G–A–C–D), and G major pentatonic/Aeolian hybrid (G–A–Bb–B–C–D–Eb–E–F) scales.

MEASURES 1–4: Following one bar of the C-major riff, a three-measure phrase is played over the IV (F) and I (C) chord changes. The passages begins with ascent of the extended form of the F major pentatonic scale, followed in measure 3 by a country-style phrase that is derived from the C major pentatonic scale and features an oblique bend. In measure 4, the C composite blues scale provides the notes for a phrase that revolves around a pair of whole-step bends.

MEASURES 5–8: The second appearance of the IV chord (measure 5) is indicated by the F-major riff and further emphasized via a run up the F major pentatonic scale (measure 6). The final note of the run, F, the root of the IV chord, facilitates an efficient, half-step transition to the 3rd of the I (C) chord, E. Here, a C major arpeggio pattern and the C major pentatonic scale are used to outline the new (C) harmony, followed by a restatement of the C-major riff (measure 8).

MEASURES 9–12: To outline the V (G) chord in measure 9, an ascending phrase, derived from the G major pentatonic/Aeolian hybrid scale, is played in a repetitive, eighth note/16th-note triplet rhythm that emphasizes chord tones (G and D) on each downbeat. This passage leads to a legato phrase that descends the F major pentatonic scale (measure 10), followed by a restatement of the C-major riff and a G/D dyad for the I–V change of the turnaround, respectively.

CHAPTER 11: FOLK/ROCK STRUMMING AND EMBELLISHMENT
THE RESOURCES

CHORDS

G

C/G

C

Cadd4

Cadd2

D

Dsus4

Dsus2

SCALES

G Major Pentatonic (Open Position):
G–A–B–D–E
(1–2–3–5–6)

G Major Pentatonic (Extended Form)

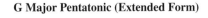

3fr

G Composite Blues Scale (Open Position):
G–A–B♭–B–C–D♭–D–E–F
(1–2–♭3–♮3–4–♭5–♮5–6–♭7)

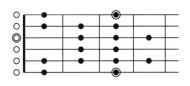

G Composite Blues Scale (2nd Position)

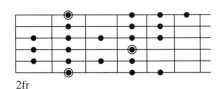

2fr

G Composite Blues Scale (Extended Form)

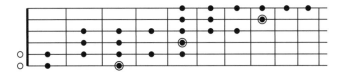

G Major:
G–A–B–C–D–E–F♯
(1–2–3–4–5–6–7)

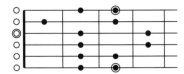

C Major Pentatonic (Open Position):
C–D–E–G–A
(1–2–3–5–6)

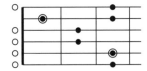

C Major Pentatonic (5th Position)

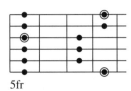

5fr

C Major Pentatonic (Extended Form)

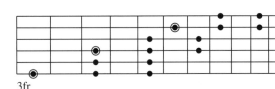

3fr

C Composite Blues Scale (Open Position):
C–D–E♭–E–F–G♭–G–A–B♭
(1–2–♭3–♮3–4–♭5–♮5–6–♭7)

C Composite Blues Scale (4th Position)

C Major:
C–D–E–F–G–A–B
(1–2–3–4–5–6–7)

D Major Pentatonic (Open Position):
D–E–F♯–A–B
(1–2–3–5–6)

D Major Pentatonic (2nd Position)

D Major Pentatonic (7th Position)

D Composite Blues Scale:
D–E–F–F♯–G–A♭–A–B–C
(1–2–♭3–♮3–4–♭5–♮5–6–♭7)

JAM #61: THE 16-BAR FORM

This arrangement deviates slightly from the 12-bar blues of the previous Jams. While standard I–IV–V changes are used, played here in the key of G (G–C–D), the length of some of the changes has been extended. Instead of one-bar intervals of the V and IV chords in measures 9 and 10, respectively, standard practice in a 12-bar blues, the chords are held for two measures apiece.

Also extended is the final appearance of the I chord, which increases from two measures to four. The result is a 16-bar form: I (four bars), IV (two bars), I (two bars), V (two bars), IV (two bars), and I (four bars). Although each chord change contains brief embellishment, the underlying harmony remains constant. For example, although the G chord is briefly embellished by a C/G voicing, the harmony (G major) remains static.

MEASURES 1–4: The Jam opens with a two-bar strumming pattern that features a common open G chord, brief embellishment (the C/G chord), and a bass-string riff. The short, three-note riff leads to another repetition of the summing pattern (measures 3–4), creating a repetitive E–G–E–G bass-string melody. The G note, of course, is the root of the G chord voicing and should be fretted with your ring finger throughout.

MEASURES 5–8: In measures 5–6, an open C chord (the IV chord) mimics the G-chord strumming pattern, with a Cadd4 voicing providing the embellishment. Also, a short Cadd2–C–Cadd2 progression is played in lieu of the single-note riff. In measures 7–8, the G-chord pattern returns for one repetition before segueing to the V (D) chord (measure 9).

MEASURES 9–12: The D-chord strumming pattern is similar to that used for the C chord. With an open D chord supplying the underlying harmony, a Dsus4 chord provides the embellishment in the first measure of the pattern. Meanwhile, a Dsus2–D–Dsus2 progression is substituted for the bass-string riff that was featured in the G-chord pattern. In measures 11–12, the C-chord pattern returns for one more repetition.

MEASURES 13–16: The Jam concludes with two repetitions of the G-chord pattern. Unlike some of the previous Jams, the V chord does not make an appearance for the turnaround. Instead, the I (G) chord is played for four measures.

JAM #62: ONE-BAR LEAD/RHYTHM ALTERNATIONS

This Jam applies the folk/rock strumming pattern to a series of one-bar alternations. After opening with one measure of lead, the first measure of the two-bar strumming pattern is played, with the two parts alternating throughout. Due to the one-bar intervals, the second half of the strumming patterns are unnecessary, yet the truncated patterns work well nonetheless. Meanwhile, the lead parts are played (mostly) in open position and culled from the G major pentatonic (G–A–B–D–E), C major pentatonic (C–D–E–G–A), and D major pentatonic (D–E–F#–A–B) scales.

MEASURES 1–4: The Jam opens with back-to-back alternations of G major pentatonic phrases and one-bar versions of the G-major strumming pattern. Beats 1–3 of the opening lick are restated in measure 3 before the latter continues its descent of the scale, arriving on the open low E string for its transition to the G-major strumming pattern (measure 4).

MEASURES 5–8: The C major pentatonic lick in measure 5 opens with a nod to measure 1's phrase before continuing its ascent of the scale. The open high E string is played on the "and" of beat 4 to facilitate transition to the C-major strumming pattern (E is the 3rd of C major). In measure 7, the lick from measure 1 is restated to lend continuity to the Jam and followed by another measure of the G-major strumming pattern.

MEASURES 9–12: In measures 9–10, the arrival of the V (D) chord is implied by a run up the D major pentatonic scale and one measure of the D-major strumming pattern, respectively. Meanwhile, the IV (C) chord is implied via a slippery legato phrase rooted in the C major pentatonic scale (measure 11) and one measure of the C-major strumming pattern (measure 12).

MEASURES 13–16: The Jam concludes with ascending and descending G major pentatonic phrases that alternate with one measure of the G-major strumming pattern. In both instances, the chord's 5th, D, is used as the transitional note. In measure 13, the D note at fret 3 of second string connects the lead and rhythm parts, whereas the open D string links measures 15–16.

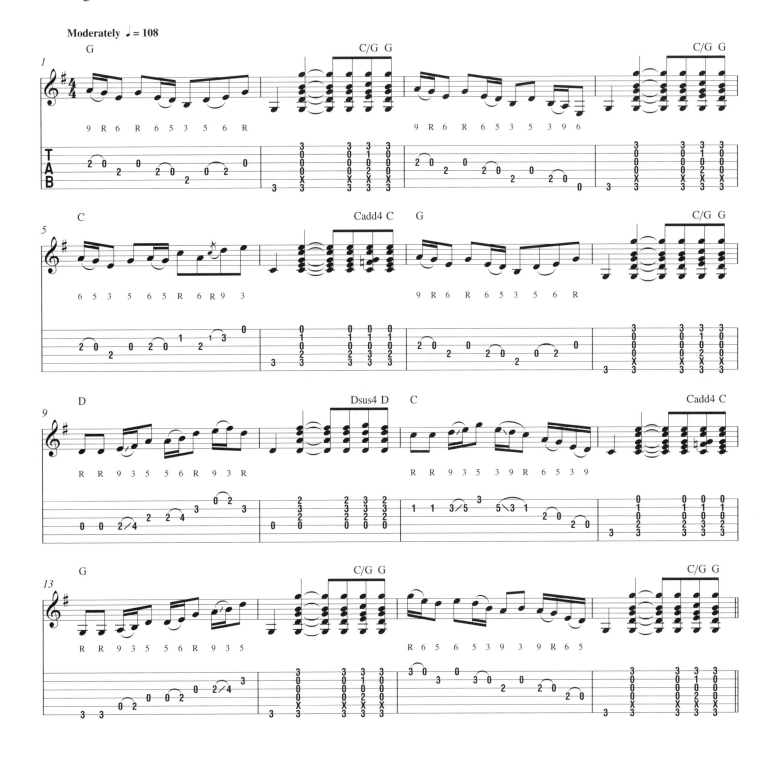

JAM #63: TWO-BAR LEAD/RHYTHM ALTERNATIONS

In this example, the one-bar lead/rhythm alternations from Jam #62 have been extended to two bars. As a result, the rhythm parts are performed as their original, two-bar patterns. Meanwhile, the lead phrases feature a recurring pedal-steel-style oblique bend that is transposed to fit the harmony of each chord change, lending a distinct country sound to the Jam.

MEASURES 1–4: The oblique bend kicks of the Jam, outlining G major chord tones (B and D, the 3rd and 5th, respectively) before transitioning from the G major pentatonic scale (measure 1) to the G composite blues scale (measure 2). The two-bar phrase transitions to two bars of the G-major strumming pattern with assistance from the open B string.

MEASURES 5–8: The extended form of the C major pentatonic scale provides the pitches for the two-bar phrase that implies the IV-chord change in measures 5–6. After a one-octave excursion up the scale, the oblique-bend makes another appearance, played here in the key of C. In measure 7–8, the G-major strumming pattern is employed to handle the return of the I (G) chord.

MEASURES 9–12: In measures 9–10, a two-bar phrase begins with a climb up the D composite blues scale (D–E–F–F♯–G–A♭–A–B–C) before transitioning to the oblique-bend motif, which is derived from the D major pentatonic scale (D–E–F♯–A–B). This phrase is followed by the first (and only) appearance of the C-major strumming pattern (measures 11–12).

MEASURES 13–16: The final four measures of the Jam kick off with an ascending/descending line that, outside of one B♭ note (the minor 3rd), is derived entirely from the extended form of the G major pentatonic scale (G–A–B–D–E). (*Note:* The inclusion of B♭, played here at fret 6 of the sixth string, briefly hints at the G composite blues scale.) Again, notice the presence of the oblique-bend motif in measure 14, which perpetuates the theme that was first established in measure 1. In measures 15–16, the Jam wraps up with another repetition of the G-major strumming pattern.

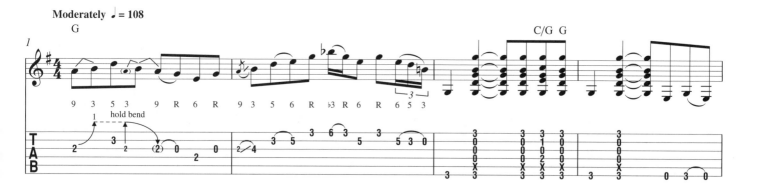

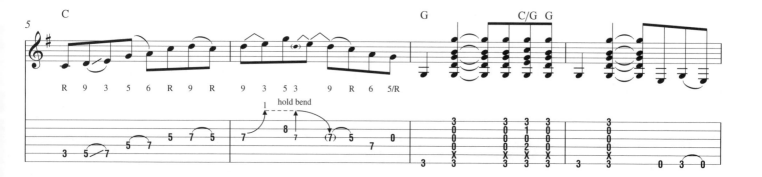

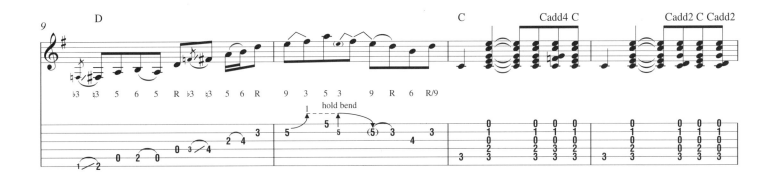

🔊 JAM #64: ONE-BAR RHYTHM/LEAD ALTERNATIONS

The rhythm/lead alternations that comprise this Jam are inversions of the one-bar lead/rhythm alternations from Jam #62. The strumming patterns are truncated versions of the two-bar patterns that were introduced in Jam #61, while the leads are mostly played in open position and derived from a plethora of scales, including G major (G–A–B–C–D–E–F♯), G composite blues (G–A–B♭–B–C–D♭–D–E–F), C major (C–D–E–F–G–A–B), C composite blues (C–D–E♭–E–F–G♭–G–A–B♭), and D composite blues (D–E–F–F♯–G–A♭–A–B–C).

MEASURES 1–4: Following one bar of the G-major strumming pattern, a double-stop motif, culled from the G major scale, is introduced in measure 2. A variation of this phrase is played in measure 4, following another measure of the strumming pattern. What differentiates this phrase, however, is the second half of the passage, which briefly moves to third position for a G composite blues scale lick.

MEASURES 5–8: The IV (C) chord harmony is handled by a measure of the C-major strumming pattern (measure 5) and a variation of the double-stop motif, played here with notes from the C major scale (measure 6). Note the open low E string at the end of the phrase, which facilitates the transition to the G-major strumming pattern (measure 7). In measure 8, a pull-off passage juxtaposes chromatically ascending notes (A–B♭–B–C) and the open G string, leading strongly to the root of the V (D) chord (measure 9).

MEASURES 9–12: Following a measure of the D-major strumming pattern (measure 9), a D composite blues scale lick flows down strings 1–5, concluding with an A-to-B hammer-on that moves stepwise to the root of the IV (C) chord (measure 11). The C-major harmony is handled by one bar of the strumming pattern and a descending lick that mimics the phrase from two bars earlier, respectively. Similar to its predecessor, the B♭–A pull-off at the end of the phrase moves stepwise to the root of the I (G) chord (measure 13).

MEASURES 13–16: The Jam's final four measures kick off with a measure of the G-major strumming pattern, followed by a descending G composite blues scale lick that is heavy on chromaticism and open strings. Measures 15–16 bring the Jam to its conclusion via the full, two-bar version of the G-major strumming pattern—the only time the Jam doesn't alternate in one-bar intervals.

JAM #65: TWO-BAR RHYTHM/LEAD ALTERNATIONS

In this example, the one-bar alternations from Jam #64 have been extended, resulting in continuous two-measure tradeoffs of rhythm and lead parts. The rhythm parts are comprised of the two-bar G-major, C-major, and D-major strumming patterns and offset by lead phrases that seamlessly blend notes from the minor pentatonic, major pentatonic, and blues scales.

MEASURES 1–4: The Jam commences with the two-measure G-major strumming pattern. The open low E string at the end of the phrase facilitates the fret-hand shift necessary for the subsequent lead phrase, which is derived from the third-position pattern of the G composite blues scale. At the end of measure 4, a half-step hammer-on creates a three-note chromatic passage (Bb-B–C) that leads smoothly to the IV (C) chord (measure 5).

MEASURES 5–8: Following two bars of C-major strumming (measures 5–6), a six-string excursion up the fretboard commences, deriving its notes from the extended form of the G composite blues scale, with emphasis on its minor qualities (i.e., the minor 3rd, B♭). On beat 4 of measure 8, a half-step, C-to-C♯ bend creates chromatic movement to the root of the V (D) chord. Even though the latter is played two octaves lower, the transitional effect is nearly the same.

MEASURES 9–12: In measures 9–10, the two-measure D-major strumming pattern handles the V chord, followed in measure 11–12 by a slippery C composite blues scale phrase that briefly slides up to third position before descending the scale in open position. Notice how the presence of the note B♭ (the ♭7th of C) on beat 3 of measure 11 lends a dominant (C7) flavor to the passage.

MEASURES 13–16: In measures 13–14, the G-major strumming pattern is employed for the return of the I chord, followed by a two-measure run up a scale that starts with pitches from the G major pentatonic scale (measure 15) and ends with a hammer/slide/pull figure from the G composite blues scale (measure 16). Because the V chord is not used in this Jam to indicate a turnaround, the phrase resolves to the root of the G chord.

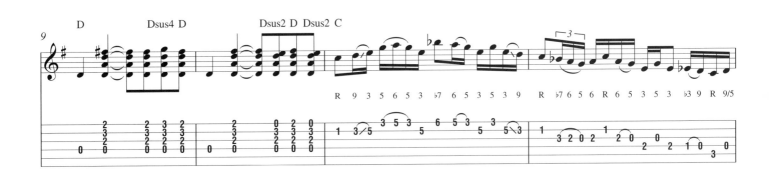

JAM #66: RANDOM RHYTHM/LEAD ALTERNATIONS

In this Jam, the alternations are arranged randomly, with heavy emphasis on lead playing. In fact, no fewer than 12 of the Jam's 16 bars contain soloing. The lead phrases themselves have a distinct country sound due, in large part, to the presence of pedal-steel-style bending. Melodically, the phrases are constructed from notes of the G composite blues (G–A–B♭–B–C–D♭–D–E–F), G major pentatonic (G–A–B–D–E), C composite blues (C–D–E♭–E–F–G♭–G–A–B♭), C major pentatonic (C–D–E–G–A), and D major pentatonic (D–E–F♯–A–B) scales.

MEASURES 1–4: The Jam commences with a pedal-steel-style phrase that is reminiscent of the one from Jam #63. Be sure to maintain the whole-step bend while you play the fretted notes on strings 1–2. On beat 3 of measure 2, the phrase transitions from open position to third position, where it concludes with a minor-sounding pull-off passage that contrasts with the major flavor of the pedal-steel passage. The three-bar lick is punctuated in measure 4 with one bar of the G-major strumming pattern.

MEASURES 5–8: Measures 5–6 feature a C composite blues scale lick that imparts a distinct dominant sound to the C major harmony via the presence of the note B♭ (the ♭7th), which is tied across the bar and re-struck on beat 2 of measure 6. To facilitate the transition to the G-major strumming pattern in measure 7, the open G string is played in lieu of the fretted G note at fret 5 of the fourth string. The strum pattern is cut short, however, in favor of a four-note line that ascends to the root of the G major harmony (beat 1 of measure 8). Here, the lick from measure 3 is mimicked before shifting up to seventh position for the forthcoming pedal-steel phrase (measure 9).

MEASURES 9–12: The pedal-steel lick in measure 9 is a note-for-note copy of the lick from measure 1, only it's played here in the key of D (for the V chord), and is followed by a bar of D major pentatonic soloing (measure 10). For the arrival of the IV (C) chord (measure 11), the pedal-steel lick is transposed down one step, to the key of C major, and followed by descent of the C major pentatonic scale (measure 12). At the end of the phrase, the open A string is played in lieu of the fretted A note at fret 5 of the sixth string to facilitate the transition to the G-major strumming pattern in measure 13.

MEASURES 13–16: Following two measures of the G-major strumming pattern (measures 13–14), an open-position bluegrass lick is carved from the G composite blues scale to bring the Jam to its conclusion. Notice that the phrase's first four notes (G, A, B♭, and B) are restated at the onset of measure 16, only an octave higher.

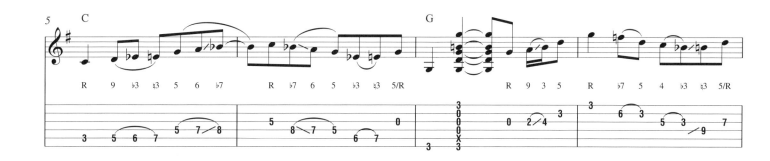

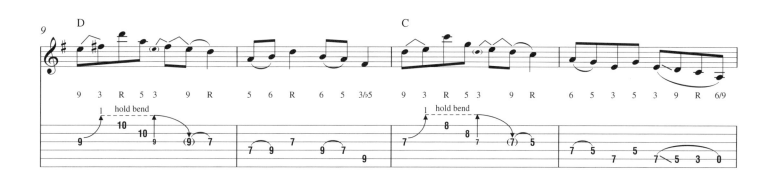

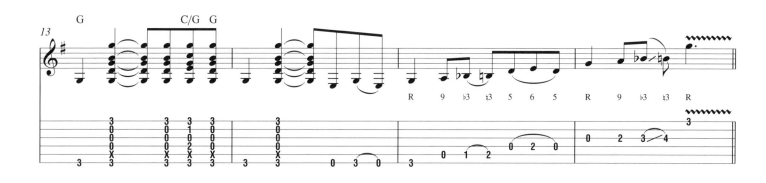

CHAPTER 12: PERCUSSIVE POP/ROCK GROOVE
THE RESOURCES

CHORDS

G5   Csus2   D   Dsus4

 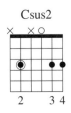  

SCALES

G Major Pentatonic (Open Position):
G–A–B–D–E
(1–2–3–5–6)

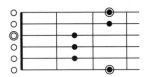

G Major Pentatonic (Extended Form)

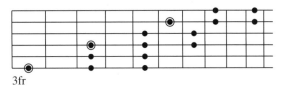

3fr

G Composite Blues Scale (Open Position):
G–A–B♭–B–C–D♭–D–E–F
(1–2–♭3–♮3–4–♭5–♮5–6–♭7)

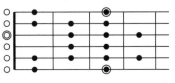

G Composite Blues Scale (2nd Position)

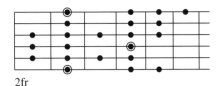

2fr

G Composite Blues Scale (11th Position)

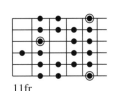

11fr

G Mixolydian:
G–A–B–C–D–E–F
(1–2–3–4–5–6–♭7)

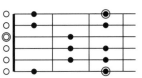

C Major Pentatonic (Open Position):
C–D–E–G–A
(1–2–3–5–6)

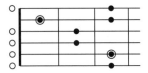

C Major Pentatonic (Extended Form)

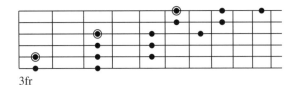

3fr

C Composite Blues Scale:
C–D–E♭–E–F–G♭–G–A–B♭
(1–2–♭3–♮3–4–♭5–♮5–6–♭7)

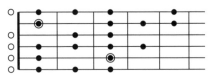

C Mixolydian:
C–D–E–F–G–A–B♭
(1–2–3–4–5–6–♭7)

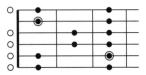

D Major Pentatonic:
D–E–F♯–A–B
(1–2–3–5–6)

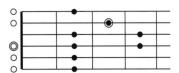

D Composite Blues Scale:
D–E–F–F♯–G–A♭–A–B–C
(1–2–♭3–♮3–4–♭5–♮5–6–♭7)

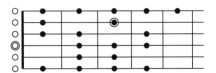

JAM #67: THE 12-BAR FORM

This example diverges a bit from previous Jams. While it does feature a standard set of 12-bar blues changes, the chords are plucked exclusively with the fingers of the pick hand, in a percussive style. Employing common open-position G5, Csus2, and D major voicings for the I, IV, and V changes, respectively, the thumb percussively strikes the sixth string on beats 2 and 4 of each measure to mimic a drummer's hi-hat. This approach enables the solo performer to keep time and establish a groove while playing the changes.

This type of playing has been used by guitarists of disparate musical styles, including Nuno Bettencourt (Extreme), John Mayer, and Andy McKee, among many others. The I (G5) and IV (Csus2) chords are voiced similarly and employ the same rhythmic pattern, while the V (D) chord includes brief embellishment (the Dsus4–D change).

MEASURES 1–4: The Jam's opening four measures contain a static G major (I chord) harmony. The rhythm is played in a repetitive two-measure pattern that features sixth-string bass (root) notes that precede chordal plucks on beats 1 and 3 of each measure, as well as percussive "slaps" on beats 2 and 4.

MEASURES 5–8: For the IV chord (measures 5–6), a Csus2 chord voicing is performed with the same rhythmic pattern that was used for the I chord. Notice that these two voicings, G5 and Csus2, differ only in their bass notes. Therefore, to change chords, simply shift your middle finger from string 6 to string 5. Following two measures of the IV chord, the G5 pattern returns for the I chord (measures 7–8).

MEASURES 9–12: In measure 9, an open D chord handles the V-chord change and features brief chordal embellishment (Dsus4–D) on beat 3. In measure 10, a shortened (one-bar) Csus2 pattern is employed for the IV-chord change, followed by two more measures of the G5 pattern, which brings the Jam to a close.

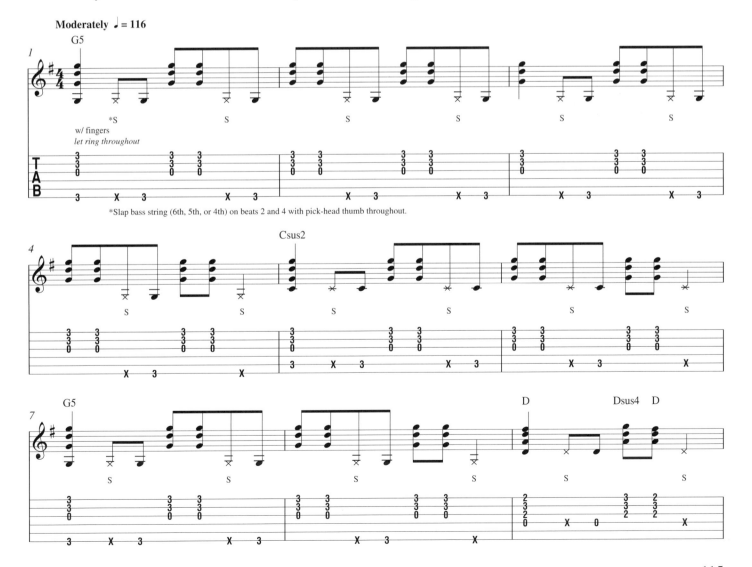

115

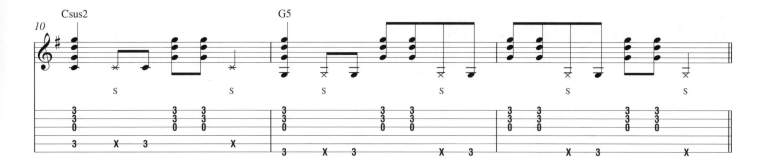

JAM #68: ONE-BAR LEAD/RHYTHM ALTERNATIONS

In this example, the percussive rhythm patterns that were introduced in Jam #67 are shortened and alternated, every measure, with one-bar lead phrases. A couple of the more notable features of the lead phrases included melodic octave shapes and dyads that are performed in quarter-note triplet rhythms, both of which are transposed and restated to lend cohesion to the Jam.

MEASURES 1–4: The Jam opens with octave shapes that perform a melody that consist entirely of Gmaj7 chord tones (G–B–D–F#). In measure 2, a one-bar version of the G5 percussive pattern is played. However, notice that, on the "and" of beat 4, a G octave shape is played as a pickup to the octave-shape melody in measure 3. Here, B-to-C octave slides bookend a D octave shape, which is held for two beats (i.e., a half note). In measure 4, the Jam returns to the G5 rhythm pattern in anticipation of the IV (Csus2) chord (measure 5).

MEASURES 5–8: In measure 5, octave shapes recreate the melody from measure 1, only it's played here in the key of C. Following a measure of a truncated Csus2 rhythm pattern (measure 6), dyads are performed exclusively along strings 3–4 to outline the I (G5) chord harmony, using notes from the G major scale (G–A–B–C–D–E–F#). The dyads are punctuated with a return to the one-bar version of the G5 rhythm pattern (measure 8).

MEASURES 9–12: The D major pentatonic scale (D–E–F#–A–B) provides the notes for the double-stop phrase that is performed over the V chord (measure 9). This lick is followed by another measure of the Csus2 percussive pattern (measure 10) and a variation of the dyad phrase from measure 7, played, once again, with notes from the G major scale. Notice that, like the original phrase, the dyads flow seamlessly into the G5 pattern (measure 12) due to the presence of the open G and D strings at the end of the phrase.

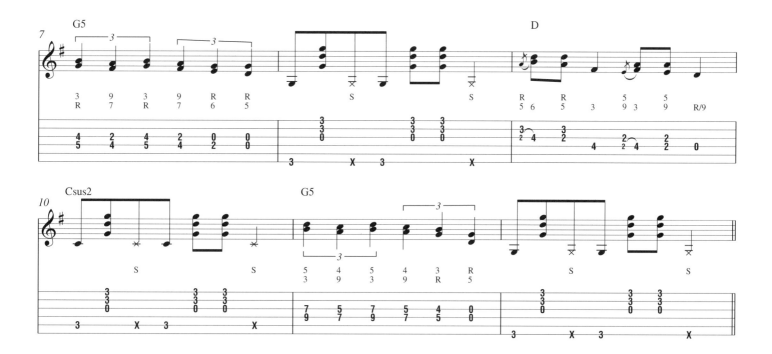

JAM #69: TWO-BAR LEAD/RHYTHM ALTERNATIONS

This Jam involves continuously alternating two bars of lead and two bars of the percussive rhythm pattern that was introduced in Jam #67. The lead phrases feature a couple of disparate approaches. The first approach is more rhythmic in natural and involves double stops sliding up and down the fretboard in a repetitive rhythm (two 16th notes followed by a dotted quarter note). The second approach is more typical of lead playing and involves single-note lines outlining the V (D) and IV (Csus2) chords (measures 9–10).

MEASURES 1–4: In measure 1, a D/G double stop is slid up and down a whole step on beats 1–2, followed on beats 3–4 by a G/D double stop that is slid along strings 3–4 (and requires a finger adjustment). Notice that the second double stop is merely an inversion of the first. In measure 2, the double-stop motif from measure 1 is transposed down one octave, resulting in slides along strings 4–5 for the D/G double stop and strings 5–6 for the G/D double stop. The final two measures of the I chord are handled by the two-measure version of the G5 percussive pattern.

MEASURES 5–8: Measures 5–6 feature a variation of the double-stop motif from measures 1–2, although the shapes have been adjust to fit the new (IV chord) harmony. To facilitate the transition to the G5 percussive pattern (measures 7–8), the open low E sting makes an appearance at the end of the double-stop passage.

MEASURES 9–12: In measure 9, the D major pentatonic scale (D–E–F♯–A–B) provides the pitches for a short single-note line that outlines the V (D) chord harmony, followed in measure 10 by a C composite blues scale (C–D–E♭–E–F–G♭–G–A–B♭) passage that handles the IV chord. To cap the Jam, the G5 percussive pattern makes a final appearance (measures 11–12).

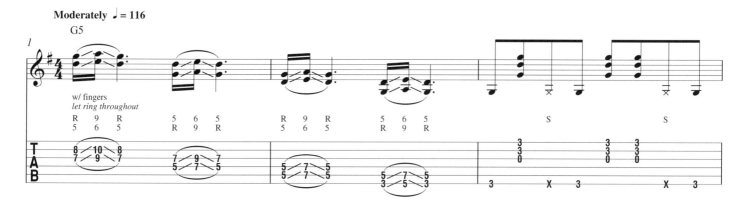

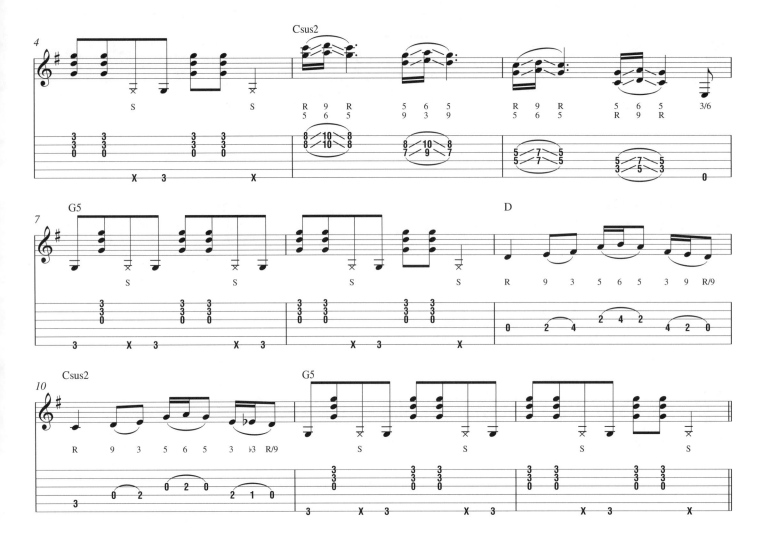

JAM #70: ONE-BAR RHYTHM/LEAD ALTERNATIONS

This Jam returns to the one-bar alternations that were featured in Jam #68, although in inverse order. Here, one-bar versions of the percussive rhythm pattern alternate with one bar of lead throughout the 12-bar form. The phrases, played over the G major and Csus2 harmonies, are rooted in the open-position and extended patterns of the G major pentatonic (G–A–B–D–E) and C major pentatonic (C–D–E–G–A) scales.

MEASURES 1–4: Following one bar of the G5 percussive pattern, an open-position G major pentatonic phrase is launched from the sixth-string root (on the "and" of beat 4). For the sake of finger efficiency, keep your ring and pinky fingers planted on fret 3 of strings 2–1, respectively, while you play the passage. In measures 3–4, one measure of the G5 pattern is followed by another open-position G major pentatonic lick. Again, keep your ring and pinky fingers in place so as to efficiently voice the forthcoming Csus2 chord.

MEASURES 5–8: The Csus2 (IV chord) harmony is handled by a measure of the percussive pattern (measure 5) and a descending C major pentatonic phrase (measure 6), respectively. Notice that the open G string at the end of the phrase anticipates the impending G5 chord. Following another measure of the G5 rhythm pattern (measure 7), a bass-string run up the extended form of the G major pentatonic scale connects the I (G5) chord to the V (D) chord. Again, note how the open D string anticipates the chord change (and helps transition to the open D chord in measure 9).

MEASURES 9–12: After the percussive pattern implies the V (D) chord change in measure 9, a run up the extended form of the C major pentatonic scale mimics the phrase from measure 8—albeit with a hint of syncopation, courtesy of the tie the connects beats 2 and 3. At the end of the phrase, the open G string is employed, once again, to anticipate the G5 pattern, which wraps up the Jam (measures 11–12).

JAM #71: TWO-BAR RHYTHM/LEAD ALTERNATIONS

The one-bar rhythm/lead alternations from Jam #70 have been extended to two bars here. Now, two bars of the percussive rhythm pattern alternate with two measures of lead playing throughout the 12-bar form. All of the lead phrases are played over the same harmony, G5, and derive their notes from the open-position, third-position, or 12th-position patterns of the G composite blues scale (G–A–Bb–B–C–Db–D–E–F).

MEASURES 1–4: After two measures of the G5 rhythm pattern introduce the Jam, a two-bar, open-position G composite blues scale lick ascends/descends strings 1–5 via hammer-ons, pull-offs, and slides. Notice that the lick actually commences on the "and" of beat 4 of measure 2, where the open B string is hammered onto the D and E notes at frets 3 and 5 of the second string, respectively.

MEASURES 5–8: The IV-chord harmony (measures 5–6) is handled by the Csus2 rhythm pattern, leading to a third-position G composite blues scale lick that revolves around a recurring third-string, Bb-to-B (minor-to-major) hammer-on. At the end of the phrase, a fourth-string pull-off flows seamlessly from the root of the I chord (G5) to the open D string—the root of the V chord.

MEASURES 9–12: The V and IV chords in measures 9–10 are played with one-bar versions of the D and Csus2 rhythm patterns, respectively, followed in measures 11–12 by a phrase that outlines the I chord. The phrase, rooted in the 12th-position pattern of the G composite blues scale, is played in a repetitive four-note sequence and resolves to the G note located at fret 12 of the third string.

JAM #72: RANDOM RHYTHM/LEAD ALTERNATIONS

The alternations in this example are arranged in random fashion. This arrangement sounds less predictable than the one- and two-bar intervals used in Jams 67–71 and is an example of the type of "on the fly" (i.e., improvised) tradeoffs that you should strive for.

Here, two measures of lead playing are followed, in order, by one bar of rhythm, two bars of lead, three bars of rhythm, three bars of lead, and one bar of rhythm. The note sources for the lead lines included the G composite blues scale (G–A–Bb–B–C–Db–D–E–F), the G Mixolydian mode (G–A–B–C–D–E–F), C composite blues scale (C–D–Eb–E–F–Gb–G–A–Bb), C Mixolydian mode (C–D–E–F–G–A–Bb), and D composite blues scale (D–E–F–F#–G–Ab–A–B–C).

MEASURES 1–4: To open the Jam, a countrified lick descends the G composite blues scale, hitting nearly every pitch of the nine-note scale. The phrase ends with the open D string, which helps in the transition to the G5 rhythm pattern (measure 3). The final note of the rhythm pattern, G (fret 3, string 6), is then tied into measure 4, where an open-position run up the entire G Mixolydian mode outlines the final bar of the I chord.

MEASURES 5–8: In measure 5, the Mixolydian lick from the previous measure is transposed to the key of C (for the IV-chord harmony). However, the open B string is played as the phrase's last note, thereby creating a chromatic (A–B♭–B) passage that leads to the root of the Csus2 chord in measure 6, where the one-bar version of the rhythm pattern is performed. In measures 7–8, the G5 pattern is reprised and played as the full, two-measure version.

MEASURES 9–12: The V (D) chord change in measure 9 is outlined with a chromatic-laden phrase that jumps from third position to first position at its midpoint. This phrase is mimicked in measure 10, where it has been transposed down one step to outline the IV (Csus2) chord. The arrival of the I chord (measures 11) is handled by an open-position G composite blues scale phrase that emphasizes open strings before giving way to one more bar of the G5 rhythm pattern (measure 12).

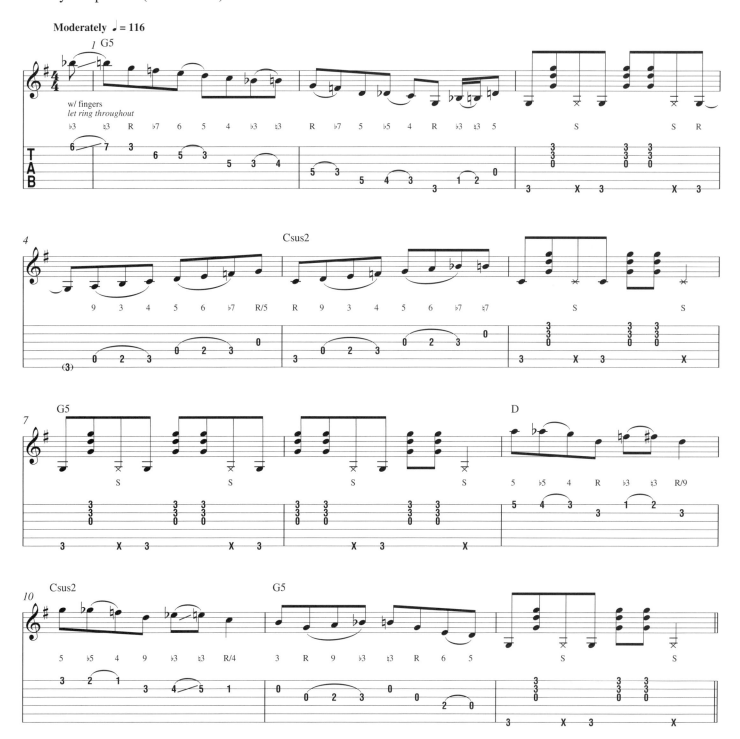

SECTION III: JAZZ

CHAPTER 13: JUMP-BLUES RIFF

THE RESOURCES

CHORDS

G6   C6   D6   E♭9   D9

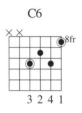
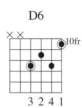
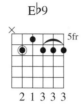
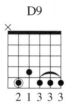

SCALES

G Composite Blues Scale (2nd Position):
G–A–B♭–B–C–D♭–D–E–F
(1–2–♭3–♮3–4–♭5–♮5–6–♭7)

G Composite Blues Scale (4th Position)

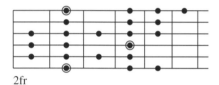

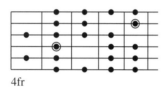

C Composite Blues Scale (2nd Position):
C–D–E♭–E–F–G♭–G–A–B♭
(1–2–♭3–♮3–4–♭5–♮5–6–♭7)

C Composite Blues Scale (7th Position)

C Composite Blues Scale (9th Position)

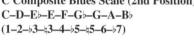

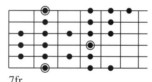

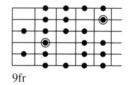

D Composite Blues Scale (4th Position):
D–E–F–F♯–G–A♭–A–B–C
(1–2–♭3–♮3–4–♭5–♮5–6–♭7)

D Composite Blues Scale (9th Position)

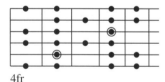

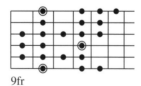

 ## JAM #73: THE 12-BAR FORM

The riff employed in the next six examples combines a single-note line with a major-sixth chord "stab," which is used to punctuate each repetition. This type of riff is wildly popular in the jump-blues idiom (a combination of traditional blues and swing/jazz). The single-note phrase is derived from the composite blues scale respective to the chord change and moves from a minor-to-major hammer-on (string 3) to a 5th-to-6th hammer-on (string 2) and, finally, to the root of the of the chord (string 1). In true jazz fashion, the major sixth chord arrives on the upbeat—the "and" of beat 2. After the riff is repeated four times for the I (G6) chord, it's moved to eighth and tenth positions for the IV (C6) and V (D6) chords, respectively.

The Jam is constructed from a standard set of blues changes (I–IV–V) and concludes with a turnaround lick that juxtaposes root notes (string 1) and a descending chromatic line (string 2), which leads to the V chord, played here as a dominant ninth (D9) voicing and preceded by a half step (E♭9). Although the turnaround implies a more sophisticated G7–G6–G+–G5–E♭9–D9 progression, the fundamental changes, I–V (G6–D6), remain intact.

MEASURES 1–4: The first four measures of the Jam feature four repetitions of the I-chord riff. Since the first repetition of the riff is preceded by a pickup, the same approach is used for the IV (C6) chord; that is, the single-note line at the end of measure 4 is shifted up to eighth position.

MEASURES 5–8: Following two repetition of the IV-chord riff (measures 5–6), the I-chord riff returns for two more repetitions (measures 7–8). Again, notice that the single-note line at the end of measure 6 is played in third position (for the I chord), and the single-note line at the end of measure 8 is played in tenth position (for the V chord).

MEASURES 9–12: For the V (D6) and IV (C6) chord changes (measures 9–10), the riff is played, once each, in tenth position and eighth position, respectively. The pickup line at the end of measure 10 leads to the turnaround lick, which is played entirely along strings 1–2 and resolves to the E♭9–D9 change to signal a return to the top of the form.

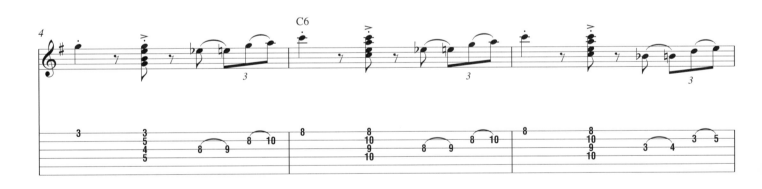

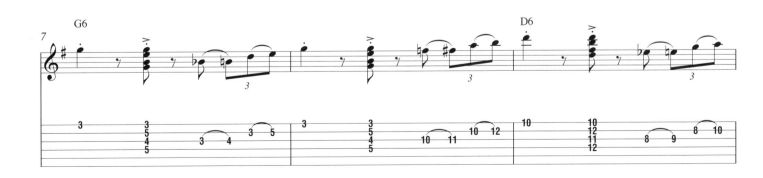

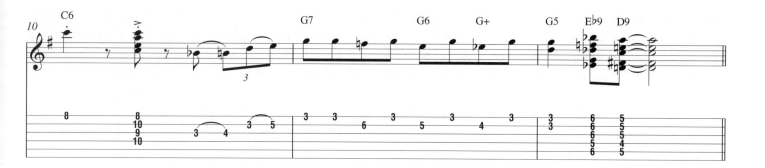

JAM #74: ONE-BAR LEAD/RHYTHM ALTERNATIONS

This first series of jump-blues alternations is played in one-bar intervals, oscillating between a measure of lead playing and a measure of "rhythm" throughout. Interestingly, in this Jam, the single-note pickups lead to soloing, rather than the staccato roots and chord stabs. In an effort to maintain the integrity of the riff, however, the "rhythm" measures are typically preceded by the riff's signature—the minor-to-major hammer-on.

This Jam showcases the versatility of the jump-blues riff; how it can weave seamlessly into either lead phrases or chord stabs that reinforce the harmonies. To accentuate the minor-against-major "rub" that exits in the riff, the lead phrases are derived from scales that contain both tonalities: G composite blues (G–A–Bb–B–C–Db–D–E–F), C composite blues (C–D–Eb–E–F–Gb–G–A–Bb), and D composite blues (D–E–F–F#–G–Ab–A–B–C).

MEASURES 1–4: The Jam opens with the pickup line, which is followed by a G composite blues scale lick that mimics its predecessor. Notice the Bb-to-B (minor-to-major) hammer-on that ends then phrase, which, again, hints at the riff's pickup line. Following the chord stab (measure 2), the pickup line leads to a lick that briefly imparts a dominant (G7) quality via a half-step (E-to-F) bend before responding to measure 1's "call" by resolving to the lower-octave root note (G) in measure 4. Here, the G6 harmony is restated with another chord stab, followed by the pickup line that leads to the IV-chord harmony.

MEASURES 5–8: The lick that comprises measure 5 is a hybrid of the licks from measures 1 and 3, lending continuity to the Jam. This phrase is followed by a chord stab and pickup line that lead back to the I chord (measure 7). Here, half-step bends, like the one from measure 3, give the one-bar phrase a dominant flavor before segueing to yet another chord stab (measure 8).

MEASURES 9–12: Following the pickup line, the V (D6) chord is outlined with a bluesy lick that commences with a pair of root notes (fret 10, first string) and ends with a half-step, Eb-to-E slide that signals the arrival of the IV (C6) chord. In measure 10, the IV-chord harmony is acknowledged via a C6 chord stab, which is followed by the G6 pickup line. The turnaround lick that was introduced in Jam #73 is used here to wrap up the example. However, in place of the Eb9–D9 change in measure 12, a Bb-to-B (minor-to-major) hammer-on resolves to the note D, the root of the V chord.

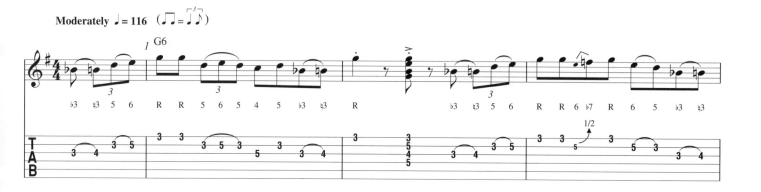

JAM #75: TWO-BAR LEAD/RHYTHM ALTERNATIONS

In this example, the one-bar alternations from Jam #74 have been extended to two bars. Like the previous Jam, the lead phrases are derived from the G composite blues (G–A–B♭–B–C–D♭–D–E–F), C composite blues (C–D–E♭–E–F–G♭–G–A–B♭), and D composite blues (D–E–F–F♯–G–A♭–A–B–C) scales, depending on the harmony being implied at the time. One deviation from the previous two Jams (73–74) occurs in measures 11–12, where the single-note turnaround lick is replaced with the jump-blues riff and chord stab, leading to the E♭9–D9 chord change.

MEASURES 1–4: Following the pickup lick, a two-measure G composite blues scale phrase makes a six-string descent, landing on the sixth-string root of the G6 chord. This phrase is followed by two repetitions of the riff/chord stab, with the requisite position shift (third to eighth) occurring at the end of measure 4.

MEASURES 5–8: The first measure of the C composite blues scale phrase (measure 5) loosely mirrors the lick from measure 1, with the whole-step bend being the most conspicuous element. Rather than continuing to descend the strings (like the opening phrase), this lick backtracks a bit in measure 6 and engages in a minor-to-major (E♭-to-E) hammer-on passage that segues to the G6 pickup line. The return of the I-chord harmony in measures 7–8 is handled by two repetition of the G6 riff, with the D6 pickup lick arriving at the end of measure 8.

MEASURES 9–12: The D composite blues scale lick that outlines the V chord (measure 9) is recreated, with a couple of alterations, over the IV chord (measure 10). Notice that the last note of the C6 phrase, G, anticipates the I chord by half a beat. In fact, the note is repeated on beat 1 of measure 11 to commence the G6 riff, which, along with the E♭9–D9 change, comprise the two-bar turnaround.

JAM #76: ONE-BAR RHYTHM/LEAD ALTERNATIONS

In this Jam, the jump-blues riff alternates, every measure, with one bar of lead playing—a reversal of the lead/rhythm sequence from Jams 74–75. A notable aspect of this Jam is how some of the eighth-note rests are strategically used to facilitate positional shifts. In some cases, the lead phrases that precede chord changes conclude in a position different from the one in which the impending chord stab is located. However, the presence of the eight-note rests allows enough time to relocate the fret hand. Like the previous jump-blues Jams, the note sources for the lead phrases include the G composite (G–A–Bb–B–C–Db–D–E–F), C composite (C–D–Eb–E–F–Gb–G–A–Bb), and D composite (D–E–F–F#–G–Ab–A–B–C) blues scales.

MEASURES 1–4: The Jam kicks off with the G6 riff, with the single-note line appearing in both the pickup measure and at the end of measure 1. In measure 2, a descending G composite blues scale lick resolves to fret 5 of the fourth string—the root of the G6 chord. Following a G6 chord stab in measure 3, the pickup line transitions seamlessly to another G composite blues scale phrase (measure 4), which resolves to the root of the new (C6) harmony (measure 5).

MEASURES 5–8: Measure 5 contains an example of the aforementioned strategic eighth rest. Here, the preceding phrase concludes in third position, on the root of the C6 harmony. However, the eighth rest allows enough time to shift the fret hand to eighth position for the C6 chord stab. At end of measure 5, the pickup line leads to a phrase that is derived from the C composite blues scale. Like measure 5, the eighth-note rest on beat 2 of measure 7 enables the fret hand to shift back to third position (for the G6 chord) without missing a beat. The chord stab is followed by the pickup line and a legato-heavy phrase that is carved from the G composite blues scale (measure 8).

MEASURES 9–12: More position-shifting occurs in measure 9, where the fret hand moves from third position to tenth position for the D6 chord stab. The pickup line at the end of the measure segues to a phrase that is a note-for-note copy of the lick from measure 8, only it's played here in the key of C. For the turnaround (measures 11–12), the G6 riff returns for one repetition before yielding to the E♭9–D9 chord change.

JAM #77: TWO-BAR RHYTHM/LEAD ALTERNATIONS

In this example, the rhythm/lead alternations from Jam #76 are played in two-bar intervals. After commencing with two bars of riffing, two bars of lead are played, a sequence that continues throughout the 12-bar form. All of the lead phrases are played over the I (G6) chord and derive their notes from the G composite blues scale (G–A–B♭–B–C–D♭–D–E–F).

MEASURES 1–4: Following two measures of the G6 riff, the pickup line at the end of measure 2 segues to a two-measure G composite blues scale lick. The phrase commences with a wide (four-fret), first-string pull-off from the scale's major 3rd (B) to its root, while the remainder of the lick is played with a combination of pull-offs, hammer-ons, and slides, concluding with a B♭–B hammer-on that move chromatically to the root of the C6 (IV) chord (measure 5).

MEASURES 5–8: Measures 5–6 feature two repetitions of the C6 riff, with the G6 pickup line occurring at the end of measure 6, leading to another two-measure G composite blues scale lick. In measure 7, the phrase features a countrified double-stop passage, followed in measure 8 by a bass-string run down the remainder of the scale. Similar to measure 4, a C–D♭ hammer-on is played at the end of measure 8 to create a line that moves chromatically to the root of the D6 (V) chord (measure 9).

MEASURES 9–12: In measure 9, a large fret-hand jump is required to reach the D6 chord stab. Fortunately, the eighth-note rest on beat 2 offers adequate time to execute the shift. After one repetition apiece of the D6 and C6 riffs, the Jam concludes with a third G composite blues scale lick. This phrase features several instances of the B♭-to-B (minor-to-major) hammer-on and briefly implies a dominant tonality (G7) via a half-step, E-to-F bend. To signal the arrival of the V chord, the passage resolves to the D note at fret 5 of the fifth string.

JAM #78: RANDOM RHYTHM/LEAD ALTERNATIONS

In this example, the alternations are arranged randomly, resulting in a Jam that unfolds as follows: one bar of rhythm, two bars of lead, two bars of rhythm, one bar of lead, one bar of rhythm, three bars of lead, and two bars of rhythm. Like previous Jams, the lead phrase are rooted in the G composite (G–A–B♭–B–C–D♭–D–E–F), C composite (C–D–E♭–E–F–G♭–G–A–B♭), and D composite (D–E–F–F♯–G–A♭–A–B–C) blues scales.

MEASURES 1–4: The Jam commences with the pickup line and chord stab. However, rather than return to the pickup line at the end of the measure, the ring finger is employed to play a trio of notes (at fret 8) that launch a two-measure G composite blues scale lick. After starting out in sixth position (measure 2), the phrase shifts down to third position at its midpoint (measure 3). In measure 4, this passage is punctuated with a return to the G6 riff.

MEASURES 5–8: The pickup lick at the end of measure 4 leads to a C6 chord stab, followed in measure 6 by a C composite blues scale lick that quickly shifts from 11th position to eighth position. Notice that a variation of the C6 pickup lick is played at the end of measure 6, leading to the G6 harmony. However, because this phrase ends on the note G (rather than C), it works well in this context. On beat 4 of measure 7, another G composite blues scale lick is launched, although this one is played exclusively in third position. A notable component of this phrase is the half-step (E–F) bend, which is mimicked in the subsequent two measures.

MEASURES 9–12: The D composite blues scale lick in measure 9 is transposed down one step, to the key of C, for the IV-chord change in measure 10. The only difference between the two licks is that, on beat 4 of measure 10, the G6 pickup line is substituted for a return to the G6 harmony (measure 11). The Jam wraps up with one repetition of the G6 riff and the chromatic E♭9–D9 change, which signals a return to the top of the form.

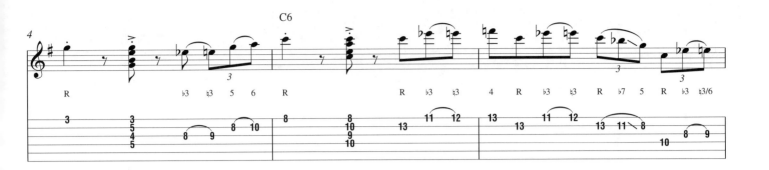

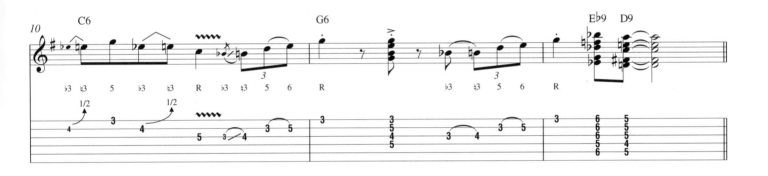

CHAPTER 14: SOUL-JAZZ RIFF
THE RESOURCES

CHORDS

G7

3fr
3 2 4 1

C7

8fr
3 2 4 1

D7

10fr
3 2 4 1

D7

3 2 4 1

SCALES

G Composite Blues Scale (2nd Position):
G–A–B♭–B–C–D♭–D–E–F
(1–2–♭3–♮3–4–♭5–♮5–6–♭7)

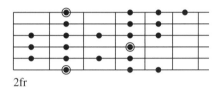
2fr

G Composite Blues Scale (4th Position)

4fr

G Composite Blues Scale (9th Position)

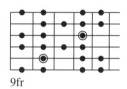
9fr

G Composite Blues Scale (11th Position)

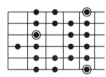
11fr

G Mixolydian (2nd Position):
G–A–B–C–D–E–F
(1–2–3–4–5–6–♭7)

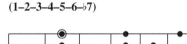
2fr

G Mixolydian (7th Position)

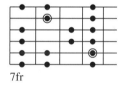
7fr

C Composite Blues Scale (2nd Position):
C–D–E♭–E–F–G♭–G–A–B♭
(1–2–♭3–♮3–4–♭5–♮5–6–♭7)

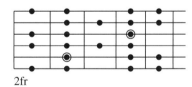
2fr

C Composite Blues Scale (7th Position)

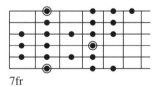
7fr

C Mixolydian:
C–D–E–F–G–A–B♭
(1–2–3–4–5–6–♭7)

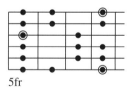
5fr

D Composite Blues Scale (4th Position):
D–E–F–F♯–G–A♭–A–B–C
(1–2–♭3–♮3–4–♭5–♮5–6–♭7)

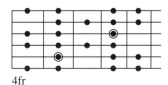
4fr

D Composite Blues Scale (9th Position)

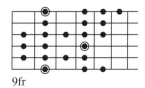
9fr

D Mixolydian:
D–E–F♯–G–A–B–C
(1–2–3–4–5–6–♭7)

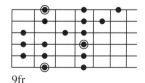
9fr

JAM #79: THE 12-BAR FORM

The riff that is utilized in the next six examples is reminiscent of the "head" to "Back at the Chicken Shack," the signature tune of "soul jazz" organist and icon Jimmy Smith. The riff is constructed from a trio of double stops (for the G7 chord: B/D, C/E, and D/F) that are played exclusively along strings 2–3 and alternated with a fourth-string root note. In true jazz (and blues) form, the major 3rd (relative to each chord change) is preceded by the minor 3rd via a grace note. This minor-against-major "rub" is one of the defining sounds of the genre and is most often implemented over dominant-seventh harmonies, like the ones used here.

Perform the riff with hybrid picking, plucking the fourth-string roots exclusively with your pick, and strings 2–3 with your ring and middle fingers, respectively. Experiment with your fret hand, as a few fingering options are available. Use whichever works best for you.

MEASURES 1–4: The first four bars of the Jam are handled by two repetitions of the G7 riff, starting with a pickup note (G). The D/F double-stop slide at the end of measures 1 and 3 defines the dominant quality of the riff (F is the ♭7th of G7) and adds a touch of syncopation to an otherwise straightforward rhythm.

MEASURES 5–8: The G7 riff is shifted from third position to eighth position for the arrival of the IV (C7) chord (measures 5–6). One repetition of the C7 riff is followed in measures 7–8 by another two measures of the G7 riff.

MEASURES 9–12: In measures 9–10, one-bar versions of the riff are implemented for the V (D7) and IV (C7) chord changes. For the turnaround (measures 11–12), a one-measure variation of the G7 riff is followed by a short lick, featuring the minor-to-major (B♭-to-B) hammer-on, and a common D7 voicing for the V chord.

 JAM #80: ONE-BAR LEAD/RHYTHM ALTERNATIONS

For this next Jam involving the soul-jazz riff, one bar of lead is continuously alternated with one bar of rhythm. Since the original riff is two measures long, only the first measure of the two-bar figure is played in this example. The lead phrases for the I (G7) and IV (C7) chords are derived from the G composite (G–A–B♭–B–C–D♭–D–E–F) and C composite (C–D–E♭–E–F–G♭–G–A–B♭) blues scales, respectively, whereas the V (D7) chord is handled by the D Mixolydian mode (D–E–F♯–G–A–B–C).

MEASURES 1–4: Following a half-step (F♯–G) lead-in, the opening phrase commences with arpeggiation of a G major triad (G–B–D), which is briefly interrupted by a second-string pull-off figure. In measure 2, the G7 riff returns for one measure before segueing to a G composite blues scale lick that imparts a dominant 13th sound via multiple appearances of the note E (the 13th). Notice that the phrase ends on G (fret 5, fourth string)—the same note that is used as the pickup to the G7 riff, which is reprised in measure 4.

MEASURES 5–8: The IV chord is handled by a C composite blues scale lick that actually begins on beat 4 of the preceding measure. The root–♭7th–root (C–B♭–C) sequence that launches the phrase hammers home the dominant quality of the C7 chord before moving up and down the scale, covering seven of the scale's nine tones and segueing to a bar of the C7 riff (measure 6). The lick in measure 7 opens by mimicking the first part of the phrase from measure 3 and ends with a reverse G major arpeggio. Again, notice that the last note of the phrase in measure 7, G, is the same note that is used as the pickup to the G7 riff (which is repeated in measure 8).

MEASURES 9–12: The ♭7th–root (C–D) hammer-on that opens the lick in measure 9 is reminiscent of the opening hammer-pull passage from measure 5 and the arpeggiations of the D major triad hark back to the lick in measure 1, both of which lend continuity to the Jam. After one repetition of the C7 riff (measure 10), the lick from measure 5 is restated in the key of G to outline the I-chord harmony (measure 11). The passage then concludes in measure 12 with two repetitions of the minor-to-major (B♭-to-B) hammer-on and resolution to the root of the V chord, D.

JAM #81: TWO-BAR LEAD/RHYTHM ALTERNATIONS

The alternations in this Jam are played in two-bar intervals, starting with two measures of lead and followed by the two-measure version of the soul-jazz riff. The lead phrases feature several lead-guitar techniques, including arpeggios, pedal tones, and legato, among others. As for the notes, the G7 phrases are derived from the G composite blues scale (G–A–Bb–B–C–Db–D–E–F) and the G Mixolydian mode (G–A–B–C–D–E–F), while the C7 and D7 phrases are culled from the C composite (C–D–Eb–E–F–Gb–G–A–Bb) and D composite (D–E–F–F#–G–Ab–A–B–C) blues scales, respectively.

MEASURES 1–4: To launch the Jam, G major and G dominant arpeggios, played in a repetitive rhythm, descend the fretboard, moving from tenth position to third position. The last note of the phrase, G, is used to signal a return to the G7 riff, which handles the second half of the I-chord harmony (measures 3–4).

MEASURES 5–8: After the first few notes of the C composite blues scale phrase (measures 5–6) mimic the C7 riff, the passage morphs into a pedal-tone lick that alternates fourth-string roots (C) with chord tones on strings 2–1 (G and C, respectively). In measure 6, the passage employs major- and minor-3rd intervals to descend strings 3–4, moving from eighth position to third position, where it segues to two bars of the G7 riff (measures 7–8).

MEASURES 9–12: In measure 9, a short D composite blues scale lick is used to outline the D7 harmony. This phrase is then moved down two frets (one whole step) to handle the IV-chord harmony. Notice, however, that the end of measures 10's phrase has been slightly altered so as to move seamlessly to the G7 riff in measure 10. After one bar of the G7 riff, the Jam concludes with a common D7 voicing (the V chord), signaling a return to the top of the form.

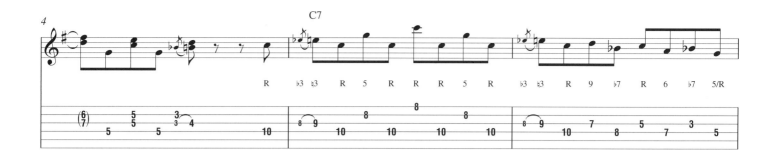

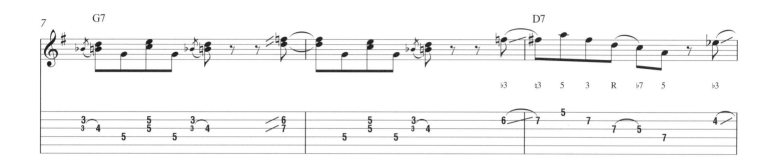

🔊 JAM #82: ONE-BAR RHYTHM/LEAD ALTERNATIONS

Compared to Jam #81, the alternations in this example are reversed and the intervals have been shortened to one bar. The result is continuous fluctuations of one bar of the soul-jazz riff and one bar of lead throughout the 12-bar form. For the lead phrases, the G composite blues scale (G–A–B♭–B–C–D♭–D–E–F) provides the pitches for the G7 harmonies, while the C Mixolydian mode (C–D–E–F–G–A–B♭) outlines the C7 changes.

MEASURES 1–4: Following one bar of the G7 riff, a G composite blues scale lick is introduced in measure 2, where it splits its time between sixth position and third position. The G7 riff returns in measure 3 before giving way to a one-measure phrase that mimics the opening of measure 2's lick. However, instead of moving down to third position, the new lick shifts up to eighth position for a smooth transition to the C7 riff in measure 5.

MEASURES 5–8: The IV-chord harmony in measures 5–6 is handled by one measure of the C7 riff and a descending C Mixolydian phrase that commences on the last eighth note of the previous measure, respectively. The phrase ends on the note G, the pickup note to the G7 riff, which is reprised in measure 7. In measure 8, a triplet-based phrase is carved from the G composite blues scale, played in the vicinity of 12th position.

MEASURES 9–12: The final note in measure 8, D, facilitates smooth transition to the D7 riff in measure 9. Following one repetition of the riff, a C Mixolydian phrase is launched in measure 10, effectively outlining the measure's dominant tonality via strategic placement (beat 1) of the ♭7th (B♭) tone. The Jam then wraps up with a combination of the G7 riff and a third-position voicing of the V (D7) chord.

JAM #83: TWO-BAR RHYTHM/LEAD ALTERNATIONS

The full, two-measure version of the soul-jazz riff returns for this Jam. Here, two bars of the riff alternate with two bars of lead playing throughout the 12-bar form. The lead phrases are performed over the I (G7) chord changes exclusively and derive their notes from a combination of the G composite blues scale (G–A–Bb–B–C–Db–D–E–F) and G Mixolydian mode (G–A–B–C–D–E–F).

MEASURES 1–4: The Jam opens with two bars of the G7 riff, followed in measure 3–4 by a long, flowing phrase culled from the G Mixolydian mode. Notice that the phrase begins immediately after the riff, replacing the eighth rests with a pull-off phrase that flows down the scale. Once the passage reaches the sixth-string root (on the "and" of beat 1), it reverses course and employs hammer-ons to ascend the scale. In measure 4, the phrase slides up to seventh position, where a reverse G major arpeggio is performed.

MEASURES 5–8: A half-step (B–C) slide is used as a lead-in to the C7 riff (measures 5–6), smoothly transitioning from lead playing to riffing. After two measures of the riff, another half-step slide is implemented to transition from the C7 riff to a two-measure phrase that commences in G Mixolydian (measure 7) and ends with a G composite blues scale passage (measure 8). Notice that the phrasing of the former is mirrored by the latter.

MEASURES 9–12: In measures 9–10, one-bar versions of the D7 and C7 riffs are used to outline the V and IV chords, respectively. In measure 11, a triplet-based phrase is employed to outline the I (G7) chord. Although it looks sophisticated, the phrase is actually a common G major chord voicing embellished with notes that are located a half step below the chord tones. In measure 12, on the "and" of beat 2, the legato passage resolves to the D note located at fret 3 of the second string—the root of the V chord—for the turnaround.

🔊 JAM #84: RANDOM RHYTHM/LEAD ALTERNATIONS

The alternations in this example are arranged in random fashion, replacing the structured, one- and two-bar arrangements of previous Jams with an arrangement that is more "off the cuff" (i.e., improvised). The spontaneous feel of these alternations is akin to how a seasoned self-accompanist would play the changes.

The lead phrases in this Jam have a jump-blues feel to them and outnumber rhythm-based measures by a 2-to-1 margin (eight measures of lead versus four measures of riffing). Melodically, the lead lines are derived from the composite blues scales relative to the changes: G composite (G–A–Bb–B–C–Db–D–E–F), C composite (C–D–Eb–E–F–Gb–G–A–Bb), and D composite (D–E–F–F#–G–Ab–A–B–C).

MEASURES 1–4: The Jam's "groove" is established from the get-go via two measures of the G7 riff. Following the riff is a four-measure phrase that outlines two measures of the I (G7) chord and two measures of the IV (C7) chord. For the I-chord harmony (measures 3–4), the notes are derived from the G composite blues scale and revolve around a pair of hammer-on figures: ♭B-to-B (string 3) and D-to-E (string 2).

MEASURES 5–8: The second half of the four-measure phrase that began in measure 3 commences with a B♭-to-C (♭7th-to-root) hammer-on, culling its notes from the second-position pattern of the C composite blues scale. The long phrase comes to a conclusion at the end of measure 6, on the G note located at fret 5 of the fourth string. This note is also the pickup note for the G7 riff, which is reprised in measures 7–8.

MEASURES 9–12: In measure 9, the D composite blues scale is the note source for the phrase used to imply the V chord. Here, a D major arpeggio (beats 1–2) is offset by a passage that recalls the legato figures from the four-bar phrase (beats 3–4). In measure 10, the D7 lick is shifted down two frets to outline the C7 chord, leading to a G7 phrase that is a variation of the previous two licks. This two-measure phrase concludes with a jagged passage that jumps between notes of a G major arpeggio before resolving to the root of the V chord, D, played here at fret 10 of the first string.

138

CHAPTER 15: GYPSY JAZZ COMPING PATTERN
THE RESOURCES

CHORDS

F$^6_9$
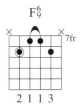

F$^6_9$/C
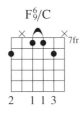

Cm7
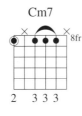

F9
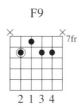

B♭6
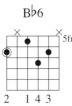

C7
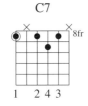

D7
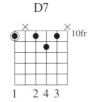

Gm9
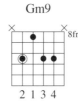

C13
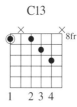

SCALES

F Major (5th Position):
F–G–A–B♭–C–D–E
(1–2–3–4–5–6–7)
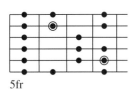
5fr

F Major (7th Position)
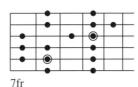
7fr

B♭ Major (5th Position):
B♭–C–D–E♭–F–G–A
(1–2–3–4–5–6–7)
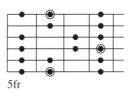
5fr

B♭ Major (7th Position)
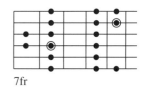
7fr

C Mixolydian (5th Position):
C–D–E–F–G–A–B♭
(1–2–3–4–5–6–♭7)

5fr

C Mixolydian (7th Position)
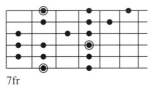
7fr

C Mixolydian (9th Position)
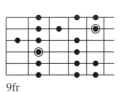
9fr

C Dorian (5th Position):
C–D–E♭–F–G–A–B♭
(1–2–♭3–4–5–6–♭7)
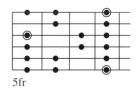
5fr

C Dorian (7th Position)
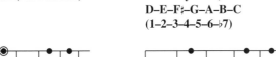
7fr

D Mixolydian (4th Position):
D–E–F♯–G–A–B–C
(1–2–3–4–5–6–♭7)

4fr

D Mixolydian (9th Position)
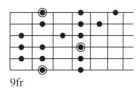
9fr

G Dorian (5th Position):
G–A–B♭–C–D–E–F
(1–2–♭3–4–5–6–♭7)
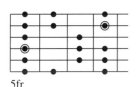
5fr

G Dorian (7th Position)
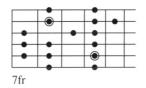
7fr

G Dorian (9th Position)
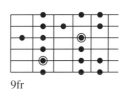
9fr

JAM #85: THE 12-BAR FORM

The next six Jams feature a rhythm-guitar approach that is best described as "gypsy-jazz comping" (*comping* is slang for "accompaniment") due to its similarities to the rhythm-guitar work of Django Reinhardt, the father of the gypsy-jazz genre. The most notable features of this style include alternating (root–5th) bass notes, major sixth and major 6/9 chord voicings, and accented chords on beats 2 and 4 of each measure, all of which are present in these next few Jams.

Harmonically, the Jam is a more sophisticated version of the 12-bar blues. If you look closely, the basic I–IV–V changes are still present; they're just voiced as F6/9 (I), Bb6 (IV), and C7 (V) chords, rather than major triads or dominant seventh voicings. The other chords of the progression are simply "transitional" chords. For example, the Cm7–F9 change in measure 3 functions as a ii–V progression in the key of Bb, treating the IV chord, Bb6, as the I chord in this ii–V–I (Cm7–F9–Bb6) progression. Meanwhile, the F6/9–D7–Gm9–C13 (I–VI–ii–V) progression in measures 11–12 is a standard jazz turnaround. In this instance, the ii–V (Gm9–C13) progression is played in the key of F, leading back to the I (F6/9) chord at the top of the form.

MEASURES 1–4:
In measures 1–3, the I chord is handled by a fairly common F6/9 voicing. In true gypsy-jazz fashion, the chord's bass note alternates between its root, F, and its 5th, C. In measure 4, a ii–V progression in the key of Bb (Cm7–F9) is substituted for F6/9 to lead to the IV chord, Bb6 (which functions as the I chord within the context of the ii–V–I progression).

MEASURES 5–8:
In measures 5–6, the IV chord arrives in the form of a Bb6 voicing. Here, the chord's bass note is plucked on beats 1 and 3, while the voicing is strummed on beats 2 and 4. In measures 7–8, the F6/9 rhythm pattern returns for two more repetitions.

MEASURES 9–12:
In measure 9, a C7 voicing functions as the V chord and is followed in measure 10 by another repetition of the Bb6 (IV) chord. For the turnaround, a I–VI–ii–V progression is employed—a common set of changes for a 12-bar jazz-blues turnaround. Although the VI chord in major keys is minor in quality, a D7 (dominant) voicing is substituted for Dm7 (a common jazz substitution in this context). The turnaround concludes with a ii–V in the key of F (Gm9–C13), sending the progression back to the top of the song form. The two tones shared by Gm9 and C13, Bb and A, contribute greatly to this change's efficient voice leading.

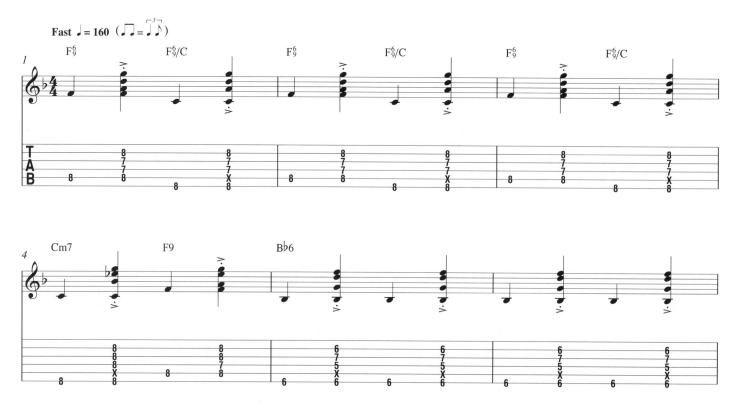

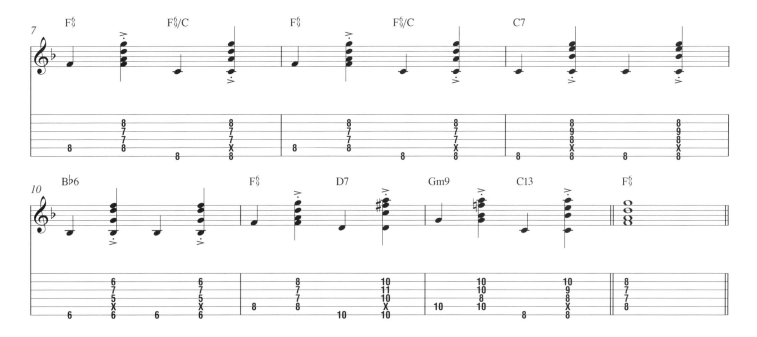

JAM #86: ONE-BAR LEAD/RHYTHM ALTERNATIONS

The alternations in this Jam oscillate between one bar of lead and one bar of the comping pattern. Although the brisk tempo (160 bpm) makes alternating the two approaches a challenge, the lead phrases are pretty straightforward, so once you're able to play the comping pattern cleanly through the entire form, executing the transitions up to tempo should come relatively quickly. For the lead lines, the major scale handles all major chords, the Mixolydian mode handles all dominant chords, and the Dorian mode is implemented for all minor chords.

MEASURES 1–4: The Jam commences with a pickup note (D) that leads to an arpeggio-based lick that outlines an F6 chord (F–A–C–D). Following one bar of comping (measure 2), an F major lick is performed in measure 3. Notice that the second half of this phrase mimics the lick from measure 1, lending continuity to the Jam. In measure 4, the comping pattern handles the ii–V (Cm7–F9) change, leading to the IV (Bb6) chord.

MEASURES 5–8: The Bb6 arpeggio in measure 5 is preceded by a pickup note, A, and is played in a two-notes-per-string pattern before sliding back down the neck and resting on the chord's 3rd, D. The second measure of the IV chord is performed with the comping pattern, followed in measure 7 by another F major lick. The E–F–E trill from measure 3 is reprised here (on beat 3) for additional continuity. In measure 8, the F6/9 comping pattern makes another appearance, leading the Jam to the V chord (measure 9).

MEASURES 9–12: In measure 9, the C Mixolydian mode is mined to imply the V (C7) chord. After moving up the scale in stepwise fashion, the lick segues to a Bb–G–Bb trill that harks back to the trills in measures 1, 3, and 7. Following a bar of Bb6 comping (measure 10), the Jam concludes with a steady stream of eighth notes to outline the I–VI–ii–V progression. The F6/9, Gm9, and C13 chords are implied by a scale sequence that is comprised of the first, second, third, and fifth tones (1–2–3–5) of the chords' respective scales. Meanwhile, the D7 chord is outlined with a D dominant seventh arpeggio (D–F#–A–C), starting from the 3rd (F#).

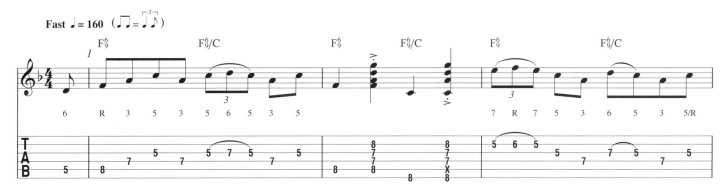

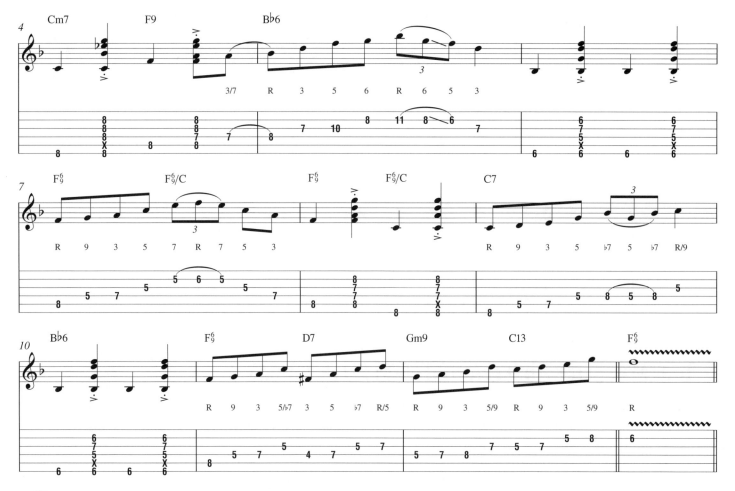

JAM #87: TWO-BAR LEAD/RHYTHM ALTERNATIONS

The one-bar alternations from the previous Jam (#86) have been extended to two measures in this example. Now, two measures of lead are continuously alternated with two measures of comping throughout the 12-bar form. The leads in the first half of the Jam emphasize root notes, while the second half involves dominant seventh (C7) and major sixth (Bb6) arpeggios.

MEASURES 1–4: The two-measure phrase that opens the Jam is derived entirely from the F major scale (F–G–A–Bb–C–D–E) and drives home the key center via multiple staccato roots. The third measure of the F6/9 harmony is handled by the comping pattern, which also is employed in measure 4, for the ii–V (Cm7–F9) progression.

MEASURES 5–8: In measures 5–6, the staccato-root-notes theme is reprised. Here, only a Bb–G pull-off stands in the way of one-and-a-half measures of uninterrupted root (Bb) notes. On beat 3 of measure 6, the phrase concludes with a Bb6 arpeggio (Bb–D–F–G) before transitioning to two bars of F6/9 comping (measures 7–8).

MEASURES 9–12: In measure 9, the C7 harmony is outlined with a melodically sequenced C dominant seventh arpeggio (C–E–G–Bb). The phrase is then restated in measure 10, with the C7 chord tones replaced by a Bb6 arpeggio (Bb–D–F–G). In measures 11–12, the entire turnaround progression (F6/9–D7–Gm9–C13) is handled by the comping pattern.

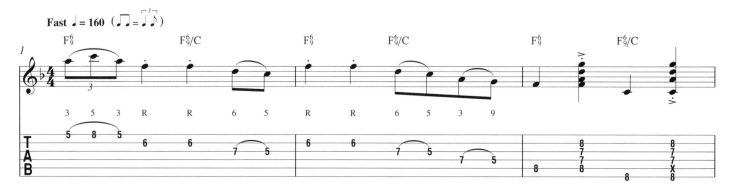

JAM #88: ONE-BAR RHYTHM/LEAD ALTERNATIONS

In this example, the sequence of the lead/rhythm alternations from the previous two Jams (86–87) is reversed. Here, one bar of gypsy-jazz comping is continuously alternated with one bar of lead playing. Rhythmically, many of the lead phrases feature a motif comprised of an eighth-note triplet and a pair of eighth notes. Melodically, the phrases for the major changes are derived from the major scale, whereas the minor and dominant changes are culled from the Dorian and Mixolydian modes, respectively.

MEASURES 1–4: Following one bar of F6/9 comping, the rhythmic motif makes its first appearance, played here within the confines of the F major scale. This phrase is followed by another bar of F6/9 comping and a lick that mimics the rhythm that was introduced in measure 2 while emphasizing chord tones of the Cm7 and F9 changes.

MEASURES 5–8: Following a bar of Bb6 comping, the motif is restated at the onset of measure 6, where tones from the Bb major scale (Bb–C–D–Eb–F–G–A) outline the Bb6 harmony. The last note of the phrase, F, facilitates smooth transition to the F6/9 comping in measure 7. The motif makes yet another appearance in measure 8, where the F6/9 harmony is implied by notes from the F major scale (F–G–A–Bb–C–D–E). The one exception is the B note at fret 7 of the first string, which is present in order to move chromatically (A–Bb–B–C) from the 3rd of F6/9, A, to the root of the impending C7 chord.

MEASURES 9–12: Following a bar of C7 comping (measure 9), a Bb6 arpeggio (Bb–D–F–G) is utilized to imply the IV (Bb6) chord. This lick leads to the first two chords of the I–VI–ii–V turnaround progression, F6/9 and D7, which are handled by the comping pattern. In measure 12, the Gm9 and C13 harmonies are outlined with a 1–2–3–5 scale (G Dorian) sequence and a C6 arpeggio (C–E–G–A), respectively.

JAM #89: TWO-BAR RHYTHM/LEAD ALTERNATIONS

The one-bar alternations from Jam #88 have been extended to two bars in this example. Now, throughout this Jam's 12 bars, two measures of gypsy-jazz comping are followed by two-bar lead passages that are played in the style of jazz icon Django Reinhardt, particularly the wide interval jumps in measures 3 and 7, where the F6/9 chord's root (F) and 5th (C) are played in two octaves. This motif is also restated in measure 11, at the onset of the I–VI–ii–V progression.

MEASURES 1–4: Following two measures of F6/9 comping, the multi-octave Django lick makes its first appearance (measure 3). Be sure to note that the first quarter note (beat 2) is performed in staccato fashion, whereas the second quarter note is held for its entire duration (one beat). In measure 4, the ii–V (Cm7–F9) progression is outlined with a lick that employs efficient voice leading—specifically, the fourth-string slide, which moves from the ♭7th of the Cm7 chord, B♭, to the 3rd of the F9 chord, A.

MEASURES 5–8: Measures 5–6 employ the comping pattern to handle the IV (B♭6) chord, followed in measures 7–8 by a restatement of the Django lick and a sequenced F6 arpeggio (F–A–C–D), respectively. The F6 arpeggio outlines all but one note of the F6/9 harmony—G, the 9th.

144

MEASURES 9–12: The V (C7) and IV (B♭6) chords are handled by the comping pattern, which leads to a two-measure, unbroken set of eighth notes that outline each change of the I–VI–ii–V (F6/9–D7–Gm9–C13) progression, similar to the phrase used in Jam #86. Here, the F6/9 passage is a variation of the Django motif and leads to a D7 arpeggio (starting from the 3rd, F♯) and a 1–2–3–5 scale sequence for both Gm9 (G Dorian) and C13 (C Mixolydian).

 # JAM #90: RANDOM RHYTHM/LEAD ALTERNATIONS

The alternations in this Jam are arranged randomly, rather than in strict one- or two-bar tradeoffs. Although the first eight measures are arranged in a consist pattern (two bars of lead and one bar of rhythm), the unbalanced nature of these tradeoffs give the Jam a more "improvised" feel, with significantly more emphasis given to lead playing. At measure 9, the Jam wraps up with one-and-a-half measures of comping and a string of eighth notes that commences at the midpoint of measure 10, flowing all the way through the I–VI–ii–V (F6/9–D7–Gm9–C13) progression in measures 11–12.

MEASURES 1–4: The two-measure phrase that opens the Jam is constructed exclusively from F6 chord tones (F–A–C–D). After juggling triplet-based trills and quarter notes, the phrase moves straight down an F6 arpeggio on beat 2 of the measure 2. In measure 3, the comping pattern handles the third bar of F6/9 harmony before segueing to a single-note line that outlines the ii–V (Cm7–F9) progression (measure 4).

MEASURES 5–8: The arrival of the IV (B♭6) chord is signaled via a reverse B♭ major arpeggio, played in sixth position. The one-bar phrase wraps up with a chord-tone-laden legato figure that is punctuated with a bar of B♭6 comping (measure 6). In measures 7–8, a repetitive, Django-style lick is constructed from an F6 arpeggio that alludes to the phrase from measure 2.

MEASURES 9–12: The comping pattern returns in measures 9–10, implying the V (C7) and IV (B♭6) chords before giving way to a two-and-a-half-measure string of eighth notes. Notice that, instead of beginning on beat 1, the single-note line begins on beat 3 of measure 10, outlining the second half of the IV-chord harmony before taking care of the I–VI–ii–V (F6/9–D7–Gm9–C13) progression. For the first three chords (B♭6, F6/9, and D7), arpeggios are employed, whereas scale tones imply the Gm9 (G Dorian) and C13 (C Mixolydian) changes in measure 12.

146

CHAPTER 16: WALKING BASS LINE: 12-BAR JAZZ-BLUES
THE RESOURCES

CHORDS

 F7

 F7/A

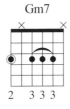 Gm7

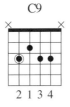 C9

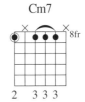 Cm7

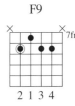 F9

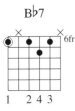 Bb7

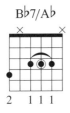 Bb7/Ab

 Am7

 D9

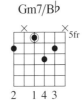 Gm7/Bb

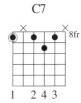 C7

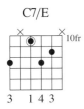 C7/E

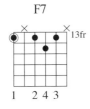 F7

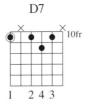 D7

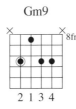 Gm9

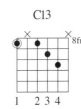 C13

SCALES

F Mixolydian (All Positions):
F–G–A–Bb–C–D–Eb
(1–2–3–4–5–6–b7)

F Composite Blues Scale:
F–G–Ab–A–Bb–Cb–C–D–Eb
(1–2–b3–b3–4–b5–b5–6–b7)

Bb Mixolydian (3rd Position):
Bb–C–D–Eb–F–G–Ab
(1–2–3–4–5–6–b7)

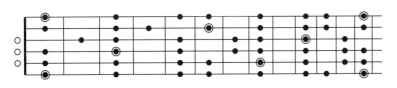

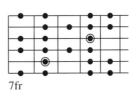
7fr

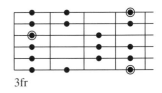
3fr

Bb Mixolydian (5th Position)

Bb Composite Blues Scale:
Bb–C–Db–D–Eb–Fb–F–G–Ab
(1–2–b3–b3–4–b5–b5–6–b7)

G Dorian (All Positions):
G–A–Bb–C–D–E–F
(1–2–b3–4–5–6–b7)

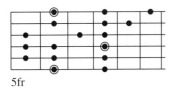
5fr

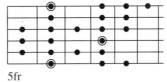
5fr

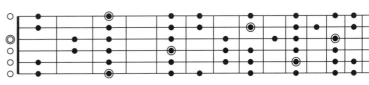

D Mixolydian (2nd Position):
D–E–F♯–G–A–B–C
(1–2–3–4–5–6–b7)

D Mixolydian (4th Position)

D Mixolydian (9th Position)

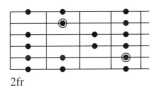
2fr

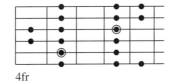
4fr

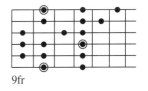
9fr

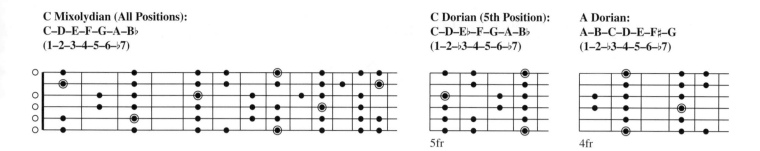

C Mixolydian (All Positions):
C–D–E–F–G–A–B♭
(1–2–3–4–5–6–♭7)

C Dorian (5th Position):
C–D–E♭–F–G–A–B♭
(1–2–♭3–4–5–6–♭7)

A Dorian:
A–B–C–D–E–F♯–G
(1–2–♭3–4–5–6–♭7)

5fr   4fr

 # JAM #91: THE 12-BAR FORM

The next six Jams are an introduction to jazz-based walking bass lines. Like the rock 'n' roll walking bass lines in Chapter 7, jazz-based walking bass lines are played in steady quarter-notes. What differentiates the jazz-based lines from the rock-based ones, however, is the incorporation of chord voicings on beats 1 and 3. The result is an accompaniment figure that involves simultaneous performance of the chord changes and the walking bass line. In other words, you're pulling double duty, playing the parts of both the bass player and the guitarist (or pianist).

The song form is a 12-bar jazz-blues, played here in the key of F. The fundamental changes (I–IV–V) replicate the ones used in Chapter 15 (Gypsy Jazz Comping Pattern), although the I and IV chords here are dominant in quality (F7 and B♭7, respectively) and more chord substitutions are involved. For example, one- and two-bar Gm7–C7 (ii–V) progressions are substituted in measures 2 and 9–10. Similarly, a Cm7–F9 progression is substituted in measure 4 (a substitution that was used in Chapter 15) and an Am7–D9 progression is substituted in measure 8.

Although the aforementioned changes are ii–V progressions, the only one that is diatonic to the Jam's key, F major, is Gm7–C7. The Cm7–F9 progression is diatonic to B♭ major (the IV chord, although played here as a dominant voicing), and Am7–D9 is diatonic to the key of G—although, in this progression, the forthcoming chord is minor in quality (Gm7), creating a series of ii–V progressions, which is extremely common in the jazz idiom.

MEASURES 1–4: Measure 1 features root-position and first-inversion F7 chords and a bass line that leads chromatically (A♭–G) to a root-position Gm7 voicing in measure 2. Here, a C9 voicing is played in place of a common dominant seventh chord. Measure 3, also approached via a half-step (G♭–F), returns to the root-position and first-inversion F7 voicings and approaches Cm7 (measure 4) by way of a half step (B–C). The ii–V (Cm7–F9) voicings in measure 4 are borrowed from measure 2, only they've been moved up five frets, to the key of B♭.

MEASURES 5–8: In measures 5–6, the IV chord (B♭7) is implied by root-position and third-inversion voicings, respectively. This two-bar figure is heavy on bass line, as the no voicings are played on beat 3 of either measure. On beat 4 of measure 6, the open low E string is utilized to approach the F7 chord (measure 7) by a half step. The pattern used here is very similar to the ones employed in measures 1 and 3, and approaches the Am7 voicing in measure 8 by a half step (B♭–A). Meanwhile, the voicings for the Am7–D9 change are the same as those used in the ii–V progressions in measures 2 and 4.

MEASURES 9–12: In measures 9–10, the two-bar ii–V progression features root-position and first-inversion Gm7 and C7 voicings, respectively. For the I–VI–ii–V turnaround, a root-position dominant seventh voicing handles both the I (F7) chord and the VI (D7) chord, followed in measure 12 by a fifth-string Gm9 voicing and a sixth-string C13 voicing, both of which are approached by a half step. (As you can see, approaching chord changes via a half step [i.e., chromatically] is a common device used by jazz guitarists and bassists when constructing walking bass lines.)

JAM #92: ONE-BAR LEAD/RHYTHM ALTERNATIONS

The alternations in this example consist of one-bar leads continuously fluctuating with one bar of walking bass line throughout the form's 12 measures. The lead phrases that are played over the dominant seventh chords, F7 and Bb7, are derived from the F Mixolydian (F–G–A–Bb–C–D–Eb) and Bb Mixolydian (Bb–C–D–Eb–F–G–Ab) modes, respectively. Meanwhile, the lone minor phrase, for the Gm7 harmony in measure 9, is rooted in the G Dorian mode (G–A–Bb–C–D–E–F).

MEASURES 1–4: The Jam kicks off with a descending lick that is derived entirely from the F Mixolydian mode, incorporating five of the scale's seven pitches. In measure 2, root-position Gm7 and C9 voicings handle the ii–V progression, with the bass line segueing to measure 3's F7 lick via a half step (Gb–F). The bass-string lick in measure 3 is a chord-tone-laden phrase that incorporates every note of the F7 harmony (F, A, C, and Eb). The measure's final note, C, is tied into measure 4, where it functions as the root of the Cm7 chord. Voice the Cm7 with an index-finger barre, fretting the Eb note at fret 4 of the second string with your middle finger. The F7 voicing (beat 3) can be voiced with a similar fingering.

MEASURES 5–8: The phrase in measure 5 is a copy of the lick from measure 3, only it's been transposed up a perfect 4th to fit the B♭7 harmony. The second bar of the IV-chord harmony (measure 6) is handled by a third-inversion B♭7 chord and a bass line that walks down string 6, from A♭ to the E, to transition to the root of the I chord, F. Here, a barre-chord-style F7 arpeggio (F–A–C–E♭) outlines the dominant harmony, using the minor 3rd, A♭, to approach the Am7 chord in measure 8 via a half step. This ii–V progression (Am7–D9) is simply the pattern from measure 2 moved up a whole step (two frets).

MEASURES 9–12: The bass-string lick in measure 9 is a minor-key variation of the licks from measures 3 and 5. To anticipate the impending chord change, the lick slides from the ♭7th of the Gm7 chord, F, to the 3rd of the C7 chord, E, on beat 4. In measure 10, the bass line simply alternates between the C9 chord's root and 5th (C and G, respectively), the latter of which is played on string 6. The bass-string motif that was established in measure 3 is restated in measure 11, where it quickly segues to a descending, two-notes-per-string D7 arpeggio (D–F♯–A–C). The arpeggio's final note, F♯, creates a half-step transition (F♯–G) to the root of the Gm7 chord in measure 12. Here, the Gm7–C9 pattern from measure 2 is reproduced, with a slight rhythmic alteration, to conclude the Jam.

150

JAM #93: TWO-BAR LEAD/RHYTHM ALTERNATIONS

In this Jam, the length of the lead and rhythm parts has been extended to two bars apiece. Now the Jam begins with a two-measure lead phrase before giving way to two bars of bass line—a sequence that continues throughout the form's 12 bars. The opening phrase is derived from the F composite blues scale (F–G–A♭–A–B♭–C♭–C–D–E♭), whereas the remainder of the dominant seventh and minor seventh chords are outlined with the Mixolydian and Dorian modes relative to the changes, respectively.

MEASURES 1–4: A minor-to-major (A♭-to-A) slide initiates the Jam and is followed by a descending F7 arpeggio (F–A–C–E♭). In measure 2, the line morphs into a scale-based passage that outlines the Gm7–C7 progression before the bass line takes over for the F9 and Cm7–F9 changes in measures 3–4. Notice that the A note at fret 7 of the fourth string precedes the bass-line pattern in measure 3, as well as the single-note line in measure 5. In the former setting, the note functions as the 3rd of the forthcoming F9 chord, whereas in the latter, it enables a half-step transition (A–B♭) to the root of the B♭7 chord—a common device is jazz soloing.

MEASURES 5–8: The lick in measure 5 emphasizes every tone of the B♭7 chord (B♭, D, F, and A♭), as does the phrase in measure 6, but with a much different approach. Here, all but one of the phrases notes are played on string 1, with the root (B♭) and ♭7th (A♭) garnering most of the attention. A fairly large fret-hand jump is required to get to the F7 chord on beat 1 of measure 7, where the I chord is accompanied by root-position and first-inversion voicings, followed in measure 8 by root-position Am7 and D9 voicings for the ii–V progression.

MEASURES 9–12: The G Dorian (G–A–B♭–C–D–E–F) phrase in measure 9 commences with a two-note pickup, which results in the minor 3rd (B♭) landing on beat 1 to emphasize the minor quality of the harmony (Gm7). Then, on beats 3–4, the lick descends strings 1–4 via a reverse G minor arpeggio (G–B♭–D), which is voiced like a common Gm chord. In measure 10, the phrase transitions to a one-bar C Mixolydian (C–D–E–F–G–A–B♭) phrase, followed in measures 11–12 by a bass line that incorporates root-position F7, D9, Gm7, and C9 voicings for the turnaround's I–VI–ii–V progression.

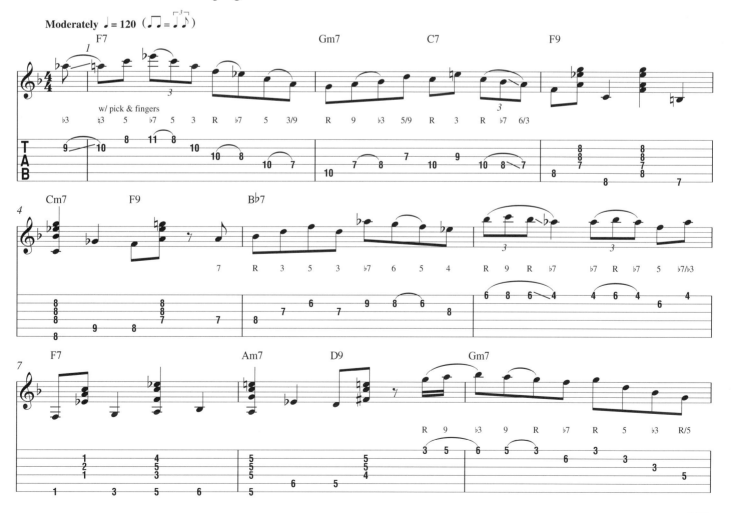

🔊 JAM #94: ONE-BAR RHYTHM/LEAD ALTERNATIONS

In this example, the sequence of the alternations from Jams 92–93 is reversed. Here, the bass line is played first, and then alternated, every measure, with one bar of lead. These one-bar intervals are maintained throughout the Jam's 12-bar form. Melodically, the lead phrases consist of short scale sequences and arpeggios, with emphasis on the latter.

MEASURES 1–4: The I-chord harmony that opens the Jam is handled by root-position and first-inversion F7 voicings. In measure 2, the ii–V progression is outlined with a bass-string lick that utilizes G minor seventh (G–Bb–D–F) and C major (C–E–G) arpeggios, connected via a slide from the former's b7th (F) to the latter's 3rd (E). The chord voicings from measure 1 are restated in measure 3 for the return of the I chord, with the bass line transitioning to measure 4's lead phrase via a half step (B–C). After the Cm7 chord is outlined with a C Dorian (C–D–Eb–F–G–A–Bb) scale sequence (1–2–3–5), the F7 chord is implied with a simple F major arpeggio (F–A–C).

MEASURES 5–8: Measure 5 consists of root-position and third-inversion Bb7 voicings and a bass line that moves chromatically along string 6 before segueing to a bluesy Bb composite blues scale (Bb–C–Db–D–Eb–Fb–F–G–Ab) lick. In measure 7, the return to the I-chord harmony is handled by an F9 voicing, with the bass line alternating between the chord's root and 5th (C), which is played on string 6. At the end of measure 7, a Bb notes is used to create a half-step transition to the A minor arpeggio (A–C–E) that commences the lick in measure 8. The A minor arpeggio is then followed by a D dominant seventh arpeggio (D–F#–A–C) for the D7 harmony.

MEASURES 9–12: In measures 9–10, the two-bar ii–V progression is implied via root-position and first-inversion Gm7 voicings and a bass-string lick that is derived from the C Mixolydian mode (C–D–E–F–G–A–Bb). The first half of the I–VI–ii–V turnaround progression (measure 11) is handled by root-position F9 and D7 voicings, followed in measure 12 by a G Dorian (G–A–Bb–C–D–E–F) scale sequence and a passage built around a C dominant seventh arpeggio (C–E–G–Bb).

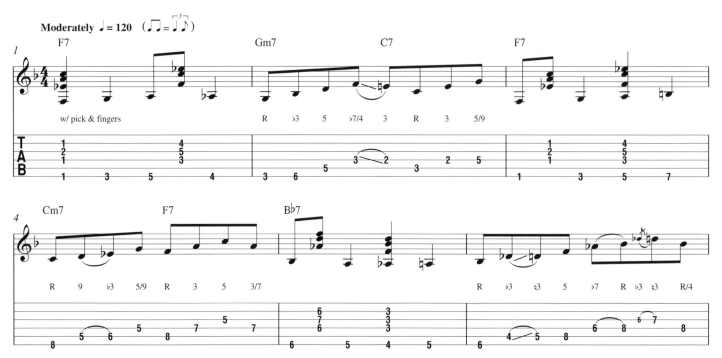

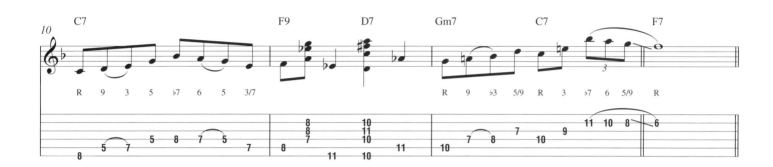

JAM #95: TWO-BAR RHYTHM/LEAD ALTERNATIONS

In this example, the alternations are extended to two measures, starting with two bars of the bass line. These two-bar rhythm/lead tradeoffs are maintained throughout the Jam's 12 bars. Like the previous Jam (#94), the lead phrases are constructed from short scale sequences and arpeggios, with emphasis on the latter. In a solo setting such as this one, arpeggio-focused playing enables you to accentuate chord tones of the harmonies that you're attempting to outline.

MEASURES 1–4: In measure 1, root-position and first-inversion F7 voicings emphasize the I chord, followed in measure 2 by root-position Gm7 and C9 voicings for the ii–V change. On the "and" of beat 4, the minor 3rd of the F7 harmony, Ab, is slid up to the major 3rd, A, which is followed by arpeggiation of F7 chord tones (F–A–C–Eb). Similarly, in measure 4, the Cm7–F7 progression is outlined with C minor seventh (C–Eb–G–Bb) and F major (F–A–C) arpeggios. Note that the C minor seventh arpeggio begins on its b7th tone (Bb), whereas the F major arpeggio begins and ends on its 3rd (A), resulting in a seamless transition between the two harmonies.

MEASURES 5–8: Measures 5–6 are heavy on bass notes, with chord voicings appearing only on beat 1 of each measure. After a root-position Bb7 voicing is played on beat 1 of measure 5, the third-inversion Bb7 chord in measure 6 is approached chromatically: Bb–A–Ab. A similar approach is used in measure 6, where the bass line moves chromatically (Ab–G–Gb) before the arrival of the open low E string (beat 4). The open string enables the fret-hand to relocate to fifth position, where an F Mixolydian (F–G–A–Bb–C–D–Eb) phrase outlines the F7 harmony. This phrase flows seamlessly into measure 8, where chord tones outline the Am7 change before sliding down to the 3rd of the D7 chord, F#. Here, the phrase shifts down to string 6, where it walks chromatically (A–Ab–G) to the root of the forthcoming Gm7 chord (measure 9).

MEASURES 9–12: In measures 9–10, the Gm7 and C7 harmonies are handled by root-position and first-inversion voicings. This two-bar bass line is followed in measures 11–12 by a single-note phrase that flows smoothly across all six strings while, at the same time, effectively outlining each chord of the I–VI–ii–V progression, using a combination of scale fragments (F7, Gm7, and C7) and an arpeggio (D7).

JAM #96: RANDOM RHYTHM/LEAD ALTERNATIONS

The alternations in this Jam are arranged in random fashion. In addition to the typical one or two bars of bass line or lead playing, this Jam illustrates how a few well-placed chord stabs can offer additional forward momentum to the rhythm/lead tradeoffs. Meanwhile, the lead lines are constructed mostly from arpeggios, but also include short phrases derived from the F composite blues scale (F–G–Ab–A–Bb–Cb–C–D–Eb) and G Dorian (G–A–Bb–C–D–E–F) and A Dorian (A–B–C–D–E–F#–G) modes.

MEASURES 1–4: In measures 1–2, a two-bar phrase begins with an arpeggio-based passage that segues to a lick derived from the F composite blues scale. On the "and" of beat 4 of the measure 1, the scale's root, F, slides up a whole step, to the root of the Gm7 harmony. Here, a G Dorian phrase is followed by a descending C dominant seventh arpeggio (C–E–G–Bb) that skips over its 3rd, E, in favor of its root. In measure 3, the I (F7) chord is outline with an F9 voicing and a bass line that fluctuates between the chord's root, F, and its 5th, C, which is fretted on string 6. This bass pattern is followed in measure 4 by a root-position Cm7 voicing and the return of the F9 voicing, which functions here as the V chord of the ii–V progression that leads to the Bb7 chord in measure 5.

MEASURES 5–8: Although the harmony in measures 5–6 is Bb7, the phrase is distinctly Bb6 (Bb–D–F–G)—that is, until the arrival of the chord stab (on the "and" of beat 3, measure 6), which consists of the upper voices of a *dominant* 13th chord. The chord stab is followed one beat later by a Gb bass note (fret 9, string 5), which transitions chromatically to a restatement (with slight rhythmic variation) of the F9 bass-line pattern from measure 3. The final bass note of this measure, Bb, approaches the single-note line in measure 8 via a half step. Here, notes from the A Dorian mode and a D dominant seventh arpeggio are combined to create a seamless bass-note run.

MEASURES 9–12: The bass-note run from measure 8 continues in measure 9, where the pattern from the phrase's first two beats is transposed and restated over the Gm7 harmony. On the "and" of beat 3, a Gm7 chord stab punctuates the 12-note passage, followed a beat later by a Db9 voicing, which moves chromatically to the C9 bass-line pattern in measure 10. This pattern is similar to the F9 pattern, only it has been moved down five frets to accommodate the new (C9) harmony. In measures 11–12, the turnaround progression (I–VI–ii–V) is outlined via a steady stream of eight notes, starting with a pickup note (E) from the preceding measure. Although the 16-note phrase moves uninterrupted from chord to chord, it's actually constructed from four four-note licks, all of which are comprised of chord tones (i.e., arpeggios).

155

CHAPTER 17: WALKING BASS LINE: RHYTHM CHANGES
THE RESOURCES

CHORDS

B♭6
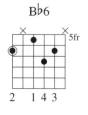
2 1 4 3

Gm7

2 3 3 3

Cm9
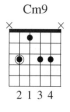
2 1 3 4

F13
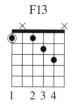
1 2 3 4

B♭⁶₉
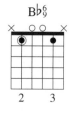
2 3

Cm7
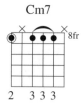
2 3 3 3

F9
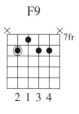
2 1 3 4

Fm9
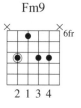
2 1 3 4

B♭13
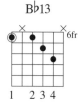
1 2 3 4

E♭maj7
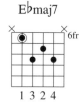
1 3 2 4

E♭m7
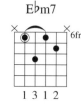
1 3 1 2

D9
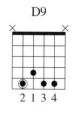
2 1 3 4

D7/C

2 1 3 1

G7
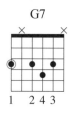
1 2 4 3

G7/B
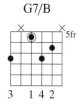
3 1 4 2

G7/D
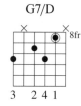
3 2 4 1

C7
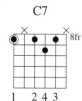
1 2 4 3

C7/B♭
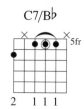
2 1 1 1

C7/G

3 2 4 1

F7
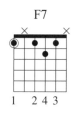
1 2 4 3

F7/A

3 1 4 2

F7/C
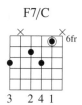
3 2 4 1

SCALES

B♭ Major (2nd Position):
B♭–C–D–E♭–F–G–A
(1–2–3–4–5–6–7)
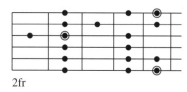
2fr

B♭ Major (5th Position)
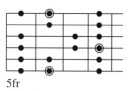
5fr

B♭ Mixolydian (5th Position):
B♭–C–D–E♭–F–G–A♭
(1–2–3–4–5–6–♭7)
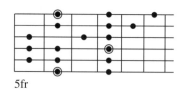
5fr

B♭ Mixolydian (7th Position)
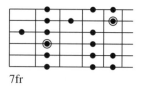
7fr

G Dorian (2nd Position):
G–A–B♭–C–D–E–F
(1–2–♭3–4–5–6–♭7)
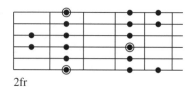
2fr

G Dorian (5th Position)
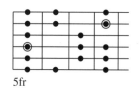
5fr

G Mixolydian:
G–A–B–C–D–E–F
(1–2–3–4–5–6–♭7)
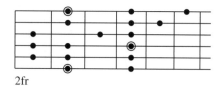
2fr

G Composite Blues Scale (2nd Position):
G–A–B♭–B–C–D♭–D–E–F
(1–2–♭3–♮3–4–♭5–♮5–6–♭7)

2fr

G Composite Blues Scale (6th Position)

6fr

F Dorian (4th Position):
F–G–A♭–B♭–C–D–E♭
(1–2–♭3–4–5–6–♭7)

4fr

F Dorian (7th Position)

7fr

F Composite Blues Scale (Extended Form):
F–G–A♭–A–B♭–C♭–C–D–E♭
(1–2–♭3–♮3–4–♭5–♮5–6–♭7)

F Mixolydian (All Positions):
F–G–A–B♭–C–D–E♭
(1–2–3–4–5–6–♭7)

D Mixolydian:
D–E–F♯–G–A–B–C
(1–2–3–4–5–6–♭7)

4fr

D Composite Blues Scale (2nd Position):
D–E–F–F♯–G–A♭–A–B–C
(1–2–♭3–♮3–4–♭5–♮5–6–♭7)

2fr

D Composite Blues Scale (4th Position)

4fr

C Mixolydian (2nd Position):
C–D–E–F–G–A–B♭
(1–2–3–4–5–6–♭7)

2fr

C Mixolydian (5th Position)

5fr

C Mixolydian (7th Position)

7fr

C Dorian (2nd Position):
C–D–E♭–F–G–A–B♭
(1–2–♭3–4–5–6–♭7)

2fr

C Dorian (5th Position)

5fr

E♭ Major:
E♭–F–G–A♭–B♭–C–D
(1–2–3–4–5–6–7)

5fr

E♭ Dorian:
E♭–F–G♭–A♭–B♭–C–D♭
(1–2–♭3–4–5–6–♭7)

5fr

157

JAM #97: THE 16-BAR (A–B) FORM

The next six Jams are an extension of the walking bass lines from Chapter 16. While the simultaneous performance of chords and bass lines is the common link, this Jam utilizes a more sophisticated set of changes. Gone is the 12-bar blues, and in its place is "Rhythm Changes," a set of chord changes based on George Gershwin's song "I Got Rhythm." However, instead of utilizing all 32 bars of the song's AABA form, this example is arranged as a 16-bar Jam, with two eight-bar sections (A and B).

The A-section, repeated in "Rhythm Changes" but played once here, features major, minor, and dominant chords that change every two beats. This Jam is arranged in the key of Bb and, as typical in "Rhythm Changes," begins with two repetitions of the I–vi–ii–V (Bb6–Gm7–Cm9–F13) progression, played here with a minor vi chord. The second half of the A-section begins with a ii–V progression in the key of Eb (Fm9–Bb13), leading to the I (Ebmaj7) chord in measure 6. Here, the quality of the chord changes from major to minor, followed in measures 7–8 by a I–V–I (Bb6–F13–Bb6/9) progression in the key of Bb.

Like a typical bridge section in a pop or jazz tune, the chord changes in the B-section arrive at a much slower pace to contrast the fast-moving changes of the A-section. In this Jam, the chords change every two measures and are all dominant in quality. After commencing with a D9 voicing, the remainder of the changes follows the "circle of 4ths"—that is, each subsequent chord is exactly a perfect 4th above its predecessor: D7–G7–C7–F7.

MEASURES 1–4: The opening I–vi–ii–V progression features root-position voicings exclusively, all of which are approached by way of a half step (i.e., chromatically). In measures 3–4, a Bb6/9 chord is substituted for the I chord, and the ii- and V-chord changes have been shifted up the fretboard and played as minor seventh and dominant ninth voicings, respectively.

MEASURES 5–8: The Fm9 voicing in measure 5 differs from its predecessor, F9, by only one note (see string 4), and a Bb13 voicing concludes this ii–V progression (Fm9–Bb13), leading to barre-chord-style voicings for the Ebmaj7 and Ebm7 changes in measure 6. The A-section concludes with a I–V–I progression that begins with a Bb6 voicing and the open low E string, which facilitates a position shift for the forthcoming F13 chord. Like measure 3, a Bb6/9 voicing is substituted in measure 8, where a root–5th bass line is followed by movement up string 5 to the D9 voicing, the first chord of the B-section.

MEASURES 9–12: Another root–5th pattern is employed in measure 9, for the D9 change. However, at the onset of measure 10, the pattern segues to a third-inversion D7 voicing, which is followed by three consecutive bass notes, leading to the G7 chord change (measure 11). The two measures of G7 harmony consist of root-position, first-inversion, and second-inversion voicings and a bass line that transitions to the C7 chord (measure 13) via a half step (Db–C).

MEASURES 13–16: In measures 13–14, the C7 harmony is stated with three different inversions of a sixth-string C7 voicing. After opening with the root inversion, the bass line descends string 6, moving to third inversion on beat 3 and to second inversion on beat 1 of measure 14. Following two repetitions of the second-inversion C7 voicing, the open low E string is used to bridge the C7 and F7 harmonies. In measures 15–16, the bass pattern from measures 11–12 has been employed, only it's been shifted down one whole step to accommodate the new (F7) harmony.

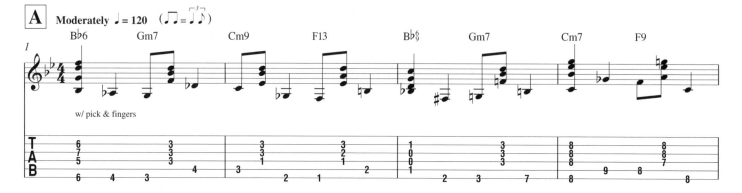

🔊 JAM #98: ONE-BAR LEAD/RHYTHM ALTERNATIONS

This first series of "Rhythm Changes" alternations involves rotating one bar of soloing with one bar of bass line. These lead/rhythm tradeoffs are maintained throughout the Jam's 16 bars. Since the changes move by quickly in the A-section, the lead phrases mostly stick to simple arpeggios and a repetitive scale pattern (1–2–3–5). In the B-section, the lead phrases are built around a pair of one-bar melodic motifs.

MEASURES 1–4: The Bb6–Gm7 progression in measure 1 is handled by a Bb major arpeggio (Bb–D–F) and a reverse G minor seventh arpeggio (G–Bb–D–F), respectively. Following one bar of bass line (measure 2), the Bb6–Gm7 progression's second appearance is outlined with a Bb major scale (Bb–C–D–Eb–F–G–A) sequence (1–2–3–5) and a G Dorian (G–A–Bb–C–D–E–F) passage, respectively. In measure 4, the bass pattern from measure 2 is repeated, with slight modifications.

MEASURES 5–8: The 1–2–3–5 scale sequence is used for both the Fm7 and the Bb7 chords in measure 5, deriving its notes from the F Dorian (F–G–Ab–Bb–C–D–Eb) and Bb Mixolydian (Bb–C–D–Eb–F–G–Ab) modes, respectively. In measure 6, barre-chord-style voicings are implemented for the Ebmaj7–Ebm7 progression bass line. In measure 7, the 1–2–3–5 scale sequence outlines the Bb6 chord and is followed by an F9 chord stab, played on the "and" of beat 3. The bass line then moves chromatically to measure 8, where a common Bb6 voicing alternates with an A bass note.

MEASURES 9–12: The one-bar phrase in measure 9 is a D dominant seventh arpeggio (D–F#–A–C) that includes the sixth degree of the D Mixolydian mode, B. The addition of the B note implies a D13 harmony. In measure 10, a root–5th bass line is paired with a D9 voicing, followed in measure 11 by a restatement of the motif from measure 9, although it's played here in the key of G—specifically, G Mixolydian. The bass line in measure 12 is also a root–5th pattern, although the location of the G7 chord's root and 5th are reversed. Here, the root is on string 6, whereas the 5th is located on string 5.

MEASURES 13–16: The C Mixolydian mode (C–D–E–F–G–A–Bb) provides the pitches for the lick in measure 13. In measure 14, the bass-line pattern from measure 10 is restated, although it's played down a whole step and contains a slight rhythmic modification. The bass-string lick in measure 15 is derived from the F composite blues scale (F–G–Ab–A–Bb–Cb–C–D–Eb) and is loosely based on the lick from measure 13. The bass line that wraps up the Jam (measure 16) commences with a first-inversion F7 voicing (rather than a root-position voicing) and travels up string 6, to the second-inversion voicing of the chord (beat 3), before resolving to the I (Bb6) chord.

🔊 JAM #99: TWO-BAR LEAD/RHYTHM ALTERNATIONS

In this Jam, the lead and rhythm components have been extended to two bars apiece. The result is an arrangement that commences with two bars of lead before shifting to two measures of bass line, with the two approaches continuously alternating throughout the Jam's 16 measures. Melodically, the Jam's lead passages employ a variety of devices, including hybrid scales, scale sequences, and arpeggios, both in ascending and descending order.

MEASURES 1–4: The B♭ major pentatonic scale (B♭–C–D–F–G) provides the framework for the entire lick in measure 1. However, if you examine the phrase closely, you'll discover that the phrase is built entirely from B♭6 (B♭–D–F–G) and Gm7 (G–B♭–D–F) chord tones. For example, the G note that is tied across beats 2 and 3 functions as the 6th of B♭6 *and* as the root of Gm7. In measure 2, the Cm7 chord is outlined with a 1–2–3–5 sequence derived from the C Dorian mode (C–D–E♭–F–G–A–B♭), while the F7 harmony is outlined with arpeggiation of a common F major voicing. Meanwhile, in measures 3–4, the second repetition of the I–vi–ii–V (B♭6–Gm7–Cm7–F7) progression is outlined with a bass line that substitutes an open-position B♭6/9 voicing for the I chord and makes a large fretboard jump when moving from the vi chord to the ii chord, thereby enabling both minor seventh harmonies to be voiced the same.

MEASURES 5–8: The Fm7–B♭7 progression in measure 5 is effectively outlined with simple F minor (F–A♭–C) and B♭ major (B♭–D–F) arpeggios. The dominant quality of the B♭7 change is implied via the A♭ note (the ♭7th), which is tied across beats 2 and 3. In measure 6, an E♭ major (E♭–G–B♭) arpeggio handles the E♭maj7 change, and a reverse E♭ minor (E♭–G♭–B♭) arpeggio handles the E♭m7 harmony, starting from the minor 3rd, G♭. In measure 7, the bass line moves from a common B♭6 voicing to a root-position F13 voicing by way of the open low E string. In measure 8, the bass line returns to the open-position B♭6/9 voicing for an alternating root–5th pattern.

MEASURES 9–12: The B-section kicks off with a long, flowing phrase derived from the D composite blues scale (D–E–F–F♯–G–A♭–A–B–C). This passage leads to a two-bar bass line that commences with a root-position G7 chord, which alternates its root (string 6) and 5th (string 5) before moving up the fretboard. In measure 12, the bass line employs first-inversion (beat 1) and second-inversion (beat 3) voicings of the G7 chord before moving chromatically to the root of the C7 harmony (measure 13).

MEASURES 13–16: The first half of the C7 lick (measure 13) is constructed from a two-octave C dominant seventh arpeggio (C–E–G–B♭) pattern. In measure 14, the lick introduces a couple of A notes to impart a C13 tonality. The fourth-string slide from B♭ to A at the end of the passage effectively shifts the Jam from lead to rhythm, as A is the 3rd of the F7 harmony (measure 15) and is included in the F9 voicing, which alternates is root and 5th (C) tones for the bass line. In measure 16, the bass line juggles a third-inversion F7 voicing and the F9 chord before resolving to the I (B♭6) chord.

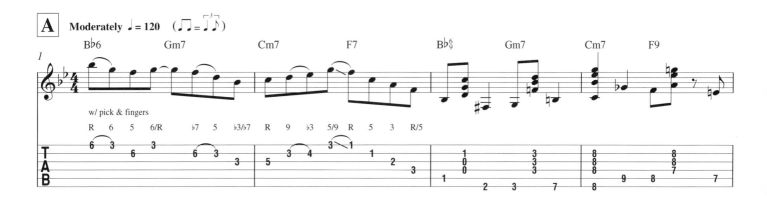

🔊 JAM #100: ONE-BAR RHYTHM/LEAD ALTERNATIONS

Compared to Jams 98–99, the sequence and length of the alternations in this example have been altered. Here, one bar of walking bass line and one bar of lead continuously alternate—in that order—throughout the form's 16 measures. Like the other "Rhythm Changes" Jams, the lead phrases in this example feature several soloing devices, including scale sequences, arpeggios, melodic motif, and legato phrasing.

MEASURES 1–4: The Jam commences with a bass line that incorporates root-position Bb6 and Gm7 voicings. In measure 2, the first lead enters the fray, utilizing the C Dorian (C–D–Eb–F–G–A–Bb) and F Mixolydian (F–G–A–Bb–C–D–Eb) modes and a 1–2–3–5 scale sequence to outline the Cm7 and F7 chords, respectively. In measure 3, an open-position Bb6/9 voicing is substituted for the I chord and followed by a Gm7 voicing for the vi chord. Similar to measure 2, the bass-string lick in measure 4 moves from C Dorian to F Mixolydian as the chords change; however, at the end of the phrase, the F7 chord's 3rd, A, is pulled off to the open low E string to facilitate the transition to the root-position Fm7 voicing (measure 5).

MEASURES 5–8: The ii–V progression in measure 5 features sixth-string, root-position Fm7 and Bb7 voicings, requiring the bass line to make a three-fret jump up the fretboard on beat 2 and an additional two frets on beat 3. In measure 6, the 1–2–3–5 pattern is applied to the Eb major scale (Eb–F–G–Ab–Bb–C–D) for the Ebmaj7 change and moves seamlessly to a four-note phrase that targets chord tones of the Ebm7 harmony. In measure 7, the Bb6 voicing that opened the Jam is employed for the I chord, followed by a common, fifth-string F9 voicing for the V chord. The bass line ends on the note B (beat 4) and moves chromatically to the arpeggio-based phrase in measure 8. Although the harmony here is Bb6, the presence of the major 7th (A), in addition to the tones of a Bb6 chord (Bb–D–F–G), implies a Bbmaj13 harmony.

MEASURES 9–12: The D9 harmony is first implied via a root–5th bass pattern that is paired with a common D9 voicing, and then by a D composite blues scale (D–E–F–F♯–G–Ab–A–B–C) lick that is heavy on second-string chromaticism. In measure 11, root-position and first-inversion G7 voicings acknowledge the change in harmony before segueing to a phrase that mimics the lick from measure 10. However, in place of chromaticism, this phrase emphasizes G7 chord tones (G–B–D–F). Notice that the phrase ends on the note E, which also functions as the 3rd of the forthcoming C7 harmony. In fact, the note is included in the voicing that commences measure 13.

MEASURES 13–16: In measures 13–14, root-position and third-inversion C7 voicings are paired with a descending bass line that segues to a single-note line that begins on the chord's 5th, G, before emphasizing chord tones (C–E–G–B♭) in the second half of the phrase. The bass line in measures 15–16 moves in the opposite direction. Here, root-position and first-inversion F7 chords are paired with an ascending bass line that segues to a two-octave, two-notes-per-string F dominant seventh arpeggio (F–A–C–E♭), starting on the chord's 5th, C.

JAM #101: TWO-BAR RHYTHM/LEAD ALTERNATIONS

In this example, the rhythm/lead alternations from Jam #100 have been extended to two bars. Now, two measures of walking bass line are continuously alternated with two bars of lead throughout the Jam's 16 bars. Like the other "Rhythm Changes" Jams, the bass lines incorporate multiple inversions of major, minor, and dominant chord types, approached by both diatonic and chromatic (non-diatonic) bass notes. Meanwhile, the lead phrases are derived from several note sources, including the major scale, the composite blues scale, and the Mixolydian and Dorian modes.

163

MEASURES 1–4: The opening bass line begins with a root-position B♭6 voicing before moving down string 6 to a root-position Gm7 voicing. In measure 2, the bass line shifts to string 5 for a Cm9 voicing, returning to string 6 for an F13 voicing to close out the two-bar pattern. After a pickup note (A), a two-bar phrase commences with a reverse B♭ major (B♭–D–F) arpeggio. When the phrase reaches string 4, it shifts to a G minor seventh arpeggio (G–B♭–D–F) sequence, signaling a change in harmony (B♭6 to Gm7). In measure 4, the C Dorian (C–D–E♭–F–G–A–B♭) and F Mixolydian (F–G–A–B♭–C–D–E♭) modes utilize a 1–2–3–5 scale sequence to imply the Cm7 and F7 harmonies, respectively.

MEASURES 5–8: The bass-line pattern from measure 2 is restated in measure 5, although it's shifted up five frets to accommodate the new harmonies (Fm9 and B♭13). In measure 6, barre-chord-style E♭maj7 and E♭m7 voicings are paired to handle the IV–iv progression, followed in measure 7 by B♭ major sixth (B♭–D–F–G) and F major (F–A–C) arpeggios. The A-section wraps up in measure 8 with a chord-tone-laden phrase derived from the B♭ major scale (B♭–C–D–E♭–F–G–A). The phrase ends on the note E♭, which creates a half-step transition to the root of the D9 harmony (measure 9).

MEASURES 9–12: The two-measure bass line played over the D9 harmony involves an alternating root–5th pattern (measure 9), followed by a third-inversion D7 voicing and a bass line that descends string 5 (measure 10). At measure 11, an F♯ pickup (bass) note is slid to the root of the G7 harmony. This two-measure phrase starts out as a two-notes-per-string G dominant seventh arpeggio (G–B–D–F) before morphing into a G composite blues scale (G–A–B♭–B–C–D♭–D–E–F) phrase at measure 11's midpoint. Notice that the E note that wraps up the two-measure phrase also functions as the 3rd of the forthcoming C7 harmony and, as such, is included in the C9 voicing that opens measure 13.

MEASURES 13–16: The C9 bass pattern in measure 13 is a restatement of the one introduced in measure 9, only it's played here a whole-step lower to accommodate the new (C7) harmony. On beat 4, the bass line jumps up to fret 7 to begin the descent of string 6, incorporating third- and second-inversion C7 voicings along the way. In measure 15, a two-bar F Mixolydian (F–G–A–B♭–C–D–E♭) phrase commences. The pattern is essentially the extended form of the F major pentatonic scale, but with the addition of the ♭7th (E♭). A melodic motif is stated in measure 15 and then restated an octave higher, with slight modifications, in measure 16, leading to the root of the B♭6 chord.

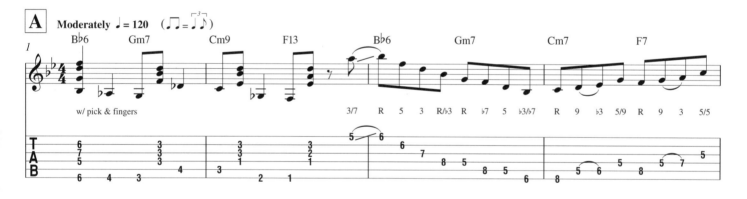

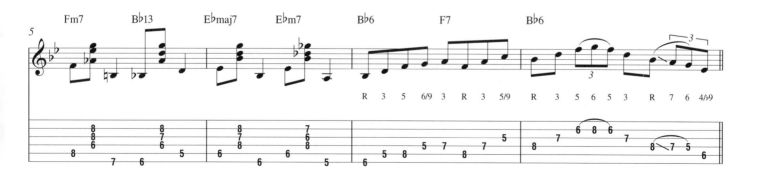

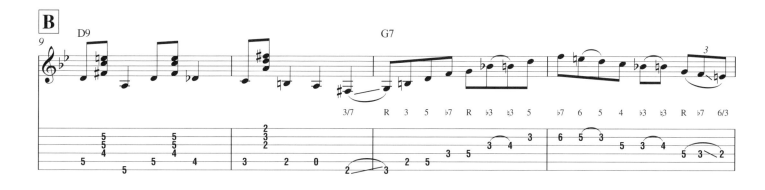

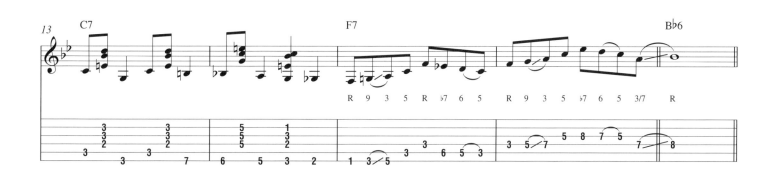

🔊 JAM #102: RANDOM RHYTHM/LEAD ALTERNATIONS

The alternations in this Jam are arranged randomly, with no predetermined one- or two-bar intervals. The unpredictable, less-structured nature of these rhythm/lead tradeoffs is more appealing to the listener and, therefore, is the approach that you should strive for.

This Jam is heavily tilted toward lead playing, as no fewer than 11 of the example's 16 bars are devoted to soloing. With so few measures dedicated to outlining the chord changes via the bass line, the burden falls on the lead phrases. Consequently, the lead passages in this Jam are heavily focused on chord tones. That way, listeners are able to identify changes in harmony, even during long stretches where the bass line and chords are absent. For example, a four-bar phrase begins at the end of the A-section, continuing through the first three measures of the B-section. During that stretch, the chords change as follows: Bb6–D7–G7. Although the bass line and chords are nowhere to be found, the lead passage is so rich in chord tones that the listener is nevertheless able to hear the changes.

MEASURES 1–4: The Jam launches with a three-bar phrase that outlines the first repetition of the I–vi–ii–V progression, as well as the second repetition of the Bb6–Gm7 change. The only note in this passage that is *not* a chord tone is the C note performed on beat 1 of measure 1 (the second note of the first-string trill). Of particular note is the chord tone that is tied across beats 2 and 3 in measure 3, Bb, which functions both as the root of Bb6 and as the minor 3rd of Gm7. At the end of measure 3, a Db bass note moves chromatically to the Cm7 chord in measure 4, where root-position voicings outline the Cm7 and F9 changes.

MEASURES 5–8: In measures 5–6, F minor seventh (F–Ab–C–Eb), Bb dominant seventh (Bb–D–F–Ab), and Eb major (Eb–G–Bb) arpeggios outline the Fm7, Bb7, and Ebmaj7 changes, respectively. Meanwhile, the Ebm7 change is handled by an Ebm7 chord stab, played on the "and" of beat 3. In measure 7, root-position voicing are paired with the bass line to outline the Bb6–F9 progression, followed in measure 8 by a phrase that is built around a Bb major sixth (Bb–D–F–G) arpeggio, which is used to signal a return to the I (Bb6) chord.

MEASURES 9–12: The phrase that began in measure 8 is sustained through the first three measures of the B-section (measures 9–11). To hammer home a change in harmony (literally!), from Bb6 to D7, the phrase shifts from F, the 5th of the former, to F#, the 3rd of the latter. While measure 9 emphasizes chord tones (D, F#, A, and C), measure 10 introduces the note G, giving the phrase a brief scalar feel. At the end of measure 10, the F# note that commenced the D7 phrase is slide up a half step, to the root of the G7 harmony. Here, a G major (G–B–D) arpeggio is used to outline the new chord, followed in measure 12 by a bass line that alternates the root and 5th (D) of a fifth-string G9 voicing.

MEASURES 13–16: The first instance in which the bass line is played in consecutive measures occurs in measure 13, where root-position and third-inversion voicings outline the C7 harmony, following the G9 bass line from measure 12. A half-step (B–C) slide commences the bass-string lick in measure 14, which is composed of pitches from the C Mixolydian mode (C–D–E–F–G–A–Bb). In measure 15, the bass line from measure 12 is restated, although it has been shifted down one whole step to accommodate the new (F7) harmony. In place of a bass note on beat 4, however, a descending F Mixolydian (F–G–A–Bb–C–D–Eb) phrase is launched, outlining the second measure of the two-bar F7 harmony before resolving to the root of the I (Bb6) chord.

CHAPTER 18: WALKING BASS LINE: COLTRANE CHANGES
THE RESOURCES

CHORDS

Bmaj9   D9   G6   B♭7   E♭maj9

  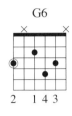 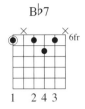 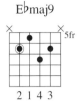

Am7   F♯9   Bmaj7   Fm9   B♭13

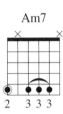 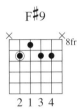 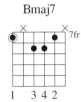 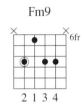 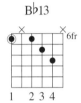

Gmaj7   C♯m9   F♯13   Fm7

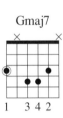  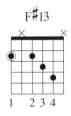 

SCALES

B Major (3rd Position):
B–C♯–D♯–E–F♯–G♯–A♯
(1–2–3–4–5–6–7)

B Major (6th Position)

B Major Pentatonic (Extended Form):
B–C♯–D♯–F♯–G♯
(1–2–3–5–6)

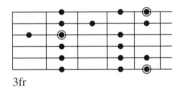 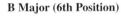 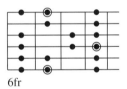 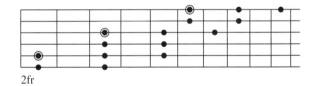

3fr   6fr   2fr

D Mixolydian (All Positions):
D–E–F♯–G–A–B–C
(1–2–3–4–5–6–♭7)

E♭ Major (3rd Position):
E♭–F–G–A♭–B♭–C–D
(1–2–3–4–5–6–7)

E♭ Major (5th Position)

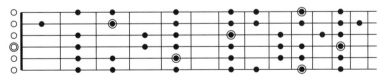 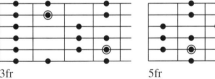 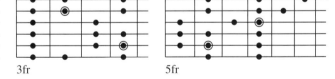

3fr   5fr

E♭ Major (10th Position)

G Major (2nd Position):
G–A–B–C–D–E–F♯
(1–2–3–4–5–6–7)

G Major (4th Position)

G Major (7th Position)

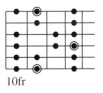 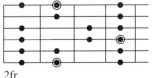 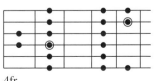 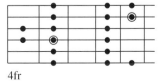

10fr   2fr   4fr   7fr

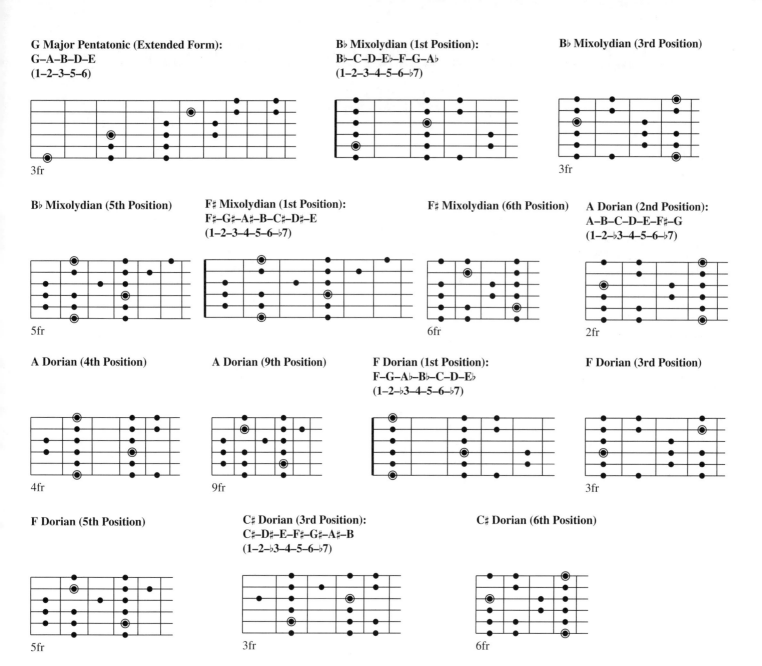

G Major Pentatonic (Extended Form):
G–A–B–D–E
(1–2–3–5–6)

B♭ Mixolydian (1st Position):
B♭–C–D–E♭–F–G–A♭
(1–2–3–4–5–6–♭7)

B♭ Mixolydian (3rd Position)

B♭ Mixolydian (5th Position)

F♯ Mixolydian (1st Position):
F♯–G♯–A♯–B–C♯–D♯–E
(1–2–3–4–5–6–♭7)

F♯ Mixolydian (6th Position)

A Dorian (2nd Position):
A–B–C–D–E–F♯–G
(1–2–♭3–4–5–6–♭7)

A Dorian (4th Position)

A Dorian (9th Position)

F Dorian (1st Position):
F–G–A♭–B♭–C–D–E♭
(1–2–♭3–4–5–6–♭7)

F Dorian (3rd Position)

F Dorian (5th Position)

C♯ Dorian (3rd Position):
C♯–D♯–E–F♯–G♯–A♯–B
(1–2–♭3–4–5–6–♭7)

C♯ Dorian (6th Position)

 # JAM #103: THE 16-BAR FORM

Although not as ubiquitous as "Rhythm Changes," "Coltrane Changes" have become a staple of jazz harmony. Coltrane Changes are a sophisticated set of chord substitutions that were introduced to the public by tenor saxophonist John Coltrane, on his seminal recording "Giant Steps" (1960).

The 16-bar tune essentially contains two eight-bar sections. The first section is comprised of a series of chord changes that move from a major chord to a dominant chord that is located a minor 3rd (three frets) above the former. This dominant chord functions here as a V chord and moves to a new tonic, or I chord, creating a V–I progression. This chord cycle is repeated in the new key, with the resultant key/tonic (measure 3) located a major 3rd (four frets) above the original tonic (measure 1). This five-chord cycle is then punctuated by a ii–V progression that leads to another new tonic (I chord)—again, located a major 3rd above the previous key/tonic. This four-bar progression (bars 1–4) is then repeated in the new key centers (bars 5–8).

The second section (bars 9–16) features a cycle of ii–V–I progressions that are separated by a major 3rd. For example, the Fm7–B♭7–E♭maj7 progression in measures 8–9 is followed by Am7–D7–Gmaj7, which is located a major 3rd above its predecessor. This cycling of ii–V–I progressions continues till the end of the song form, with the final ii–V progression, C♯m7–F♯7, leading back to measure 1 and the original I chord, Bmaj7.

The 16-bar form used in the next six Jams is based on Coltrane Change, although some basic reharmonization has been implemented in the form of chord extensions. In many cases, sixth, ninth, and 13th voicings have been substituted for basic major, minor, and dominant seventh chords. The extensions impart a more sophisticated sound without changing the structure of the progression. Meanwhile, the walking bass lines are constructed from a combination of diatonic and chromatic (non-diatonic) pitches, much like the bass lines in Chapters 16 and 17.

MEASURES 1–4: The Jam commences with Bmaj9 and D9 voicings that are paired with a bass line that walks up string 5. On beat 4 of measure 1, the bass line shifts to string 6, where the G6 and B♭7 changes are voiced with root-position chord shapes. In measure 3, the major ninth voicing returns for the E♭maj9 change, with the bass line alternating between string 5 (the root) and string 6 (the 5th). The ii–V progression in measure 5 is handled by voicings that shift from string 6 (Am7) to string 5 (D9).

MEASURES 5–8: The bass pattern in measure 5 is identical to measure 2 and segues to E♭maj9 and F♯9 voicings that are modeled after the ones from measure 1. Voice the Bmaj7 chord in measure 7 with an index-finger barre at fret 7, using your middle and ring fingers for the notes on fret 8 of strings 4 and 3, respectively. That way, your pinky can voice string 5 as the bass line fluctuates between its root and 5th, which is located at fret 9 of the fifth string. In measure 8, the ii–V progression is outlined with a fifth-string Fm9 voicing and a sixth-string B♭13 voicing, respectively.

MEASURES 9–12: The second half of the progression starts with a bass pattern that matches the two-bar phrase from measures 3–4. In measure 11, the Gmaj7 change is handled by a pattern that is modeled after the one from measure 7 (Bmaj7). Like that chord, use an index-finger barre to voice the Gmaj7 chord. Likewise, the bass pattern in measure 12 is a variation of the pattern from measure 8, although it's been relocated to accommodate the new progression, C♯m9–F♯13.

MEASURES 13–16: The Bmaj9 voicing that opened the Jam is restated in measure 13, where the bass line alternates between the chord's root (string 5) and 5th (string 6). In measure 14, a root-position Fm7 voicing is followed by the open A string, which facilitates the fret-hand shift to sixth position of the B♭7 chord. In measure 15, the root–5th pattern is paired with the E♭maj9 voicing before the bass line descends string 5 to transition to the C♯m9–F♯13 progression, which is a reproduction of measure 12.

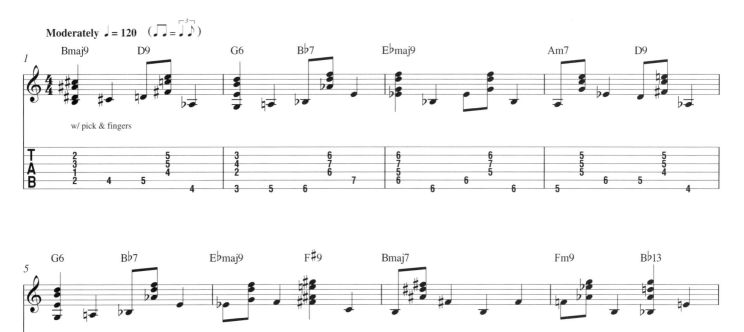

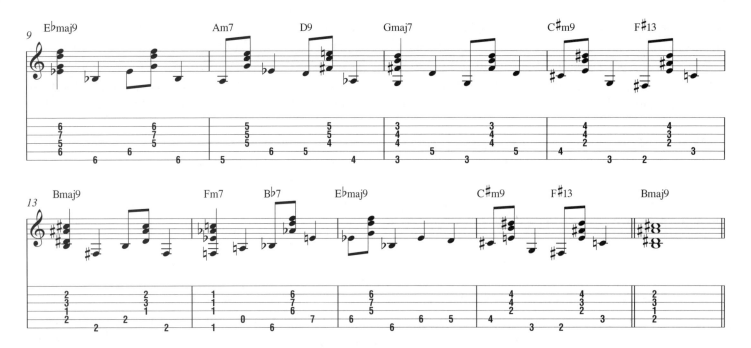

JAM #104: ONE-BAR LEAD/RHYTHM ALTERNATIONS

In this Jam, one bar of lead is continuously alternated with one bar of walking bass line. Although Coltrane performed "Giant Steps" at a blistering tempo, the tempo used in this example is a more manageable 120 beats per minute, thereby enabling clean transitions between lead and rhythm figures. The bass patterns are modeled after the ones introduced in Jam #103, with the bass notes consisting of both diatonic and non-diatonic tones. Meanwhile, the lead passages are a combination of scale phrases and arpeggios, with emphasis on the latter.

MEASURES 1–4: After outlining the Bmaj7 and D7 harmonies with descending and ascending arpeggios, respectively, the Jam transitions to the bass line for the Gmaj9–Bb7 progression. In measure 3, the Ebmaj7 harmony is implied with an arpeggio pattern that employs every note of the chord (Eb, G, Bb, and D). At the end of the measure, the lick jumps down to string 6 so as to approach the Am7 chord via a half step (Bb–A). Here, the ii–V progression is handled by root-position Am7 and D9 voicings.

MEASURES 5–8: In measure 5, the Gmaj7 chord is implied with a bass-string trill that alternates between its root (G) and major 7th (F#). This phrase leads to a Bb major (Bb–D–F) arpeggio passage that outlines the Bb7 chord. Following a measure in which Ebmaj9 and F#9 harmonies are handled by fifth-string voicings, a major seventh arpeggio is employed in measure 7 to outline the chord tones of the Bmaj7 harmony (B–D#–F#–A#). In measure 8, minor ninth and dominant 13 voicings are implemented for the ii–V (Fm9–Bb13) progression.

MEASURES 9–12: The final bass note of measure 8, E, is slid down a half step, to the root of the Ebmaj7 harmony. Here, an arpeggio-based phrase similar to the one used in measure 3 is employed to outline the Ebmaj7 chord. The C note at fret 5 of the third string is thrown into mix, as well, resulting in an implied Ebmaj13 harmony (C is the 6th/13th of Eb major). The bass pattern from measure 4 is restated in measure 10; however, in place of a bass note on beat 4, a half-step slide moves from the 3rd of D9, F#, to the root of the new Gmaj7 harmony (measure 11). This descending phrase is based around a G major sixth (G–B–D–E) arpeggio and uses its final two notes, D and C, to enclose, or "frame," the C# bass note that opens measure 12. Here, the bass pattern from measure 8 is used as the model for the ii–V (C#m9–F#13) progression.

MEASURES 13–16: In measure 13, the Bmaj7 harmony is outlined with the extended form of the B major pentatonic scale (B–C#–D#–F#–G#), starting from fret 2 of the fifth string. This phrase leads to an Fm9–Bb13 bass pattern that is nearly identical to the one from measure 8, including the slide on beat 4. Like its predecessor, the slide transitions to a lick that is built from an Eb major seventh arpeggio and includes the 6th/13th (Eb–G–Bb–C–D). At the end of measure 15, the 6th (C) is played on string 6 to move chromatically to the root of the forthcoming C#m7 chord, which is followed by the fifth-string F#9 voicing.

JAM #105: TWO-BAR LEAD/RHYTHM ALTERNATIONS

The one-bar alternations from Jam #104 have been extended to two bars in this example. Starting with two measures of lead, these two-bar tradeoffs continue throughout the Jam's 16 bars.

When John Coltrane recorded "Giant Steps" in 1959, he employed a couple of soloing devices that we've used in previous Jams—namely, arpeggios and scale sequences. These devices are great for playing over fast-moving changes due to the abundance of chord tones. Even at its blistering tempo, you can hear the chord changes in Coltrane's improvisations in "Giant Steps." Coltrane's soloing approach is implemented here, with the lead phrases comprised almost exclusively of triad and seventh-chord arpeggios and 1–2–3–5 scale sequences.

MEASURES 1–4: The two-measure phrase that opens the Jam consists of a series of four arpeggios, starting with ascending B major (B–D♯–F♯) and D major (D–F♯–A) patterns and concluding with a reverse G major (G–B–D) arpeggio and an ascending B♭ dominant seventh (B♭–D–F–A♭) pattern. In measures 3–4, the bass line enters to handle the E♭maj7 and Am7–D9 changes. The E♭maj9 pattern alternates between the chord's root (string 5) and 5th (string 6), followed in measure 4 by root-position Am7 and D9 voicings that shift from string 6 to string 5 for the latter voicing.

MEASURES 5–8:
In measure 5, the chord changes (Gmaj7–B♭7) are outlined with a G major sixth (G–B–D–E) arpeggio and a four-note phrase comprised entirely of B♭7 chord tones (F, B♭, and A♭). The E♭maj7–F♯7 progression in measure 6 is outlined with a reverse E♭ major (E♭–G–B♭) arpeggio, starting from its 3rd (G), and an ascending F♯ dominant seventh (F♯–A♯–C♯–E) arpeggio. The bass line is measures 7–8 is a reproduction of the pattern from measures 3–4, although it's been shifted down four frets to accommodate the new chords. However, instead of moving to a fifth-string dominant ninth voicing for the B♭7 change in measure 8, the bass line moves up string 6, to a root-position dominant seventh voicing. On the "and' of beat 4, a D note acts as a pickup to the forthcoming lead phrase. Over the B♭7 chord, D functions as the major 3rd, whereas over the E♭maj7 harmony, D functions as the major 7th.

MEASURES 9–12:
The phrase that outlines the E♭maj7 harmony in measure 9 is composed primarily of chord tones (E♭–G–B♭–D). The one exception is the C note on beat 4, which gives the second half of the passage a more scalar feel. A half-step (B♭–A) slide commences the phrase in measure 10. Here, the A Dorian (A–B–C–D–E–F♯–G) and D Mixolydian (D–E–F♯–G–A–B–C) modes employ the 1–2–3–5 scale sequence to outline the Am7–D7 progression, respectively. In measure 11, the root–5th bass pattern is used to outline the Gmaj7 harmony. To play this pattern, use a third-fret, index-finger barre, fretting the notes at fret 4 of the fourth and third strings with your middle and ring fingers, respectively. That way, you're able to voice the chord's 5th (fret 5, fifth string) with your pinky. The second half of the two-bar bass pattern involves a fifth-string C♯m9 voicing, which is followed by a shift to string 6 for the F♯13 chord.

MEASURES 13–16:
The A♯ note that is slid into the two-measure phrase in measures 13–14 serves two functions— it's the major 3rd of F♯13 and the major 7th of Bmaj7. This note is followed in measure 13 by an eight-note B major pentatonic (B–C♯–D♯–F♯–G♯) lick. This phrase then segues to a 1–2–3–5 scale sequence that is rooted in the F Dorian mode (F–G–A♭–B♭–C–D–E♭), followed by a four-note phrase that employs every note of the B♭7 chord (B♭–D–F–A♭). The B♭7 chord's 3rd, D, is then slide up a half step, to the root of the E♭maj9 chord (measure 15). Here, the voicing is paired with the alternating root–5th bass line, followed in measure 16 by a pattern that is modeled after the one from measure 12.

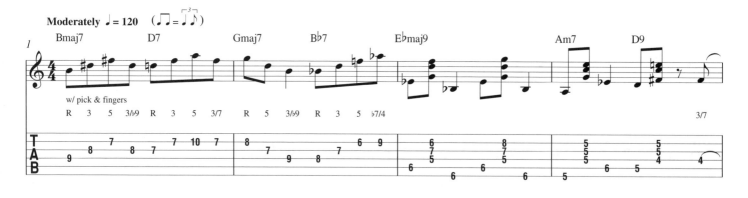

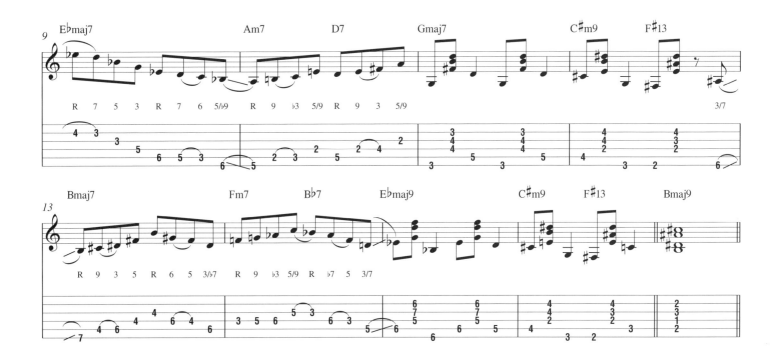

JAM #106: ONE-BAR RHYTHM/LEAD ALTERNATIONS

Compared to the previous two examples, the sequence and length of the alternations in this Jam have been modified. Here, the Jam commences with one bar of walking bass line before transitioning to a measure of lead—a pattern that is repeated throughout the 16 measures. Like the previous Jams involving Coltrane Changes, the lead phrases are mainly comprised of short scale sequences and arpeggios, with much of the soloing relegated to the guitar's bass strings.

MEASURES 1–4: After a bass line involving root-position Bmaj9 and D9 voicings ascends string 5 for three beats, the pattern shifts to string 6 on beat 4 of measure 1, where it segues to a G major pentatonic (G–A–B–D–E) lick that outlines the Gmaj7 harmony. This four-note phrase is followed by a Bb major sixth arpeggio (Bb–D–F–G). In measure 3, the bass pattern alternates the Ebmaj9 chord's root (string 5) and 5th (string 6), followed in measure 4 by an A minor seventh (A–C–E–G) arpeggio, which is approached from a half step (G#–A), and a second-string legato figure that resolves to the root of the D7 harmony.

MEASURES 5–8: In measure 5, the bass line incorporates root-position G6 and Bb7 voicings as it ascends string 6, followed in measure 6 by an Eb major phrase that is approached by the note D, which serves as the major 3rd of Bb7 and the major 7th of Ebmaj7. This four-note phrase is followed by an F# major (F#–A#–C#) arpeggio, which effectively outlines the F#7 harmony. Instead of ending with a chord tone, however, the phrase employs a C#-to-D# hammer-on, the latter of which is the major 3rd of the impending Bmaj7 chord, creating a strong pull toward the chord's root. To play the bass pattern in measure 7, use a seventh-fret, index-finger barre, fretting the notes at fret 8 of the fourth and third strings with your middle and ring fingers, respectively. That way, you're able to voice the chord's 5th (fret 9, fifth string) with your pinky. In measure 8, scale sequences are derived from the F Dorian (F–G–Ab–Bb–C–D–Eb) and Bb Mixolydian (Bb–C–D–Eb–F–G–Ab) modes for the Fm7 and Bb7 changes, respectively.

MEASURES 9–12: The bass pattern from measure 3 is incorporated, with a different ending, into measure 9 and segues to a single-note run up strings 6–4 (measure 10). The first four notes of the sequence are derived from the A Dorian mode (A–B–C–D–E–F#–G) and transitions seamlessly to a D Mixolydian (D–E–F#–G–A–B–C) phrase. Both of these four-note phrases are comprised of the first, second, third, and fifth degrees (1–2–3–5) of their respective scales. In measure 11, the bass pattern from measure 7 is replicated over the Gmaj7 change, followed in measure 12 by a 1–2–3–5 sequence, derived from C# Dorian (C#–D#–E–F#–G#–A#–B), over the C#m7 change and an F# dominant seventh (F#–A#–C#–E) arpeggio over the F#7 change.

MEASURES 13–16: The bass pattern from measure 7 is duplicated in measure 13 for the Bmaj7 harmony. The final bass note of the pattern, F♯, is then slid down to the root of the forthcoming Fm7 chord, creating a half-step (F♯–F) transition. In measure 14, the ii–V (Fm7–B♭7) progression is outlined with F minor seventh (F–A♭–C–E♭) and B♭ major (B♭–D–F) arpeggios, respectively. In measure 15, a barre-chord-style E♭maj7 chord is used to create an alternating root–5th bass line. On beat 4, the impending single-note line (measure 16) gets a one-beat head start. Here, the first note, B♭, functions as part of the root–5th bass line, and the second note, C, creates a half-step transition to the root of the forthcoming C♯m7 chord. The phrase in measure 16 starts with a C♯ minor (C♯–E–G♯) arpeggio before segueing to a 1–2–3–5 sequence derived from the F♯ Mixolydian mode (F♯–G♯–A♯–B–C♯–D♯–E).

🔊 JAM #107: TWO-BAR RHYTHM/LEAD ALTERNATIONS

The Coltrane Changes in this Jam are performed with alternations that fluctuate between two bars of walking bass line and two bars of lead. These two-bar intervals are maintained throughout the Jam's 16 bars. Like the previous Coltrane Changes Jams, the bass lines are constructed from diatonic and non-diatonic tones alike and incorporate

174

various major, major, and dominant chord inversions and extensions. Meanwhile, the lead phrases are comprised of arpeggios and scale passages derived from the major scale (major chords), Dorian mode (minor chords), and Mixolydian mode (dominant chords).

MEASURES 1–4: The first two measures of walking bass line feature fifth-string Bmaj9 and D9 voicings (measure 1) and sixth-string G6 and B♭7 voicings (measure 2), all of which are voiced with their root in the bass. In measure 3, a descending lick, comprised mostly of chord tones, outlines the E♭maj7 harmony, followed in measure 4 by a four-note A Dorian (A–B–C–D–E–F♯–G) phrase, which segues to a D major (D–F♯–A) arpeggio.

MEASURES 5–8: The bass-line voicings in measure 5 shift from string 5 (Gmaj9) to string 6 (B♭7) before returning to string 5 for the E♭maj9–F♯9 pattern (measure 6), which is modeled after the pattern from measure 1. On the "and" of measure 6, the F♯9 chord's 3rd, A♯, is used as a pickup to the Bmaj7 phrase (measure 7). This one-bar phrase, a descending/ascending B major seventh arpeggio (B–D♯–F♯–A♯), transitions chromatically (F♯–F) to the scale pattern played over the Fm7 harmony (measure 8). Here, a 1–2–3–5 sequence is derived from the F Dorian mode (F–G–A♭–B♭–C–D–E♭), followed on beats 3–4 by a four-note passage that descends the B♭ Mixolydian mode (B♭–C–D–E♭–F–G–A♭).

MEASURES 9–12: The E♭maj9 harmony in measure 9 is handled by a bass pattern that alternates between the chord's root (string 5) and its 5th (string 6). In measure 10, the bass line outlines the ii–V progression with a sixth-string Am7 voicing and a fifth-string D9 voicing, respectively. In measure 11, the Gmaj7 harmony is effectively outlined with a two-notes-per-string G major seventh (G–B–D–F♯) arpeggio. This phrase transitions chromatically to the C♯m7 passage by moving from the Gmaj7 chord's 5th, D, to the root of the C♯m7 chord, played at fret 6 of the third string. The C♯m7 phrase is a 1–2–3–5 scale pattern derived from the C♯ Dorian mode (C♯–D♯–E–F♯–G♯–A♯–B) and is followed by a reverse F♯ major (F♯–A♯–C♯) arpeggio, voiced here as a common triad shape.

MEASURES 13–16: A variation of the root–5th bass pattern from measure 9 is implemented over the Bmaj9 harmony in measure 13. This pattern is followed in measure 14 by root-position Fm7 and B♭7 voicings, with the open A string facilitating the five-fret jump. In measure 15, the E♭ major scale (E♭–F–G–A♭–B♭–C–D) provides the notes for a passage that moves (mostly) in stepwise fashion up the scale, following an E♭–D–E♭ trill on beat 1. The note that concludes the passage, E♭, the root of the E♭maj7 chord, is slid up a half step, to E, the ♭3rd of the C♯m7 chord, resulting in a chromatic transition. In measure 16, the C♯m7 phrase moves stepwise from the chord's ♭3rd to its ♭7th: E–D♯–C♯–B. On beat 3, the passage transitions to a five-note phrase that incorporates three of the F♯7 chord's four tones (A♯, C♯, and E), resulting, once again, in a half-step (B–A♯) transition.

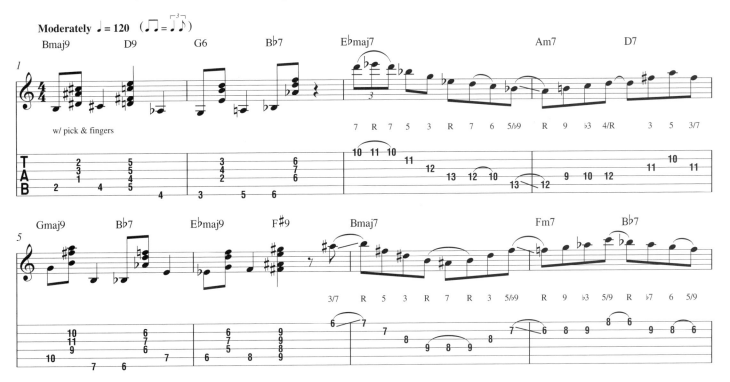

175

🔊 JAM #108: RANDOM RHYTHM/LEAD ALTERNATIONS

In this Jam, the final one involving Coltrane Changes, the alternations have been arranged randomly, with heavy emphasis on lead playing. In fact, no fewer than 11 of the Jam's 16 measures are devoted to soloing. Heck, the walking bass line doesn't make its first appearance until measure 7!

With the Jam kicking off with six straight bars of soloing, establishing the chord changes in the first half of the example is left almost entirely to the lead phrases. The solution is to construct passages ripe with arpeggios and scale sequences that emphasis chord tones on strong beats (i.e., downbeats). If chord tones are not emphasized in a solo setting, listeners have difficulty following along and anticipating what's to come. With that in mind, the following Jam features lead passages replete with chord tones.

MEASURES 1–4: The lead phrases in measures 1–2 outline the opening Bmaj7–D7–Gmaj7–Bb7 progression with arpeggios (Bmaj7, Gmaj7, and Bb7) and a scale sequence (D7). The Bmaj7 and Gmaj7 changes are implied with reverse B major (B–D#–F#) and G major (G–B–D) arpeggios, respectively, while the D7 change is handled by a 1–2–3–5 scale sequence derived from the D Mixolydian mode (D–E–F#–G–A–B–C), and the Bb7 change is implied with an ascending Bb dominant seventh (Bb–D–F–Ab) arpeggio. In measure 3, the Ebmaj7 chord is outlined with just two chord tones, G and Eb, which break up the monotony of a (mostly) eighth-note rhythm. In measure 4, A minor (A–C–E) and D dominant seventh (D–F#–A–C) arpeggios are employed for the ii–V progression, respectively.

MEASURES 5–8: After a four-note phrase (B–A–G–A) is played over the Gmaj7 change, a reverse Bb major (Bb–D–F) arpeggio handles the Bb7 harmony. In measure 6, an ascending Eb major (Eb–G–Bb) arpeggio and a descending F# dominant seventh (F#–A#–C#–E) arpeggio are combined for the Ebmaj7–F#7 progression. The bass line makes its first appearance in measure 7, for the Bmaj7 harmony. To voice this chord, employ a seventh-fret, index-finger barre, using your middle and ring fingers to fret the notes at fret 8 of the fourth and third strings, respectively. That way, your pinky is free to voice the bass notes at fret 9 of the fifth string (F#, the 5th). The bass line is maintained in measure 8, where the ii–V progression is played with a fifth-string Fm9 chord and a sixth-string Bb13 voicing, respectively.

MEASURES 9–12: The Eb major scale (Eb–F–G–Ab–Bb–C–D) supplies the notes for the nine-note phrase that outlines the Ebmaj7 chord in measure 9. This phrase leads to a pair of arpeggios that outline the ii–V progression in measure 10: A minor seventh (A–C–E–G) and D dominant seventh (D–F♯–A–C). Notice that the former ends on its ♭7th, G, while the latter begins on its 3rd, F♯, resulting in an efficient, half-step transition. The bass line return in measure 11. This pattern is identical to the one from measure 7, only it's been shifted down four frets to accommodate the new (Gmaj7) harmony. Likewise, the bass pattern in measure 12 is a restatement of the one from measure 8, played here as C♯m9 and F♯13 changes (i.e., four frets lower).

MEASURES 13–16: The bass line is maintained in measure 13, where an alternating root–5th pattern is paired with a Bmaj9 voicing. In measure 14, a bass-string run is constructed from the 1–2–3–5 scale sequence, starting with the F Dorian mode (F–G–A♭–B♭–C–D–E♭) and concluding with the B♭ Mixolydian mode (B♭–C–D–E♭–F–G–A♭). The E♭ major scale returns in measure 15, where an eight-note phrase works its way up the strings before transitioning to a pair of arpeggios, C♯ minor (C♯–E–G♯) and F♯ dominant seventh (F♯–A♯–C♯–E), for the C♯m7–F♯7 progression in measure 16.

177

THE RESOURCES

CHORDS

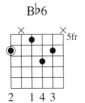

Bb6

Am7b5

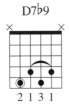

D7b9

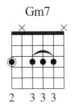

Gm7

C9

Fm7

Bb9

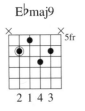

Ebmaj9

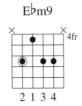

Ebm9

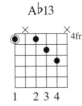

Ab13

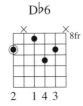

Db6

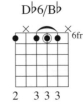

Db6/Bb

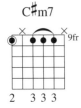

C#m7

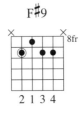

F#9

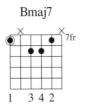

Bmaj7

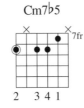

Cm7b5

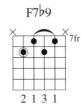

F7b9

Dm9

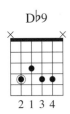

Db9

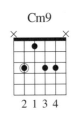

Cm9

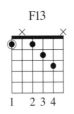

F13

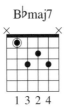

Bbmaj7

SCALES

Bb Major:
Bb–C–D–Eb–F–G–A
(1–2–3–4–5–6–7)

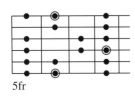

5fr

Bb Mixolydian (3rd Position):
Bb–C–D–Eb–F–G–Ab
(1–2–3–4–5–6–b7)

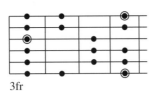

3fr

Bb Mixolydian (5th Position)

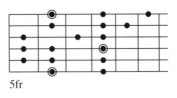

5fr

G Dorian:
G–A–Bb–C–D–E–F
(1–2–b3–4–5–6–b7)

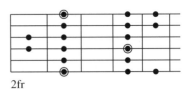

2fr

F Dorian (1st Position):
F–G–Ab–Bb–C–D–Eb
(1–2–b3–4–5–6–b7)

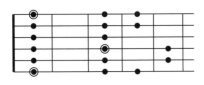

F Dorian (5th Position)

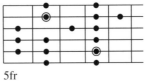

5fr

F Mixolydian (1st Position):
F–G–A–Bb–C–D–Eb
(1–2–3–4–5–6–b7)

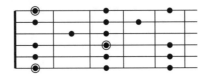

F Mixolydian (7th Position)

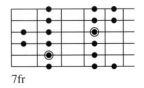

7fr

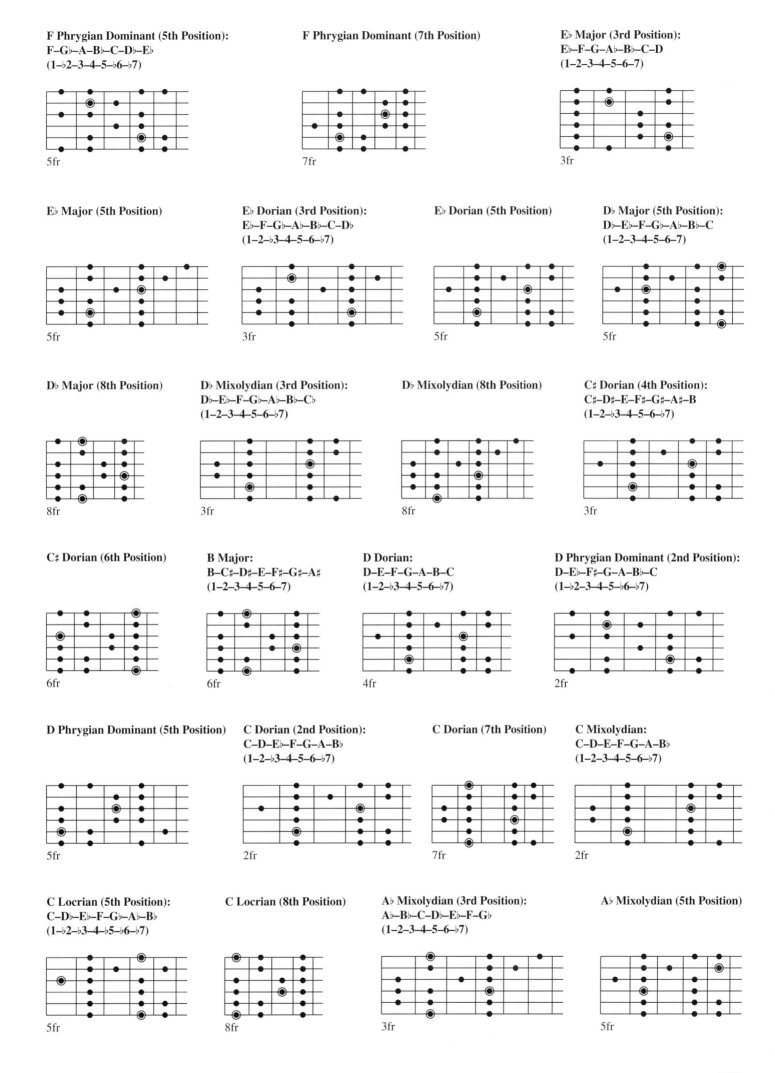

F♯ Mixolydian (4th Position):
F♯–G♯–A♯–B–C♯–D♯–E
(1–2–3–4–5–6–♭7)

F♯ Mixolydian (6th Position)

A Locrian:
A–B♭–C–D–E♭–F–G
(1–♭2–♭3–4–♭5–♭6–♭7)

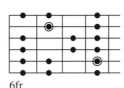

3fr

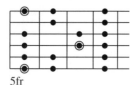

6fr

5fr

 # JAM #109: THE 24-BAR FORM

Up to this point, all of the walking bass lines have been performed in common time (4/4 meter). Well, that's about to change! The next six Jams are arranged in 3/4 time, resulting in a rhythmic feel that is most commonly labeled a "jazz waltz."

The change in meter has a significant impact on the way the walking bass lines are performed. In addition to one less bass note (obviously!), the chord accents are now played exclusively on beat 1, followed by bass notes on beats 2 and 3. Although this isn't a hard-and-fast rule, limiting the chord accents to beat 1 will reinforce the 3/4 feel and, in turn, eliminate any rhythmic ambiguity that might result from constantly shifting where the chords fall, as well as create more efficient transitions between chords.

This Jam is based on the famous jazz waltz "Bluesette" and, like that tune, consists of one 24-bar section. Although written in the key of B♭, harmonically, the Jam is structured around a quartet of key centers: B♭, E♭, D♭, and B. Offsetting these key centers are a series of ii–V and ii–V–I progression, as well as one common (tritone) substitution.

MEASURES 1–6: Harmonically, the first six measures of the Jam feature two bars of the tonic chord, B♭6, followed by ii–V progressions in minor (Am7♭5–D7♭9) and major (Gm7–C9) keys. In measures 1–2, a common B♭6 voicing is paired with bass notes that double as chord tones (B♭, D, and F). In measures 3–4, the Am7♭5 and D7♭9 changes are voiced with sixth- and fifth-string voicings, respectively, while the bass notes are a combination of diatonic and non-diatonic tones. A similar approach is employed in measures 5–6, although the ii–V progression is major in quality (they're diatonic to F major).

MEASURES 7–12: In measures 7–8, an Fm7–B♭9 progression concludes the Jam's first series of ii–V progressions. This bass pattern is similar to the pattern that preceded it (measures 5–6), although the bass line ascends string 5 at the end of measure 8, rather than descend string 6. The Fm7–B♭9 progression resolves to the IV chord in measures 9–10, where an E♭maj9 voicing is paired with a bass line that alternates the chord's root (string 5) and 5th (string 6), using the D note at fret 5 of the fifth string as a transitional note. Another ii–V progression appears in measures 11–12, voiced here as E♭m9 and A♭13 chords, respectively.

MEASURES 13–18: The D♭6 change is voiced with both the root in the bass (measure 13) and the 6th (B♭) in the bass (measure 14). Meanwhile, the bass line descends and ascends the sixth string, segueing to the C♯m7 change at measure 15. The C♯m7 and F♯9 changes are played as common sixth- and fifth-string voicings, respectively. In measures 17–18, voice the Bmaj7 chord with a seventh-fret, index-finger barre, using your middle and ring fingers to fret the notes at fret 8 of the fourth and third strings, respectively. That way, your pinky is free to voice the bass notes at fret 9 of the fifth string (F♯, the 5th).

MEASURES 19–24: The Jam concludes with a series of ii–V progressions that lead back to the tonic (B♭) chord. After starting with a minor ii–V (Cm7♭5–F7♭9), the progression moves on to major ii–Vs in the key of C (Dm9–D♭9) and key of B♭ (Cm9–F13). Technically, the Dm9–D♭9 change isn't a ii–V progression; instead, tritone substitution has been used, whereby G7 (the V chord) has been replaced by a dominant chord that is located a diminished 5th (tritone) above that chord. In this case, D♭9 has been subbed for G7 (the distance/interval between G and D♭ is a diminished 5th). As you can see in the example, the tritone substitution results in a progression that moves chromatically, Dm9–D♭9–Cm9, in measures 21–23 before the F13 chord arrives in measure 24 to initiate resolution to the I (B♭) chord.

JAM #110: ONE-BAR LEAD/RHYTHM ALTERNATIONS

In this Jam, the jazz waltz is performed with alternations that juggle one bar of lead with one bar of walking bass line. These one-bar tradeoffs are maintained throughout the Jam's 24-bar form.

Although the Jam is played at a moderate tempo (100 bpm), the 3/4 meter results in chord changes that can seem unrelenting at times. After all, one less beat means the chord changes occur at a rate that is 25% faster than in 4/4 time. To help facilitate the alternations, the lead phrases in this Jam have been mostly arranged on the bass strings, enabling smoother transitions between lead and rhythm approaches. Melodically, the lead passages are derived from the major scale (major chords), Dorian mode (minor chords), and Locrian mode (half-diminished chords).

MEASURES 1–6: The Jam kicks off with a six-note line that descends the Bb major scale (Bb–C–D–Eb–F–G–A). The second measure of I-chord harmony is handled by the bass line, which features a sixth-string Bb6 voicing. In measure 3, the A Locrian mode (A–Bb–C–D–Eb–F–G) provides the pitches for the lick that is played over the

Am7♭5 harmony, touching on all four chord tones (A–C–E♭–G). This phrase then moves chromatically (E♭–D) to the bass-line pattern in measure 4. The lick that outlines the Gm7 harmony in measure 5 is comprised almost entirely of chord tones: G, B♭, D, and F. In measure 6, the bass pattern from measure 4 is implemented in measure 6, although the new chord is a dominant ninth voicing (C9), rather than an altered dominant chord (D7♭9).

MEASURES 7–12: The lick in measure 7 is a variation on the melodic motif from measure 5, played here with notes from the F Dorian mode (F–G–A♭–B♭–C–D–E♭). Following a bass line that walks up string 5 (measure 8), the E♭ major scale (E♭–F–G–A♭–B♭–C–D), played in a 1–2–3–5 pattern, outlines the E♭maj7 harmony, which is implied with a bass pattern in measure 10. The scale pattern from measure 9 is employed in measure 11, where notes from the E♭ Dorian mode (E♭–F–G♭–A♭–B♭–C–D♭) outline the E♭m7 harmony. Notice that, in both cases, the chord's 3rd is emphasized on beat 3 (G for the E♭maj7 chord, and G♭ for the E♭m7 chord), thereby reinforcing the chord's quality. This phrase leads to a measure of bass line, which outlines the V chord of the two-measure ii–V (E♭m7–A♭7) progression.

MEASURES 13–18: In measure 13, a D♭ major sixth arpeggio (D♭–F–A♭–B♭) is employed for the D♭6 harmony, followed in measure 14 by a root–5th (D♭–A♭) bass pattern that moves to the chord's 7th, C, on beat 4 to set up a chromatic transition to the C♯m7 chord. Here, the C♯ Dorian mode (C♯–D♯–E–F♯–G♯–A♯–B) is played in a chord-tone-laden 1–2–3–5–7–5 pattern, leading to a bass pattern that employs a fifth-string F♯9 voicing. In measure 17, a variation of the scale pattern from measure 15 is played over the Bmaj7 harmony, using notes from the B major scale (B–C♯–D♯–E–F♯–G♯–A♯). The second measure of Bmaj7 harmony is handled by a root-5th bass pattern that incorporates a common Bmaj7 voicing. To voice this chord, employ a seventh-fret, index-finger barre, fretting the notes at fret 8 of the fourth and third strings with your middle and ring fingers, respectively. That way, you're able to voice the chord's 5th (fret 9, fifth string) with your pinky.

MEASURES 19–24: In measure 19, a five-note bass-string lick is derived from the C Locrian mode (C–D♭–E♭–F–G♭–A♭–B♭), with special attention given to the Cm7♭5 chord's ♭5th, G♭. The F7♭9 harmony (measure 20) is outlined with a fifth-string voicing and a bass line that descends the string to arrive in fifth position, where a six-note, chord-tone-centric lick is derived from the D Dorian mode (D–E–F–G–A–B–C) to outline the Dm7 harmony (measure 21). In measure 22, a common D♭9 voicing is paired with a bass line that alternates the chord's root (string 5) and its 5th (string 6). Then, the phrase from measure 21 is restated in measure 23, although it has been moved down one whole step (two frets) to accommodate the new (Cm7) harmony. The Jam concludes in measure 24 with a root-position F7 voicing and a bass line that walks chromatically (C–B–B♭) down string 5 to the I (B♭maj7) chord.

182

JAM #111: TWO-BAR LEAD/RHYTHM ALTERNATIONS

In this example, the one-bar alternations from Jam #110 have been extended to two bars. As a result, two bars of lead and two bars of walking bass line are continuously recycled—in that order—throughout this Jam's 24-bar form. Unlike the previous example, however, this Jam features more treble-string playing due to a decrease in the rapidity of the alternations. Melodically, the lead phrases for the major, minor, and dominant chord changes are derived from the major scale, Dorian mode, and Mixolydian mode, respectively.

MEASURES 1–6: The Jam commences with a two-bar B♭ major scale (B♭–C–D–E♭–F–G–A) phrase that introduces a motif in measure 1 and then plays a variation of it in the lower octave in measure 2. The minor ii–V progression in measures 3–4 is outlined with chromatic bass lines that incorporate root-position voicings on strings 6 and 5, respectively. In measures 5–6, a 12-note phrase starts out as a G Dorian (G–A–B♭–C–D–E–F) lick before seamlessly transitioning to a C Mixolydian (C–D–E–F–G–A–B♭) phrase for the C7 harmony.

MEASURES 7–12: The ii–V progression in measures 7–8 is implied with root-position Fm7 and B♭9 voicings and a bass line that is mostly confined to string 5, transitioning chromatically (D–E♭) to the E♭maj7 phrase in measures 9–10. This two-bar passage emphasizes chord tones (E♭, G, and B♭) while creating a repetitive rhythmic motif that pairs eight notes and an eighth-note triplet. In measures 11–12, E♭m9 and A♭13 voicings outline the ii–V change with the help of a bass line comprised of diatonic and non-diatonic pitches alike.

MEASURES 13–18: The D♭ major scale (D♭–E♭–F–G♭–A♭–B♭–C) lick in measures 13–14 traverses all six strings on its way to the D♭ note at fret 9 of the first string, which also functions as the root of the forthcoming C♯m7 chord (D♭ and C♯ are the same note, or "enharmonic equivalents"). The ii–V progression in measures 15–16 is outlined with root-position C♯m7 and F♯9 chords and a bass lines that flow chromatically down strings 5 and 6, the latter of which leading to a two-bar B major scale (B–C♯–D♯–E–F♯–G♯–A♯) phrase (measures 17–18). Here, the scale moves in (mostly) stepwise fashion from string 6 to string 4, where it reverses course and walks back down the scale.

MEASURES 19–24: In measures 19–20, root-position Cm7♭5 and F7♭9 voicings are paired with chromatic bass lines that walk down string 5, leading to a two-measure phrase that outlines the Dm7–D♭7 progression. The five-note phrase in measure 21 is derived from the D Dorian mode (D–E–F–G–A–B–C) and followed by a D♭ Mixolydian (D♭–E♭–F–G♭–A♭–B♭–C♭) phrase that mimics its predecessor. In measures 23–24, the Jam concludes with a bass pattern that combines root-position Cm9 and F13 voicings with bass lines that approach each subsequent chord (F13 and B♭maj7) chromatically.

JAM #112: ONE-BAR RHYTHM/LEAD ALTERNATIONS

Instead of starting the Jam with one or two bars of lead, this example begins with a measure of walking bass line, followed by a measure of soloing. This rhythm/lead sequence is maintained throughout the Jam's 24-bar form. Melodically, the lead phrases are comprised of arpeggios and short scale passages derived from a number of sources, including the major scale (major chords), Mixolydian mode (dominant chords), and Phrygian dominant scale (altered dominant chords).

MEASURES 1–6: The Jam opens with a one-bar bass pattern in which a common Bb6 voicing is paired with a bass line that moves exclusively among chord tones: Bb–F–D. In measure 2, a short Bb major scale (Bb–C–D–Eb–F–G–A) phrase is implemented to outline the second bar of I–chord harmony. The minor ii–V progression in measures 3–4 is implied with a bass pattern that employs a root-position Am7b5 voicing and a bass line that moves chromatically (C–C#–D) up string 5 to arrive at the D7b9 arpeggio (D–F#–A–C–Eb) for the V chord. Similarly, in measure 5, a root-position Gm7 voicing is paired with a descending fifth-string bass line that moves chromatically (D–C#–C) to the root of the C dominant seventh arpeggio (C–E–G–Bb) pattern (measure 6).

MEASURES 7–12: After a root-position Fm7 voicing is played on beat 1 of measure 7, the bass line moves up string 6 *diatonically* (G–A♭–B♭) to arrive at the root of the sequenced B♭ Mixolydian (B♭–C–D–E♭–F—G–A♭) pattern in measure 8. The E♭maj9 harmony is outlined with a chord-tone-centric (E♭–B♭–D) bass line, followed in measure 10 by a six-note run up the E♭ major scale (E♭–F–G–A♭–B♭–C–D). In measure 11, an E♭m9 voicing is paired with a sixth-string bass line that moves chromatically (B♭–A–A♭) to the root of an A♭ Mixolydian (A♭–B♭–C–D♭–E♭–F–G♭) lick that incorporates six of the mode's seven tones while effectively outlining the A♭7 harmony.

MEASURES 13–18: In measure 13, the D♭6 harmony is implied with a root-position voicing and a bass line that moves from the chord's root to its 5th (A♭) before moving chromatically (C–D♭) to the root of the D♭ major scale (D♭–E♭–F–G♭–A♭–B♭–C) run in measure 14. This lick is followed by a C♯m7 chord, which is paired with a chromatically descending (G♯–G–F♯) bass line that moves from the 5th of the chord (G♯) to the root of the F♯7 lick in measure 16. Here, a chord-tone-laden phrase outlines the V chord of the ii–V (C♯m7–F♯7) progression. The two bars of Bmaj7 harmony (measures 17–18) are handled by a root-position voicing and a bass line that moves from the chord's root to its 5th (F♯) and 7th (A♯), which moves chromatically to a two-octave, triplet-based B major seventh arpeggio (B–D♯–F♯–A♯).

MEASURES 19–24: The minor ii–V progression in measures 19–20 is handled by a root-position Cm7♭5 voicing whose bass line moves chromatically (G–G♭–F) to the root of the F7♭9 phrase. This passage is derived from the F Phrygian dominant scale (F–G♭–A–B♭–C–D♭–E♭) and disrupts the arpeggio-based pattern with a string skip on beat 2. In measure 21, voice the Dm7 chord with an index-finger barre, which will free your ring finger for the fifth-string bass note (A). In measure 22, the D♭7 harmony is implied with a D♭ dominant ninth arpeggio (D♭–F–A♭–C♭–E♭), which is followed in measure 23 with a bass line that is identical to the one from measure 19, although the chord quality here is minor, rather than half diminished. In measure 24, the Jam concludes with an F Mixolydian (F–G–A–B♭–C–D–E♭) phrase that emphasizes chord tones while outlining the F7 harmony. To voice the adjacent-string, tenth-fret notes, simply roll your pinky from string 4 to string 3.

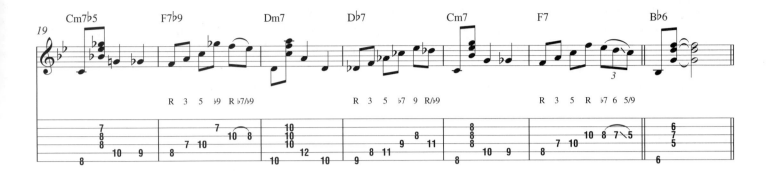

🔊 JAM #113: TWO-BAR RHYTHM/LEAD ALTERNATIONS

The one-bar alternations from Jam #112 have been extended to two bars in this example. Here, the Jam opens with two measures of bass line before segueing to two bars of lead, maintaining these two-bar intervals throughout the 24-bar form. The lead phrases in this example are derived from a multitude of sources, including the Dorian mode (minor chords), Mixolydian mode (dominant chords), Locrian mode (half-diminished chords), and Phrygian dominant scale (altered dominant chords).

MEASURES 1–6: The opening two measures outline the Jam's tonic (B♭) chord with a root-position B♭6 voicing and a bass line that is constructed from a trio of chord tones (B♭, D, and F; the root, 3rd, and 5th, respectively). In measures 3–4, the minor ii–V progression is implied with an ascending, chord-tone-laden phrase the moves from the A Locrian mode (A–B♭–C–D–E♭–F–G) to the D Phrygian dominant scale (D–E♭–F♯–G–A–B♭–C). This phrase transitions to a two-bar bass pattern that outlines the Gm7–C9 (major ii–V) progression (measures 5–6). Here, root-position Gm7 and C9 voicings are paired with bass lines that move chromatically (D–D♭–C) to the latter chord before walking diatonically (D–E–F) to the forthcoming Fm7 harmony.

MEASURES 7–12: In measure 7, the F Dorian mode (F–G–A♭–B♭–C–D–E♭) provides the pitches for the 1–2–3–5–7–5 scale sequence that outlines the Fm7 harmony. This phrase is followed in measure 8 by a B♭ dominant seventh arpeggio (B♭–D–F–A♭) pattern that outlines the V chord (of the ii–V progression). The repetitive bass pattern in measures 9–10 features a root-position E♭maj9 voicing and a bass line that moves from the chord's root to its 5th (B♭) and 7th (D). The five-note phrase in measure 11 is derived from the E♭ Dorian mode (E♭–F–G♭–A♭–B♭–C–D♭) and emphasizes the E♭m7 chord's minor 3rd, G♭, before giving way to a six-note, chord-tone-centric A♭ Mixolydian (A♭–B♭–C–D♭–E♭–F–G♭) phrase.

MEASURES 13–18: The bass pattern from measures 9–10 is restated in measures 13–14, although it's been shifted down a whole step (two frets) to accommodate the new (D♭maj9) harmony. In measures 15–16, the 1–2–3–5–7–5 scale pattern from measure 7 is applied to the C♯ Dorian (C♯–D♯–E–F♯–G♯–A♯–B) and F♯ Mixolydian (F♯–G♯–A♯–B–C♯–D♯–E) modes to outline the C♯m7–F♯7 progression. To voice the Bmaj7 chord in measures 17–18, employ a seventh-fret, index-finger barre, fretting the notes at fret 8 of the fourth and third strings with your middle and ring fingers, respectively. That way, you're able to voice the chord's 5th (fret 9, fifth string) with your pinky.

MEASURES 19–24: The two-bar phrase in measures 19–20 is a replica of the passage from measures 3–4, moving this time from the C Locrian mode (C–D♭–E♭–F–G♭–A♭–B♭) to the F Phrygian dominant scale (F–G♭–A–B♭–C–D♭–E♭). To perform the Dm7 and D♭7 bass patterns in measures 21–22, respectively, employ an index-finger barre for both, fretting each chord's 5th (string 5) with your ring finger. In the case of the D♭7 voicing, simply slide the index-finger barre down one fret (to fret 9) and add your middle finger to fret 10 of the third string (again, using your ring finger to voice the 5th). The Jam concludes with a C minor seventh arpeggio (C–E♭–G–B♭) that moves seamlessly to an F dominant seventh arpeggio (F–A–C–E♭) in measure 24, where, on beat 3, a D-to-C pull-off resolves the phrase to the I (B♭6) chord.

🔊 JAM #114: RANDOM RHYTHM/LEAD ALTERNATIONS

This final jazz-waltz Jam features randomly arranged alternations. The Jam launches with four uninterrupted measures of soloing before segueing to four measures of walking bass line. The remainder of the example is performed as follows: four bars of soloing, two bars of bass line, two bars of soloing, two bars of bass line, and, finally, six full measures of soloing. Like the previous jazz waltzes, the lead phrases are composed from a variety of note sources, including the major scale (major chords), Dorian mode (minor chords), Mixolydian mode (dominant chords), Locrian mode (half-diminished chords), and Phrygian dominant scale (altered dominant chords).

MEASURES 1–6: Following a pickup note (A), the opening phrase outlines the B♭6 harmony with a two-bar B♭ major sixth arpeggio (B♭–D–F–G) pattern that features a string skip (beat 1 of measure 2) and an efficient, half-step (B♭–A) transition to the Am7♭5 harmony. Here, a six-note phrases is carved from the A Locrian (A–B♭–C–D–E♭–F–G) mode, leading seamlessly to a passage derived from the D Phrygian dominant scale (D–E♭–F♯–G–A–B♭–C). At measure 5, the walking bass line makes its first appearance, employing root-position Gm9 and C13 chords to imply the ii–V progression.

MEASURES 7–12: The bass line continues in measures 7–8, where the pattern from measures 5–6 is reproduced a whole-step lower to accommodate the new ii–V progression, Fm9–B♭13. In measures 9–10, a five-string ascending/descending E♭ major seventh arpeggio (E♭–G–B♭–D) is employed to outline the E♭maj7 harmony. The only non-chord tone appears on the "and" of beat 3 of measure 10, where the note F is used to transition chromatically

(F–Gb) to the Ebm7 phrase (measure 11). This phrase commences on the Ebm7 chord's b3rd, Gb, before traversing the remainder of the strings with tones from the Eb minor seventh arpeggio: (in order) Bb, Db, Eb, Gb, and Bb. At the end of measure 11, a first-string slide shifts from the 5th of Ebm7, Bb, to the root of Ab7. This transition is followed in measure 12 by a chord-tone-centric Ab Mixolydian (Ab–Bb–C–Db–Eb–F–Gb) phrase.

MEASURES 13–18: In measures 13–14, the Dbmaj9 harmony is handled by a root-position Dbmaj9 voicing and a bass line that moves from the chord's root to its 5th (Ab) and 7th (C). Following two repetitions of the Dbmaj9 bass pattern, a two-measure phrase moves seamlessly from a C# Dorian (C#–D#–E–F#–G#–A#–B) phrase to an F# dominant seventh arpeggio (F#–A#–C#–E), starting from the chord's b7th, E. To voice the Bmaj7 chord in measures 17–18, employ a seventh-fret, index-finger barre, fretting the notes at fret 8 of the fourth and third strings with your middle and ring fingers, respectively. That way, you're able to voice the chord's 5th (fret 9, fifth string) with your pinky.

MEASURES 19–24: In measure 19, a chord-tone-centric C Locrian (C–Db–Eb–F–Gb–Ab–Bb) phrase outlines the ii chord of the minor ii–V progression (Cm7b5–F7b9). This phrase slides into the root of the V chord, F, by way of the b5th, Gb, creating a half-step (Gb–F) transition. In measure 20, an F7b9 arpeggio (F–A–C–Eb–Gb) pattern implies the V chord, transitioning to the Dm7 harmony (measure 21) via a half-step slide that moves from the b7th of the F7b9 chord, Eb, to the root of Dm7. Here, an ascending D minor seventh arpeggio (D–F–A–C) is played on the treble strings before segueing to a descending Db dominant seventh arpeggio (Db–F–Ab–Cb) for the Db7 harmony. For the Jam's final ii–V progression, Cm7–F7, a six-note C Dorian (C–D–Eb–F–G–A–Bb) phrase is paired with an F Mixolydian (F–G–A–Bb–C–D–Eb) passage (measure 24) before resolving to the Bb note at fret 3 of the third string—the root of the I chord.

188

SECTION IV: COUNTRY

CHAPTER 20: BLUEGRASS "BOOM-CHUCKA" STRUMMING PATTERN
THE RESOURCES

CHORDS

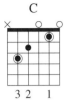

SCALES

C Composite Blues Scale (Open Position):
C–D–E♭–E–F–G♭–G–A–B♭
(1–2–♭3–♮3–4–♭5–♮5–6–♭7)

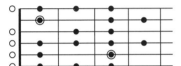

C Composite Blues Scale (2nd Position)

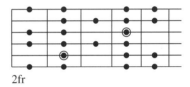

2fr

C Composite Blues Scale (Extended Form)

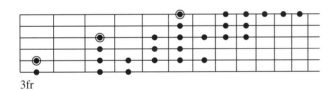

3fr

F Composite Blues Scale (Open Position):
F–G–A♭–A–B♭–C♭–C–D–E♭
(1–2–♭3–♮3–4–♭5–♮5–6–♭7)

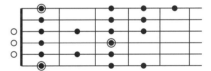

F Composite Blues Scale (Extended Form)

G Composite Blues Scale:
G–A–B♭–B–C–D♭–D–E–F
(1–2–♭3–♮3–4–♭5–♮5–6–♭7)

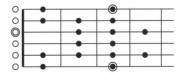

 ## JAM #115: THE 12-BAR FORM

This Jam represents the book's first foray into bluegrass and, by extension, country music. The rhythm figure used in the next six examples, the "boom-chucka" strumming pattern, is the most popular rhythm-guitar approach in country music, particularly in more traditional forms such as bluegrass.

The boom-chucka technique involves playing bass notes (the "boom") on beats 1 and 3 of each measure, followed by eighth-note chord strums (the "chucka") on beats 2 and 4. The bass notes most often consist of the root and 5th of the chord (the 3rd is another popular choice) and mimic the cut-time pattern that is performed by the bass player. In addition to the cut-time pattern, this example employs short, two- and three-note bass lines to approach each new chord change. Meanwhile, the chord strums, performed on the guitar's treble strings, reinforce the song's chord changes.

The chords used in the Jam are open-position C (I chord) and G7 (V chord) voicings, as well as a first-position F major (IV chord) barre-chord shape. These chords are arranged as a standard 12-bar blues, a common song form in country and bluegrass. Also, this example is written in "cut time," which means each half note receives one beat. If you set your metronome to the Jam's tempo (84 bpm), the bass notes fall precisely on each "click," whereas the chord strums fall on the upbeats (think 16th notes that fall on the upbeats in 4/4 time).

MEASURES 1–4: Following a three-note (G–A–B) pickup, the boom-chucka strumming pattern is applied to an open C chord, with the 5th (G) voiced on string 6 (simply shift your ring finger from string 5 to string 6 to voice the sixth-string bass note, leaving your other fingers stationary). This C-chord pattern is played three times. In measure 4, the pattern is cut in half in order to create a chromatic bass-note walk-down (G–Gb–F) to the root of the IV chord, F.

MEASURES 5–8: Played twice (measures 5–6), the F-chord pattern reverses the location of the bass notes. Here, the root is played on string 6, whereas the 5th (C) is played on string 5. No finger movement is required to perform the F-chord pattern, as both bass notes are part of the voicing. In measures 7–8, the C-chord pattern returns for one-and-a-half repetitions before yielding to a diatonic walk-down (B–A–G) to the root of the V chord, G.

MEASURES 9–12: The V chord is voiced as an open-position G7 voicing, resulting in a more challenging root–5th bass pattern. In this voicing, the root is fretted on string 6, while the 5th is performed with the open D string. Meanwhile, the chord strums employ the top three strings, with the only fretted pitch being the chord's b7th, F, which is found at fret 1 of the first string. The F-chord pattern reappears in measure 10 and is followed by another repetition of the C-chord pattern (measure 11). Measure 12 is comprised entirely of bass notes. After the root note (C) is plucked on beat 1, the pickup notes from the beginning of the Jam are used to bring the example back to the top.

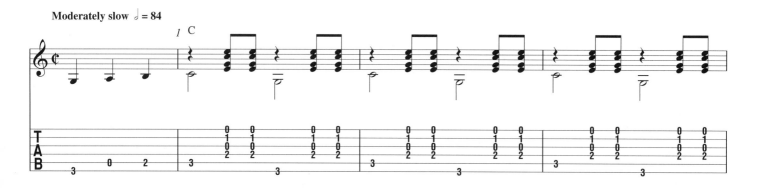

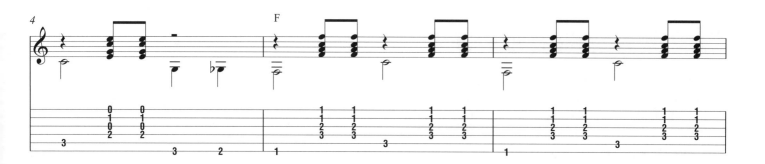

190

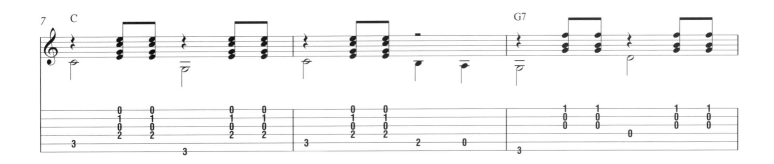

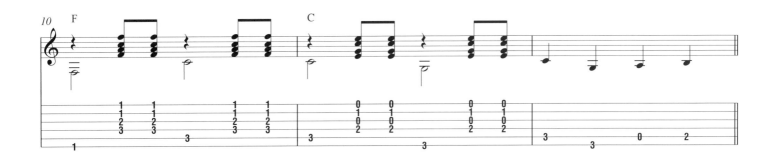

🔊 JAM #116: ONE-BAR LEAD/RHYTHM ALTERNATIONS

This bluegrass Jam is comprised entirely of one-bar alternations. After the three-note walk-up, the arrangement unfolds with a bar of lead and a bar of the boom-chucka strumming pattern—tradeoffs that are maintained throughout the Jam's 12-bar form. Melodically, the lead phrases outline the C, F, and G7 changes with notes from the C composite (C–D–Eb–E–F–Gb–G–A–Bb), F composite (F–G–Ab–A–Bb–Cb–C–D–Eb), and G composite (G–A–Bb–B–C–Db–D–E–F) blues scales, respectively.

MEASURES 1–4: Following the three-note (G–A–B) pickup, the first bar of lead features a phrase that was popularized by bluegrass guitar legend Lester Flatt. The seven-note run is derived from the C composite blues scale and features both the minor 3rd (Eb) and the major 3rd (E) of the scale. In measure 2, the C-chord strumming pattern makes its first appearance and is followed in measure 3 by a descending C composite blues lick that "responds" to the "call" of the opening lick. In measure 4, the C-chord pattern is modified to include a chromatic walk-down (G–Gb–F) to the root of the IV (F) chord (measure 5).

MEASURES 5–8: The lick in measure 5 is a variation of the phrase from measure 1, only it's played here in the key of F and is not confined to open position. Instead, the phrase shifts from first position to third position on beat 2. In measure 6, the F-chord pattern is assigned to the second bar of IV-chord harmony, followed in measure 7 by a C composite blues scale lick that jumps octaves (C to C) on beat 1 before loosely mimicking the passage from measure 3. This phrase is followed in measure 8 by a variation of the C-chord strumming pattern. After one repetition of the boom-chucka pattern, the figure segues to a bass-note line (B–A–G) that walks diatonically to the root of the V (G7) chord (measure 9).

MEASURES 9–12: In measure 9, a bass-string lick, derived from the G composite blues scale, implies the G7 harmony. This phrase is followed by another repetition of the F-chord pattern (measure 10) and a lead phrase that borrows elements from the lick in measure 7 before a second-string Eb-to-D slide resolves to the C chord's root (measures 11–12).

JAM #117: TWO-BAR LEAD/RHYTHM ALTERNATIONS

The lead and rhythm alternations in this example are two bars apiece, a one-bar increase from Jam #116. Like the previous example, a three-note (G–A–B) pickup opens the Jam, followed by alternations that fluctuate between two bars of lead playing and two bars of rhythm throughout the 12-bar form. Melodically, the lead phrases are derived from the composite blues scales relative to the C, F, and G7 chord changes—C composite (C–D–Eb–E–F–Gb–G–A–Bb), F composite (F–G–Ab–A–Bb–Cb–C–D–Eb), and G composite (G–A–Bb–B–C–Db–D–E–F), respectively.

MEASURES 1–4: Following the three-note pickup, measure 1 features the Lester Flatt run that was introduced in Jam #116. However, instead of transitioning to a bar of the C-chord strumming pattern, this version of the run segues to a restatement of the phrase in the higher octave, featuring a position shift and a modified ending. In measures 3–4, the C-chord pattern is played one-and-a-half times before bass notes descend chromatically (G–Gb–F) to the root of the IV (F) chord.

MEASURES 5–8: The two-bar phrase that outlines the IV (F) chord commences with the sixth-string root (fret 1) before jumping to string 1, where a bluesy phrase is carved from the F composite blues scale. The phrase in measure 6 restates the motif that was introduced in the previous measure—most conspicuously, the legato passage on beats 2–3 (played on beats 1–2 in measure 6)—and utilizes the open G string to transition to the C-chord strumming pattern (measure 7). Similar to measures 3–4, the C-chord pattern in measures 7–8 is played one-and-a-half times; however, because the next chord in the progression is G7 (the V chord), the bass notes walk diatonically (B–A–G) to the root of the new chord.

MEASURES 9–12: In measure 9, the Lester Flatt run is played in the key of G, effectively outlining the V chord. This phrase is restated in measure 10, although it has been relocated to strings 4–2 to fit the new (F) harmony. The Jam concludes in measures 11–12 with a repetition of the C-chord pattern and a restatement of the G–A–B pickup, which returns the Jam to the top of the form.

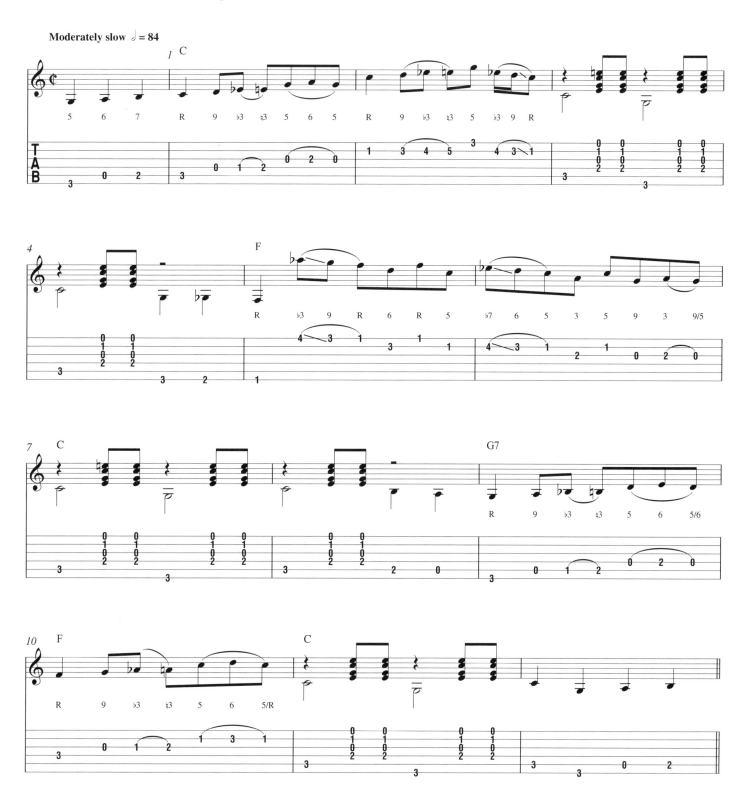

193

JAM #118: ONE-BAR RHYTHM/LEAD ALTERNATIONS

In this example, the lead/rhythm alternations from the previous two Jams (116–117) are reversed. In addition to the new sequence, the alternations are played here in one-bar intervals, which are maintained throughout the 12-bar form. Similar to the previous two examples, the lead parts are played (mostly) in open position and get their notes from the composite blues scales relative to the C, F, and G7 chord changes—C composite (C–D–Eb–E–F–Gb–G–A–Bb), F composite (F–G–Ab–A–Bb–Cb–C–D–Eb), and G composite (G–A–Bb–B–C–Db–D–E–F), respectively.

MEASURES 1–4: Following the three-note (G–A–B) pickup, the C-chord strumming pattern is played for one bar before yielding to a bar of lead (measure 2). Here, an open-position C composite blues scale phrase emphasizes the harmony's minor 3rd (Eb) and major 3rd (E) and features a one-octave jump (C to C) on beat 2. In measure 3, the C-chord pattern returns for one repetition, followed in measure 4 by another C composite blues scale phrase. This lick opens in third position before quickly shifting to open position on the "and" of beat 2.

MEASURES 5–8: The F-chord strumming pattern occupies measure 5 and is followed in measure 6 by an F composite blues scale lick that incorporates seven of the scale's nine tones. Notice the strategic placement of the open D string (on the "and" of beat 4), which facilitates the transition to the C-chord pattern in measure 7. Following one repetition of the strumming pattern, a treble-string lick emphasizes the C major harmony's root (C), 9th (D), minor 3rd (Eb), and major 3rd (E) before giving way to an A-to-G pull-off (beat 4), which seamlessly transitions to the G7 strumming pattern (measure 9).

MEASURES 9–12: Following one repetition of the G7 pattern, an ascending bass-string lick is derived from the F composite blues scale to outline the IV (F) chord harmony (measure 10). The Jam concludes with one repetition of the C-chord pattern (measures 11) and the G–A–B pickup (measure 12), which leads back to the top of the form.

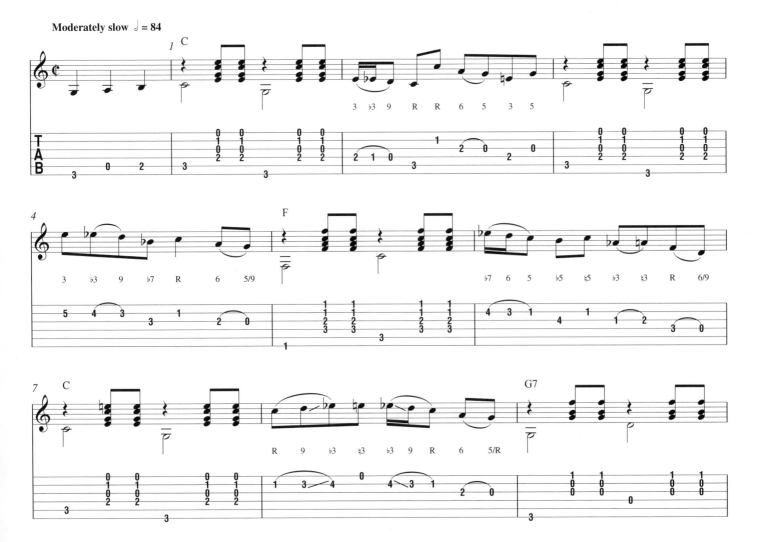

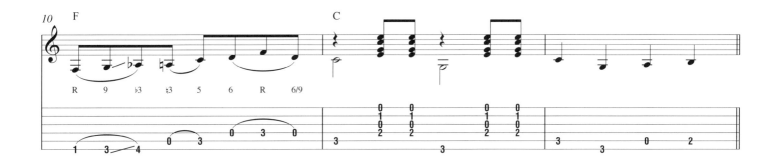

JAM #119: TWO-BAR RHYTHM/LEAD ALTERNATIONS

The one-bar rhythm/lead alternations from Jam #118 have been extended to two bars in this example. Here, the Jam opens with two measures of the boom-chucka strumming pattern before transitioning to two measures of lead playing, maintaining these two-bar tradeoffs throughout the 12-bar form. As for the lead playing, all of the phrases are played over the I (C) chord and are derived from the C composite blues scale (C–D–Eb–E–F–Gb–G–A–Bb).

MEASURES 1–4: The Jam opens with the three-note (G–A–B) pickup and two repetitions of the C-chord boom-chucka pattern. In measure 3, a descending lick is derived from the C composite blues scale. After juggling the open high E string and a pair of fretted tones (G and F), a chromatic passage is played along string 2, moving from the C chord's 9th (D) to its root (C). In measure 4, the lick continues its descent of the scale, incorporating fretted pitches and open strings alike.

MEASURES 5–8: The boom-chucka strumming pattern returns with the arrival of the IV (F) chord (measures 5–6). Following two repetitions of the F-chord pattern, an ascending C composite blues scale lick is employed to outline the two bars of I-chord harmony. In measure 7, the Lester Flatt run is played in the key of C, followed in measure 8 by a restatement of the run an octave higher, requiring a shift from open position to third position.

MEASURES 9–12: The V (G7) and IV (F) chord changes in measures 9–10 are handled by the boom-chucka strumming pattern, followed in measures 11–12 by an open-position C composite blues scale run that hovers around the bass strings before making its way up to the second-string root for resolution. Notice how the C major harmony is reinforced via multiple, strategic repetitions of the root note, including on beats 1 and 3 of measure 11, as well as on beat 1 of measure 12.

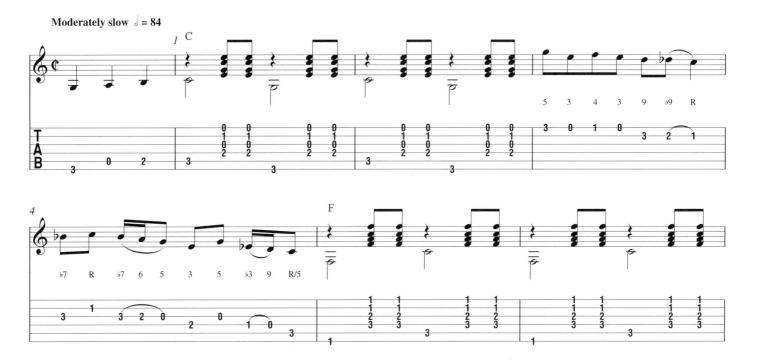

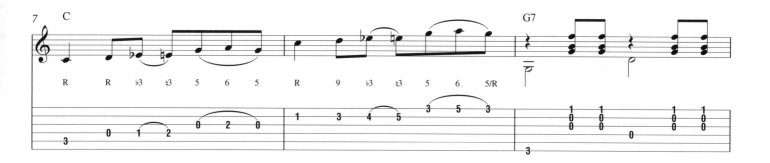

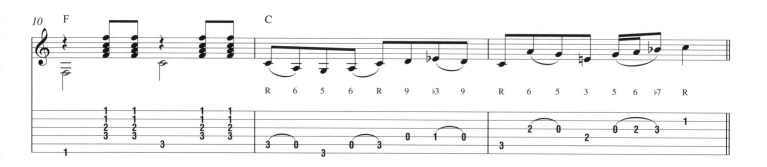

🔊 JAM #120: RANDOM RHYTHM/LEAD ALTERNATIONS

This bluegrass Jam forgoes predetermined one- or two-bar alternations in favor of a random arrangement. Although the alternations are arranged symmetrically—that is, two measures of strumming vacillating with four-bar leads—they still retain an impromptu feel. In fact, this Jam contains twice as many measures of lead playing as measures of chord strumming, which contributes greatly to its improvised nature. While the chord strumming is relegated to the I (C) chord, the leads are played over all three chord changes—C, F, and G7—deriving their notes from the C composite (C–D–Eb–E–F–Gb–G–A–Bb), F composite (F–G–Ab–A–Bb–Cb–C–D–Eb), and G composite (G–A–Bb–B–C–Db–D–E–F) blues scales.

MEASURES 1–4: After the three-note (G–A–B) pickup, two repetitions of the C-chord strumming pattern introduce the Jam and are followed by a four-measure lead phrase that outlines two bars of I-chord (C) harmony and two bars of IV-chord (F) harmony. A repetitive legato figure kicks off the phrase (measure 3) and is followed by a bass-string lick that incorporates both the minor 3rd (Eb) and the major 3rd (E) of the C major harmony (measure 4). Note the inclusion of the open A string at the end of the phrase, which creates a seamless transition to the F composite blues scale portion of the four-bar phrase (measures 5–6).

MEASURES 5–8: In measure 5, the two-bar F composite blues scale phrase commences with the root note (fret 1) before shifting to third position via a sixth-string slide. Maintaining its presence on the bottom two strings, the passage lands on Eb (the b7th) on beat 1 of measure 6, imparting a dominant tonality (F7) to the major harmony. At the end of measure 6, a fifth-string slide moves from the 6th of the F chord, D, to the root of the C chord to transition back to the C-chord strumming pattern (measures 7–8). This pattern is played one-and-a-half times before yielding to a bass-string walk-down (B–A–G) to the root of the V (G7) chord.

MEASURES 9–12: The V–IV–I (G7–F–C) progression in measures 9–12 is outlined entirely by a four-measure phrase that is confined to the bass strings, much like the passage from measures 5–6. Following a one-bar, open-position G composite blues scale lick, the phrase moves to an F composite blues scale phrase that mimics its predecessor before a sixth-string, Ab–G–E pull-off transitions to the I chord (measure 11). Here, the C composite blues scale supplies the notes to a phrase that is characterized by its minor-against-major "rub"—that is, the juxtaposition of the minor 3rd (Eb) and major 3rd (E).

Moderately slow ♩ = 84

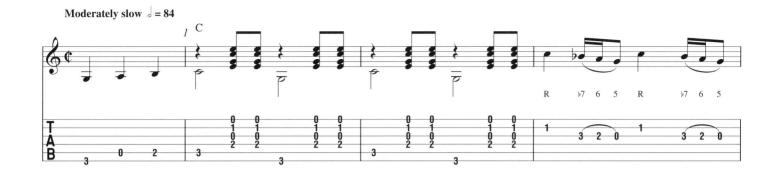

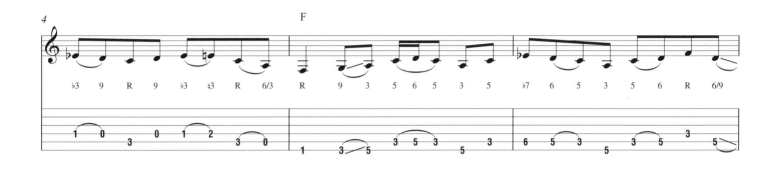

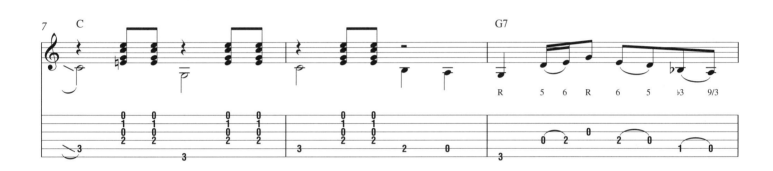

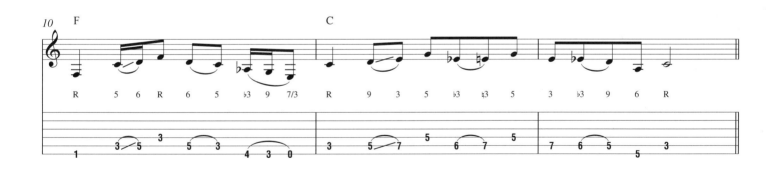

CHAPTER 21: COUNTRIFIED BOOGIE BASS LINE
THE RESOURCES

CHORDS

E5

A5

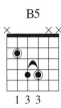

B5

SCALES

E Composite Blues Scale (Open Position):
E–F♯–G–G♯–A–B♭–B–C♯–D
(1–2–♭3–♮3–4–♭5–♮5–6–♭7)

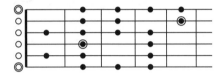

E Composite Blues Scale (9th Position)

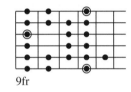

9fr

E Major Pentatonic (Extended Form):
E–F♯–G♯–B–C♯
(1–2–3–5–6)

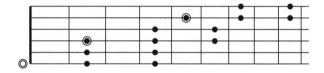

A Composite Blues Scale (Open Position):
A–B–C–C♯–D–E♭–E–F♯–G
(1–2–♭3–♮3–4–♭5–♮5–6–♭7)

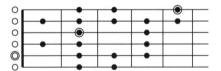

A Composite Blues Scale (2nd Position)

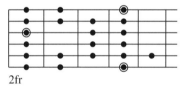

2fr

A Composite Blues Scale (4th Position)

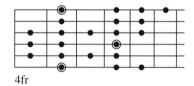

4fr

B Composite Blues Scale (4th Position):
B–C♯–D–D♯–E–F–F♯–G♯–A
(1–2–♭3–♮3–4–♭5–♮5–6–♭7)

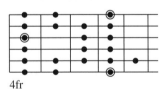

4fr

B Composite Blues Scale (Extended Form)

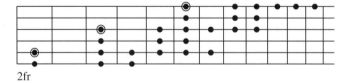

2fr

 JAM #121: THE 12-BAR FORM

The bass line that is utilized in the next six Jams is the country version of the blues-rock boogie bass line from Chapter 8. Some of the similarities include the key signature (E major), the juxtaposition of minor 3rd and major 3rd tones, and the syncopation created by notes tied across the bar. Unlike the blues-rock pattern, however, this bass line features a one-octave jump on beat 1, excludes the ♭7th tone in favor of a major 6th harmonic flavor, and is played in a more straight-ahead (i.e., less syncopated) fashion in its second half.

The song form is a standard 12-bar blues in the key of E major. Although no chords are employed, the bass line effectively implies the I (E), IV (A), and V (B) chord changes with a combination of open strings and fretted pitches from the E composite (E–F♯–G–G♯–A–B♭–B–C♯–D), A composite (A–B–C–C♯–D–E♭–E–F♯–G), and B composite (B–C♯–D–D♯–E–F–F♯–G♯–A) blues scales, respectively.

MEASURES 1–4: The initial four measures of the Jam are comprised of two repetitions of the two-bar bass line, played here over the I (E) chord. The bass line commences with a one-octave (E-to-E) jump and a G-to-G♯ (minor-to-major) hammer-on. On beats 3–4, a hammer/pull figure incorporates the E composite blues scale's 5th (B) and 6th (C♯) tones, leading to the root (E) note at fret 2 of the fourth string. Meanwhile, the second half of the bass line works its way back down the scale in a similar manner, closing with a G-to-F♯ pull-off.

MEASURES 5–8: In measures 5–6, the bass line is transposed to the key of A for the IV chord, which is achieved by shifting the pattern up one string set, from strings 6–4 to strings 5–3. Then, with the return of the I chord in measures 7–8, the E-chord pattern is played one more time.

MEASURES 9–12: The arrival of the V (B) chord requires a slightly different approach. With no open string available for the root, the bass line must be relocated to the B note at fret 2 of the fifth string. Also, because the V chord occupies just one measure, the bass line must be adjusted accordingly. To perform this pattern, start with your index on the root note, fretting the octave (string 3) with you ring finger. Then employ your pinky for the fifth-string slide, thereby putting your index finger in an advantageous position for the fourth-string legato figure. This one-bar pattern is restated in measure 10, although it's shifted to open position for the IV (A) chord change. Finally, the Jam concludes with one last repetition of the I-chord boogie pattern.

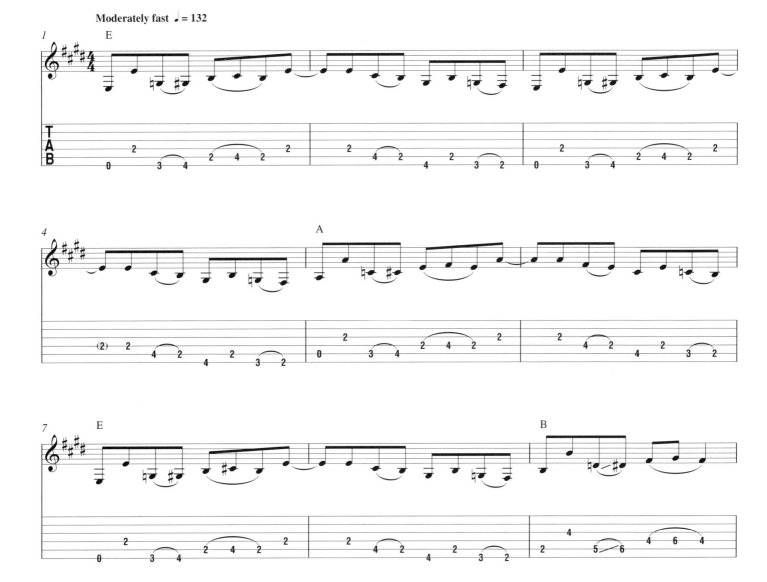

JAM #122: ONE-BAR LEAD/RHYTHM ALTERNATIONS

These first alternations involving the countrified boogie bass line rotate in one-bar intervals, starting with one bar of lead. As a result, the original two-bar bass lines are shortened to one bar apiece. These one-bar tradeoffs are maintained through the Jam's first 10 measures. Then, in measures 11–12, the Jam is capped with a two-bar lead passage, rather than ending with one measure of the bass line.

In a fitting tribute to the countrified bass line, the lead phrases are (mostly) comprised of a pedal-steel-style bend motif and performed with hybrid picking—a combination of your pick and middle, ring, and pinky fingers—an approach favored by country pickers. Melodically, the phrases are derived from the composite blues scales relative to the E, A, and B chord changes—E composite (E–F♯–G–G♯–A–B♭–B–C♯–D), A composite (A–B–C–C♯–D–E♭–E–F♯–G), and B composite (B–C♯–D–D♯–E–F–F♯–G♯–A), respectively.

MEASURES 1–4: The Jam opens with an oblique bend that targets the 5th (B) and ♭7th (D) tones of the E major harmony, briefly imparting a dominant tonality. After a couple of additional double stops, including a minor-to-major (G-to-G♯) hammer-on, the lick transitions to the one-bar version of the E-chord bass line (measure 2). The lick in measure 3 is a variation of the opening phrase. Note the presence of the open low E string on beat 1, which emphasizes the E major harmony and displaces the lick by half a beat. In measure 4, the I-chord bass line returns for one more repetition.

MEASURES 5–8: The lick in measure 5 is a variation of the licks from measures 1 and 3, although it's played here in the key of A, with the double-stop bend targeting the key's 3rd (C♯) and 5th (E) tones. A unique aspect of this phrase is the double-stop slide on beat 4. Here, an F♯/C (6th/♭3rd) dyad is slide up a half step, to a G/C♯ (♭7th/3rd) double stop—again, briefly implying a dominant tonality. In measure 6, the A-chord version of the bass line is played once before segueing to a phrase that is a variation of the E-chord licks. In this case, the phrase ends with a single note line that is derived from the E composite blues scale and resolves to a sixth-string, minor-to-major (G-to-G♯) slide, leading to another bar of the E-chord bass line (measure 8).

MEASURES 9–12: The lick in measure 9 begins as a run up the extended form of the B major pentatonic scale; however, at the top of the phrase, the minor 3rd (D) is introduced, implying the B composite blues scale. After a measure of the A-chord bass line (measure 10), the Jam concludes with a two-bar single-note phrase that incorporates six notes of the nine-note E composite blues scale. Note, once again, the presence of the open low E string on beat 1, effectively signaling the return of the I (E) chord.

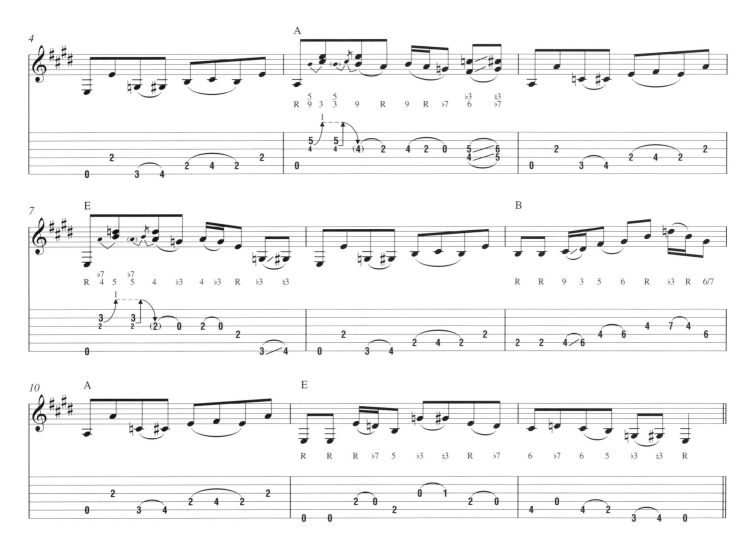

JAM #123: TWO-BAR LEAD/RHYTHM ALTERNATIONS

Whereas the leads in Jam #122 focused on oblique bends and double-stop passages, the soloing in this example emphasizes single-note playing. Further, the one-bar alternations from the previous example have been extended to two bars in this Jam. These two-bar tradeoffs are maintained throughout the Jam's 12-bar form. As a result, the bass lines are now played in their original, two-bar form, rather than as truncated one-bar patterns. Meanwhile, the lead phrases are constructed from notes of the E composite (E–F♯–G–G♯–A–B♭–B–C♯–D), A composite (A–B–C–C♯–D–E♭–E–F♯–G), and B composite (B–C♯–D–D♯–E–F–F♯–G♯–A) blues scales.

MEASURES 1–4: The two-bar phrase that opens the Jam includes every note of the nine-note E composite blues scale. Played in ninth-position, the chromatic-laden passage introduces a rhythmic motif in measure 1 and repeats it, with variations, in measure 2. This phrased is followed in measures 3–4 by the two-bar version of the E-chord bass line.

MEASURES 5–8: The motif that was introduced in measure 1 is transposed to the key of A and restated in measure 5. The first two beats of the phrase are a note-for-note reproduction of the original motif, but the remainder of the passage chooses a different course as it descends the A composite blues scale. In measures 7–8, the bass line returns for the second occurrence of the I (E) chord.

MEASURES 9–12: The two-bar phrase that outlines the V (B) and IV (A) chords is a case study in efficient voice leading. Following a run up the fourth-position B composite blues scale, the phrase seamlessly transitions to a fifth-position A composite blues scale lick via a half-step (G♯-to-A) slide. By landing on the root (A) on beat 1 of measure 10, followed closely by additional chord tones (C♯ and E), the phrase makes a clear distinction between the two harmonies (B and A). Then, on beat 4, a second-string, G-to-G♯ slide anticipates the arrival of the I chord in measures 11–12, where the E-chord bass line makes its third appearance, capping the 12-bar form.

🔊 JAM #124: ONE-BAR RHYTHM/LEAD ALTERNATIONS

The soloing in this Jam is one part blues and one part country, played in an arrangement that alternates, in order, one-bar versions of the bass line and one bar of lead. These one-bar tradeoffs are maintained through the first 10 measures of the 12-bar form. In measures 11–12, the original, two-bar version of the E-chord bass line is employed to cap the Jam. Meanwhile, all of the lead passages are played in the vicinity of open position and are derived from the E composite (E–F♯–G–G♯–A–B♭–B–C♯–D), A composite (A–B–C–C♯–D–E♭–E–F♯–G), and B composite (B–C♯–D–D♯–E–F–F♯–G♯–A) blues scales.

MEASURES 1–4: Following one measure of the E-chord bass line, a bluesy open-position lick is culled from the E composite blues scale in measure 2. The bass line returns in measure 3, followed in measure 4 by a lick that loosely mimics the phrase from measure 2. Notice that, on beat 4, a G-to-A hammer-on anticipates the IV (A) chord change in measure 5.

202

MEASURES 5–8: In measure 5, the bass line moves to strings 5–3 for the IV (A) chord harmony. In measure 6, a descending, open-position, legato-based phrase outlines the second bar of IV-chord harmony, utilizing a repetitive rhythm and the dominant qualities of the A composite blues scale—that is, the specific notes of the lick spell out the A Mixolydian mode (A–B–C♯–D–E–F♯–G). Measures 7–8 begin with another bar of the E-chord bass line before segueing to a descending open-position lick that recalls the lick from measure 6. Like that phrase, the pitches are derived from either the E composite blues scale or the E Mixolydian mode (E–F♯–G♯–A–B–C♯–D), as they're present in both scales.

MEASURES 9–12: Following one bar of the B-chord bass line (measure 9), a treble-string lick is performed over the IV-chord harmony (measure 10). Basically, this phrase is derived from the upper portion of the A composite blues scale pattern that was used for the lick in measure 6. In measures 11–12, the Jam concludes with the complete, two-bar pattern of the E-chord bass line.

JAM #125: TWO-BAR RHYTHM/LEAD ALTERNATIONS

In this example, the one-bar rhythm/lead alternations from Jam #124 have been extended to two measures. Now, the bass lines are performed as their full, two-bar patterns and are followed by two bars of soloing, a rotation that is maintained throughout the Jam's 12-bar form. As for the lead phrases, all of them are performed over the I (E) chord and are rooted in the E composite blues scale (E–F♯–G–G♯–A–B♭–B–C♯–D).

MEASURES 1–4: Following one repetition of the E-chord bass line (measures 1–2), an open-position E composite blues scale phrase handles the second half of the I-chord harmony (measures 3–4). To emphasize the E major tonality, the lick opens with the open low E string, followed by a two-octave jump to the open high E string. From there, the lick weaves its way down the scale to the E (root) note at fret 2 of the fourth string, where the lick abruptly reverses course and concludes with a C-to-C♯ slide, signaling the arrival of the IV (A) chord (measure 5).

MEASURES 5–8: In measures 5–6, the bass line is relocated to strings 5–3 for the IV (A) chord, followed in measures 7–8 by a country-inspired double-stop passage. Here, syncopated double stops, rooted in the E composite blues scale, effectively outline the I (E) chord as they descend strings 2–3 and are offset by fifth-string "ghost notes," which help guide the fret hand. Notice the strategic placement of the open B string at the end of the phrase, which anticipates the arrival of the V (B) chord and helps transition to the B-chord bass line in measure 9.

MEASURES 9–12: In measures 9–10, one-bar versions of the B- and A-chord bass lines outline the V and IV chords, respectively. These bass-line patterns are followed in measures 11–12 by a descending, legato-based passage that juxtaposes open strings and E composite blues scale tones before resolving to the E note at fret 2 of the fourth string.

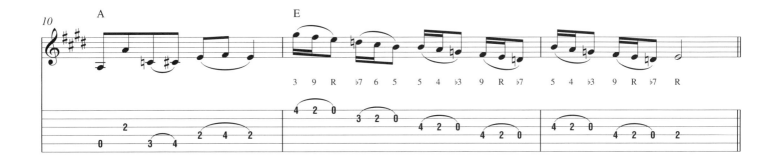

JAM #126: RANDOM RHYTHM/LEAD ALTERNATIONS

The alternations in this Jam are arranged in random fashion, with considerable emphasis on lead playing. In fact, no fewer than nine of the Jam's 12 measures are devoted to soloing, with the bass line making only sporadic appearances to help keep the arrangement moving forward. Meanwhile, the lead phrases have a distinct country sound and feature a heavy dose of major-pentatonic soloing, as well as countrified oblique bending and open-position playing.

MEASURES 1–4: The Jam kicks off with an oblique bend that is common to country pickers: While maintaining a second-string whole-step bend, C♯ and B notes (the 6th and 5th, respectively) are played on frets 9 and 7 of the first string, respectively. Following the bend and release, the phrase moves down the extended form of the E major pentatonic scale (E–F♯–G♯–B–C♯), flowing seamlessly into one repetition of the E-chord bass line (measure 3). A similar type of transition occurs while moving back into the lead phrase in measure 4. Here, the last note of the bass line, E, functions simultaneously as the first note of the lead phrase, another E major pentatonic lick. Note that, on beat 4, the B-to-A slide signals the arrival of the IV (A) chord (measure 5).

MEASURES 5–8: Following a bar of the A-chord bass line (measure 5), the lead phrase in measure 6 continues to ascend the treble strings, flowing unencumbered from open position to fifth position via notes from the A major pentatonic scale (A–B–C♯–E–F♯). (*Note:* The A-chord bass line is derived from the A composite blues scale [A–B–C–C♯–D–E♭–E–F♯–G], so the lead phrase in measure 6 could be considered an extension of that scale, as every note of the lick is found in both scales.) In measure 7, a two-bar E composite blues scale (E–F♯–G–G♯–A–B♭–B–C♯–D) lick commences in third position, shifting to open position at the onset of measure 8. Seven of the scale's nine tones are woven into the fabricate of this lead passage, which ends with a fourth-string, E-to-D pull-off to facilitate the transition to the B-chord bass line in measure 9.

MEASURES 9–12: Following one bar of the B-chord bass line, the A-chord bass line commences in measure 10; however, after the bass line's first two notes are performed, it abruptly transforms into a lead phrase for the remainder of the measure. On beat 4, a third-string, G-to-G♯ hammer-on resolves to the root of the I (E) chord in measure 11. Here, the open low E string emphatically signals a change in harmony (A major to E major) and is followed by a bass-string run up the E composite blues scale that resolves to the E note at fret 5 of the second string.

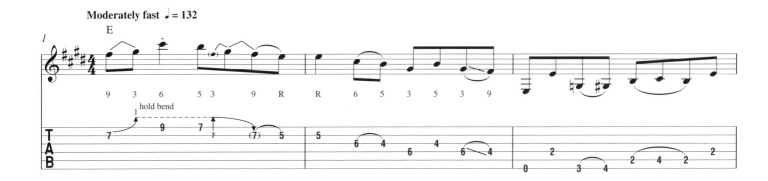

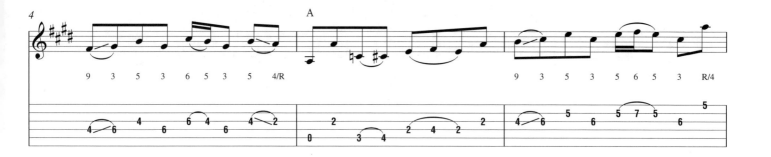

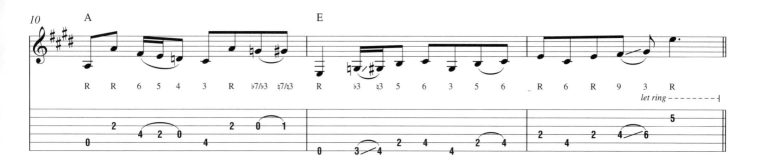

206

CHAPTER 22: TRAVIS PICKING: SEVENTH CHORDS WITH ALTERNATING BASS NOTES

THE RESOURCES

CHORDS

C7

C7/G

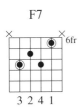

F7

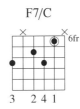

F7/C

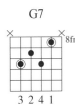

G7

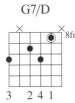

G7/D

SCALES

C Composite Blues Scale (Open Position):
C–D–E♭–E–F–G♭–G–A–B♭
(1–2–♭3–♮3–4–♭5–♮5–6–♭7)

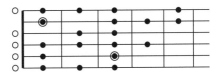

C Composite Blues Scale (2nd Position)

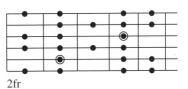

2fr

C Composite Blues Scale (5th Position)

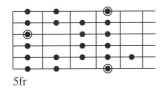

5fr

C Composite Blues Scale (Extended Form)

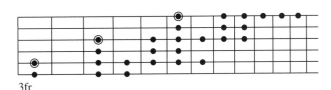

3fr

C Major Pentatonic/Aeolian Hybrid Scale:
C–D–E♭–E–F–G–A♭–A–B♭
(1–2–♭3–♮3–4–5–♭6–♮6–♭7)

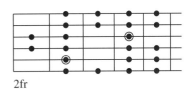

2fr

C Major Pentatonic (Extended Form):
C–D–E–G–A
(1–2–3–5–6)

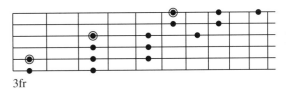

3fr

F Composite Blues Scale (Open Position):
F–G–A♭–A–B♭–C♭–C–D–E♭
(1–2–♭3–♮3–4–♭5–♮5–6–♭7)

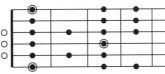

F Composite Blues Scale (5th Position)

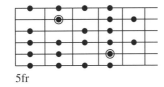

5fr

F Composite Blues Scale (Extended Form)

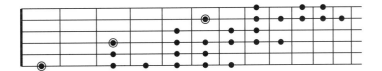

F Mixolydian Mode:
F–G–A–B♭–C–D–E♭
(1–2–3–4–5–6–♭7)

F Major Pentatonic (Extended Form):
F–G–A–C–D
(1–2–3–5–6)

G Composite Blues Scale:
G–A–Bb–B–C–Db–D–E–F
(1–2–b3–♮3–4–b5–♮5–6–b7)

G Mixolydian:
G–A–B–C–D–E–F
(1–2–3–4–5–6–b7)

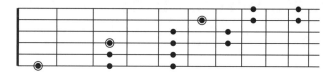
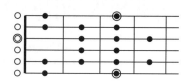
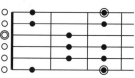

🔊 JAM #127: THE 12-BAR FORM

In this chapter, a single dominant-seventh chord voicing is used for all three chords of the 12-bar blues form—in this case, C7 (I chord), F7 (IV chord), and G7 (V chord). In addition to the seventh chords, this Jam gets its unmistakably country sound from its combination of alternating and walking bass lines, cut-time feel, and Travis-picking pattern.

Travis picking, named after legendary country singer/guitarist Merle Travis, is a fingerstyle technique whereby the thumb is assigned to alternating, quarter-note bass tones on the guitar's bass strings, while the index, middle, and ring fingers pluck a syncopated pattern on the treble strings. Travis picking can also be performed with a combination of pick and fingers (i.e., hybrid picking), which is suggested for the next six examples due to the presence of lead lines, which will require flatpicking.

MEASURES 1–4: Following a three-note (G–A–B) pickup, the Travis-picked C7 chord involves quarter-note alternations of the chord's root (C, string 5), 3rd (E, string 4), and 5th (G, string 6). For these alternations, keep your index, middle, and pinky fingers stationary while your ring finger fluctuates between string 5 and string 6 on beats 1 and 3, respectively. Also noteworthy is the staccato "pinch" one beat 2 of measure 1, imparting the Jam with additional country authenticity. This two-measure picking pattern is played one-and-a-half times (measures 1–3) before segueing to a three-note (C–D–E), fifth-string walk-up to the IV (F7) chord.

MEASURES 5–8: The picking pattern in measure 5 is a replica of the one from measure 1, played here, of course, with an F7 voicing. In measure 6, a three-note (F–E–D), fifth-string bass line walks back down to the I (C7) chord. Here, the C7 picking pattern is performed as its full, two-bar pattern (measures 7–8).

MEASURES 9–12: For the V and IV chord changes (measures 9–10), the picking pattern from measure 1 is applied to the G7 and F7 voicings. These one-bar patterns are followed by a return to the C7 pattern, which is shortened to one bar in order to include the G–A–B pickup for a return to the top of the song form.

JAM #128: ONE-BAR LEAD/RHYTHM ALTERNATIONS

In this Jam, the Travis-picked seventh chords are paired with short, one-bar lead phrases. After a three-note (G–A–B) pickup and a one-bar lick, a one-bar version of the C7 pattern is performed. This lead/rhythm sequence is maintained throughout the Jam's first 10 measures. In measures 11–12, a two-bar lead phrase is performed over the I (C7) chord to cap the Jam. The pitches for the lead phrases are supplied by the composite blues scales relative to the C7, F7, and G7 chord changes—C composite (C–D–Eb–E–F–Gb–G–A–Bb), F composite (F–G–Ab–A–Bb–Cb–C–D–Eb), and G composite (G–A–Bb–B–C–Db–D–E–F), respectively.

MEASURES 1–4: Following the three-note (G–A–B) pickup, a variation of the Lester Flatt run, featured prominently in Chapter 20, is played in measure 1. To facilitate the transition to the C7 picking pattern (measure 2), a pull-off passage is played on beat 4, moving from the chord's major 3rd (E) to the minor 3rd (Eb) and the 9th (D)—voiced here as the open D string. In measure 3, a descending phrase in employed to "respond" to the lick from measure 1. This phrase flows smoothly to a truncated version of the C7 picking pattern (measure 4). On beat 3, the pattern transitions to a two-note (D–E) walk-up to the root of the IV (F) chord (measure 5).

MEASURES 5–8: The lick in measure 5 is the full version of the Lester Flatt run, played here in fifth position and in the key of F. This lick is followed by a truncated version of the F7 picking pattern, which employs a two-note (E–D) bass line on beats 3–4 to walk down to the root of the C7 chord (measure 7). Here, the C major pentatonic (C–D–E–G–A) qualities of the C composite blues scale are utilized to create a jagged legato-based passage to outline the I (C7) chord. (*Note:* Every tone of the C major pentatonic scale is found in the nine-note C composite blues scale, so the phrase can be considered a derivative of either one.) This phrase is followed in measure 8 by a repetition of the one-bar version of the C7 picking pattern.

MEASURES 9–12: In measure 9, a legato-base G composite blues scale lick is performed on the treble strings to outline the V-chord harmony, followed in measure 10 by a repetition of the one-bar version of the F7 picking pattern. Note the pull-off passage at end of measure 9, which, like the one from measure 1, facilitates the transition (i.e., multi-fret jump) to the impending picking pattern. In measures 11–12, a two-bar C composite blues scale lick is performed in fifth position, eliminating the need to jump back to open position. As the phrase descends the strings, seven of the scale's nine tones are employed, ultimately resolving to the root note at fret 5 of the third string.

JAM #129: TWO-BAR LEAD/RHYTHM ALTERNATIONS

The one-bar alternations that were utilized in Jam #128 have been extended to two bars in this example. Throughout the 12-bar form, two measures of lead are alternated with two bars of the Travis-picked seventh chords. The picking patterns are now played in their original, two-bar forms, and the leads consist of two-measure phrases that contain healthy doses of chromaticism and are culled from the C major pentatonic/Aeolian hybrid scale (C–D–Eb–E–F–G–Ab–A–Bb), F composite blues scale (F–G–Ab–A–Bb–Cb–C–D–Eb), and G composite blues scale (G–A–Bb–B–C–Db–D–E–F).

MEASURES 1–4: The first five notes of measure 1 introduce a motif that is reproduced with the subsequent five notes, all from the C composite blues scale. Notice that both quarter-note "pauses" are chord tones—G and C, respectively—which help to emphasize the C7 harmony among the heavy chromaticism. In measures 3–4, one repetition of the C7 picking pattern is followed by a three-note (C–D–E) walk-up to the IV (F7) chord.

MEASURES 5–8: In measures 5–6, the IV-chord harmony is outlined with a (mostly) descending phrase that slips back and forth between sixth and eighth positions before working its way down the F composite blues scale. At the end of the passage, the open D string is employed to facilitate the transition back to the C7 picking pattern, which handles the two bars of I-chord harmony in measures 7–8.

MEASURES 9–12: In measure 9, an open-position G composite blues scale lick, characterized by an ascending/descending chromatic (A–B♭–B) passage, is played over the G7 chord. This phrase is then mimicked in measure 10, over the F7 chord, using notes from the F composite blues scale. In measures 11–12, the C7 picking pattern returns for the I-chord harmony and utilizes the three-note pickup to take the Jam back to the top of the form.

211

JAM #130: ONE-BAR RHYTHM/LEAD ALTERNATIONS

Like Jam #128, the alternations in this example are performed in one-bar intervals, only the order in which they occur is reversed, resulting in a rhythm/lead sequence. Since the alternations are now only one bar long, the Travis-picking patterns have been adjusted accordingly. Meanwhile, the one-bar lead phrases outline the I (C7) and IV (F7) chords (the V chord is rhythm only) with notes from several scales, including C composite blues (C–D–Eb–E–F–Gb–G–A–Bb), C major pentatonic (C–D–E–G–A), and F composite blues (F–G–Ab–A–Bb–Cb–C–D–Eb).

MEASURES 1–4: Following the three-note (G–A–B) pickup, the one-bar version of the C7 picking pattern is performed in measure 1, followed in measure 2 by an open-position C composite blues scale lick that opens with a chromatic (E–Eb–D) passage before briefly pausing on the C note (root) at fret 1 of the second string (beat 3). Following a three-note pull-off (beat 4), the C7 picking pattern makes its second appearance (measure 3). Then, in anticipation of the sixth-position F7 chord voicing in measure 5, the phrase in measure 4 makes a run up the extended form of the C composite blues scale (this could also be considered a C major pentatonic phrase, with the minor 3rd, Eb, making a brief appearance on beat 4).

MEASURES 5–8: Following a repetition of the one-bar F7 picking pattern (measure 5), an F composite blues scale phrase incorporates chromaticism and a slide to work its way down the fretboard, using the open high E string to transition to the C7 picking pattern in measure 7. Following one bar of the Travis-picked C7 chord, a variation of the phrase from measure 4—this time, fully rooted in C major pentatonic—is employed to position the fret hand for the impending G7 chord (measure 9).

MEASURES 9–12: One bar of the G7 picking pattern (measure 9) is followed by a phrase that is somewhat reminiscent of the one from measure 6. Notice how the last note of the G7 picking pattern slides seamlessly into the lick in measure 10. Also, similar to the lick in measure 6, the open B string is used strategically at the end of the phrase to transition to the C7 picking pattern in measure 11, which is shortened by three beats in order to include the G–A–B pickup for a return to the top of the form.

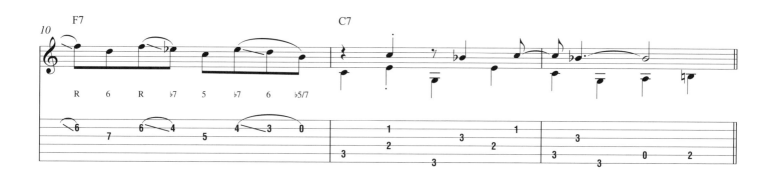

JAM #131: TWO-BAR RHYTHM/LEAD ALTERNATIONS

Since the alternations in this Jam occur in two-bar intervals, the full, two-bar versions of the Travis-picking patterns are implemented. After opening with two bars of Travis picking, the Jam shifts to two bars of soloing—a sequence that is maintained throughout the 12-bar form. All of the leads are performed over the I (C7) chord and derive their notes from the C composite blues scale (C–D–E♭–E–F–G♭–G–A–B♭), played in multiple positions of the fretboard.

MEASURES 1–4: After opening with the three-note (G–A–B) pickup, the Jam segues to two bars of the C7 picking pattern (measures 1–2). In measures 3–4, the I-chord harmony is maintained via a two-bar C composite blues scale phrase that is relegated to the treble strings and played in a (mostly) eighth-note rhythm.

MEASURES 5–8: After voicing the final note of measure 4's phrase with your ring finger, a quick, three-fret jump must be executed in order to arrive in sixth position for the F7 picking pattern. Following one bar of the Travis-picked pattern (measure 5), a three-note (F–E–D) bass line descends string 5 to arrive at the root of the C7 chord (measure 7). Here, the ubiquitous Lester Flatt run is performed in the key of C, in a pattern that moves horizontally (rather than vertically) up the fretboard. When the phrase arrives at the C note at fret 5 of the third string (measure 8), the passage is restated an octave higher.

MEASURES 9–12: In measures 9–10, the Travis-picked pattern handles the V (G7) and IV (F7) chord changes, followed by a two-measure passage that works its way from the root (C) at fret 8 of the first string to the root at fret 5 of the third string via notes of the C composite blues scale. This phrase is characterized by its major-against-minor "rub," which is created by the juxtaposition of the scale's minor 3rd (E♭) and major 3rd (E).

🔊 JAM #132: RANDOM RHYTHM/LEAD ALTERNATIONS

In this Jam, the lead and rhythm parts alternate in random fashion. After the two-bar version of the C7 picking pattern introduces the Jam, a five-measure lead phrase commences, moving from the I (C7) chord to the IV (F7) chord and, finally, back to the I chord. At measure 8, the C7 picking pattern makes a brief (one-bar) appearance before giving way to a two-measure phrase that outlines the V (G7) and IV (F7) chords. In measures 11–12, the Jam concludes with another repetition of the C7 picking pattern, which is capped with the G–A–B pickup to send the example back to the top.

The lead phrases are played over all three harmonies—C7, F7, and G7. The C7 changes are outlined with notes from the C composite blues scale (C–D–Eb–E–F–Gb–G–A–Bb), while the F7 and G7 changes are implied with tones from the F Mixolydian (F–G–A–Bb–C–D–Eb) and G Mixolydian (G–A–B–C–D–E–F) modes, respectively.

214

MEASURES 1–4: Following the G–A–B pickup and two measures of the C7 picking pattern, a C composite blues scale phrase is employed to imply the second half of the I-chord harmony (measures 3–4). This descending passage is performed in a (mostly) eighth-note rhythm and incorporates eight of the scale's nine tones.

MEASURES 5–8: In measure 5, as the harmony shifts to the IV (F7) chord, the lead phrase likewise transitions to a run up the extended form of the F major pentatonic scale (F–G–A–C–D). To emphasize the harmony's dominant quality, however, the scale incorporates the note E♭ (the ♭7th) on beat 2 of measure 6, briefly implying the F Mixolydian mode. In measures 7–8, the C7 harmony is outlined with an open-position C composite blues scale lick (a variation of the Lester Flatt run) and one bar of the C7 picking pattern, respectively.

MEASURES 9–12: In measure 9–10, the V and IV chords are outlined with one-bar phrases derived from the G Mixolydian and F Mixolydian modes, respectively. Although not a note-for-note reproduction, notice how the contour of measure 9's phrase is mimicked in measure 10. The C7 picking pattern returns in measure 11 and is followed in measure 12 by the three-note (G–A–B) pickup.

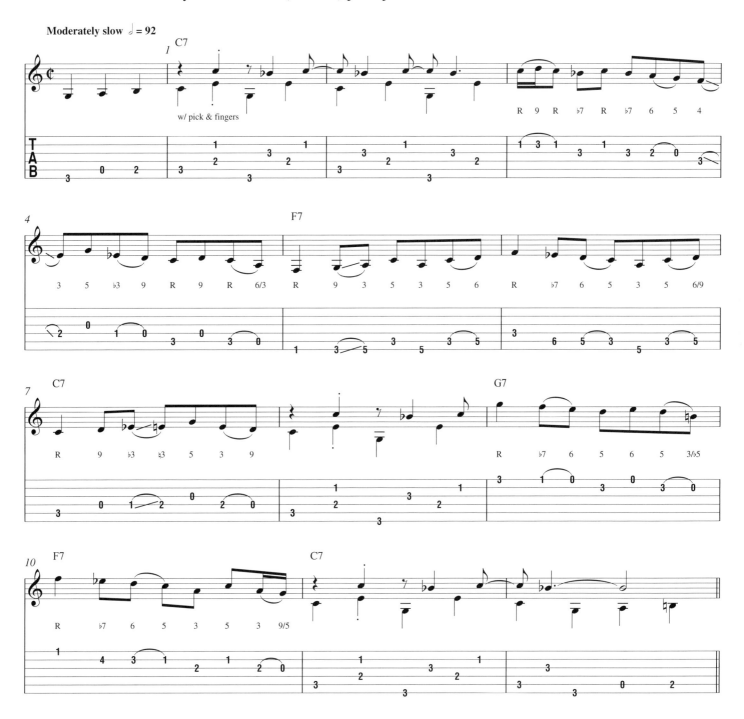

CHAPTER 23: TRAVIS PICKING: CHET ATKINS-STYLE CHORD MELODY
THE RESOURCES

CHORDS

G7

1 3 1 2 1 1

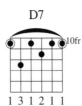

C7

8fr

1 3 1 2 1 1

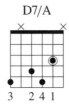

D7

10fr

1 3 1 2 1 1

D7

3 2 4 1

D7/A

3 2 4 1

SCALES

G Composite Blues Scale (Open Position):
G–A–B♭–B–C–D♭–D–E–F
(1–2–♭3–♮3–4–♭5–♮5–6–♭7)

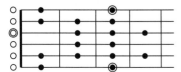

G Composite Blues Scale (2nd Position)

2fr

G Composite Blues Scale (4th Position)

4fr

G Composite Blues Scale (Extended Form)

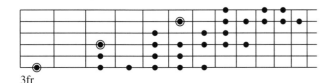

3fr

G Major Pentatonic (Extended Form):
G–A–B–D–E
(1–2–3–5–6)

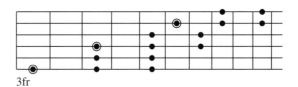

3fr

G Major Pentatonic/Aeolian Hybrid Scale (Extended Form):
G–A–B♭–B–C–D–E♭–E–F
(1–2–♭3–♮3–4–5–♭6–♮6–♭7)

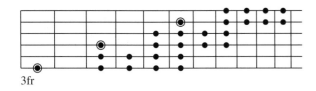

3fr

C Major Pentatonic (Extended Form):
C–D–E–G–A
(1–2–3–5–6)

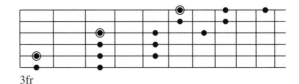

3fr

C Mixolydian:
C–D–E–F–G–A–B♭
(1–2–3–4–5–6–♭7)

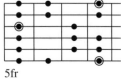

5fr

C Composite Blues Scale (Open Position):
C–D–E♭–E–F–G♭–G–A–B♭
(1–2–♭3–♮3–4–♭5–♮5–6–♭7)

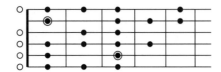

C Composite Blues Scale (2nd Position)

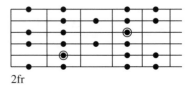

2fr

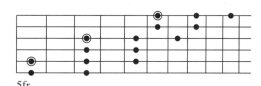

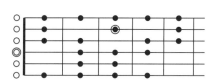

5fr   5fr

🔊 JAM #133: THE 12-BAR FORM

The rhythm approach used in the next six examples is an extension of the Travis picking from Jams 127–132 and influenced by the masterful fingerpicking of the late guitar legend Chet Atkins. Unlike the previous examples, the alternating bass notes in these Jams require no finger shifting, as each chord's root and 5th are included in the six-string dominant-seventh voicing (one exception is the D7 chord used in the turnaround, which is a holdover from the previous Travis-picking Jams). However, while the index and ring fingers remain stationary, the middle and pinky fingers do require some movement in order to voice the chord melodies that are performed on the treble strings.

The song form is a standard 12-bar blues in the key of G, with dominant voicings (G7, C7, and D7) played in lieu of basic major triads. In true country fashion, each chord features a grace-note hammer-on from the minor 3rd to the major 3rd, creating the desirable major-against-minor "rub." Meanwhile, the treble-string melodies imply a variety of chord types (major triad, major sixth, dominant seventh, etc.) without changing the chords' fundamental (dominant) tonalities.

MEASURES 1–4: The Jam's opening bars feature a four-measure picking pattern that is created from a standard G7 barre-chord shape. In addition to the alternating root–5th bass line and the minor-to-major (B♭-to-B) hammer-on, the pattern employs a treble-string melody that incorporates several pitches from the G Mixolydian mode (G–A–B–C–D–E–F), including the root (G), 3rd (B), 5th (D), 6th (E), and ♭7th (F). Notice that, although played as a four-bar pattern, measure 3 is simply a restatement of measure 1.

MEASURES 5–8: The picking pattern from measures 1–2 is restated in measures 5–6, only it's played in eighth position—with the C7 shape—to outline the IV-chord harmony. This C7 pattern is followed in measure 7–8 with a return to the G7 pattern for the I chord.

MEASURES 9–12: In measures 9–10, the pattern from measure 1 is restated in tenth and eighth positions for the V (D7) and IV (C7) chords, respectively. Then, for the turnaround (measures 11–12), the G7 pattern returns for one bar before segueing to an alternate voicing for the V chord, resulting in a root–5th bass line that moves from string 5 to string 6, rather than from string 6 to string 5.

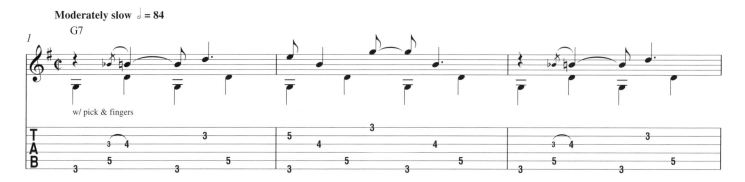

 JAM #134: ONE-BAR LEAD/RHYTHM ALTERNATIONS

In this example, short, one-bar lead phrases are continuously alternated with the Chet Atkins–style Travis picking. Consequently, the two- and four-measure picking patterns from Jam #133 are shortened to one bar. These one-bar tradeoffs are maintained throughout the Jam's first 10 measures. Then, in measures 11–12, a two-bar lead passage is employed to cap the example.

The leads are derived from several note sources—played in various locations along the neck—including the G composite blues scale (G–A–Bb–B–C–Db–D–E–F), the C major pentatonic scale (C–D–E–G–A), and the D major pentatonic scale (D–E–F♯–A–B). While the Travis-picking pattern can be performed exclusively with your fingers, the presence of lead passages in this Jam requires hybrid picking—a combination of your pick and fingers.

MEASURES 1–4: The Jam commences with a jangly G composite blues scale lick that juxtaposes fretted pitches and the open G and open D strings, using the latter to facilitate the transition to the G7 picking pattern in measure 2. In measure 3, another descending lick is carved from the G composite blues scale; however, this time, the phrase is played in third position and is characterized by multiple repetitions of adjacent 5th (D) and b5th (Db) tones. In measure 4, the G7 picking pattern (from measure 2) makes its second appearance.

MEASURES 5–8: In anticipation of the C7 picking pattern (measure 6), a C major pentatonic lick climbs the neck via pitches from the extended form of the scale, starting from the third-string root (fret 5). Similarly, in measure 7, the extended form of the G composite blues scale supplies the notes for a descending phrase that bridges the eighth-position C7 picking pattern and the third-position G7 picking pattern, which is restated in measure 8.

MEASURES 9–12: In measure 9, the extended form of the D major pentatonic scale simultaneously outlines the V (D7) chord and shifts the fret hand up the neck for the impending C7 picking pattern (measure 10). Although the last note of the phrase, C, is not found in the scale, it functions here as both the ♭7th of the D7 harmony (implying D Mixolydian) and the root of the forthcoming C7 chord. In measure 11, a slippery G composite blues scale lick handles the I-chord harmony, shifting to string 1 for the arrival of the V (D7) chord. Technically, the V-chord phrase is rooted in the G composite blues scale, although the notes—D, F, and B—function here as the root, ♭3rd, and 6th, respectively.

🔊 JAM #135: TWO-BAR LEAD/RHYTHM ALTERNATIONS

The lead/rhythm alternations in this example occur in two-measure intervals—a one-bar increase from Jam #134. As a result, the Travis-picking patterns in this example contain more robust chord melodies, which were missing in the one-bar versions. These two-bar tradeoffs are maintained throughout the Jam's 12 bars, starting with two measures of lead playing. The licks are played over all three chord changes—G7, C7, and D7—and derive their notes from a variety of sources, including the G composite blues scale (G–A–B♭–B–C–D♭–D–E–F), C composite blues scale (C–D–E♭–E–F–G♭–G–A–B♭), C Mixolydian mode (C–D–E–F–G–A–B♭), and D composite blues scale (D–E–F–F♯–G–A♭–A–B–C).

MEASURES 1–4: The lead phrase in measures 1–2 commences on the note B♭, the minor 3rd of the G7 harmony, and flows gradually down the G composite blues scale, eventually arriving at the G7 picking pattern (measure 3). Here, a two-bar version of the pattern handles the second half of the I-chord harmony, featuring a melody that moves as follows: B–D–F–B–E–D (3rd–5th–♭7th–3rd–6th–5th).

MEASURES 5–8: The phrase in measures 5–6 is a countrified double-stop passage that starts as a run up the extended form of the C major pentatonic scale, but quickly transitions to a C Mixolydian phrase that blends a C/E double stop with pitches that alternate on the fourth string, B♭ and A (the ♭7th and 6th, respectively). Slide into the double-stop passage with your ring finger, using index finger to voice the double stop and your ring and middle fingers for the alternating pitches. This phrase is followed in measures 7–8 by two bars of the G7 picking pattern. Be careful here, though—the second bar is different from the one used in the initial G7 pattern.

MEASURES 9–12: In measure 9, the D7 harmony is outlined with a descending D composite blues scale lick that moves from the second-string root to the open D string, which facilitates the transition to the C composite blues scale lick in measure 10. Other than the one-octave jump on beat 1, the contour and feel of this phrase is much like its predecessor. In measures 11–12, the Jam concludes with one bar of the G7 picking pattern and a third-position D7 voicing (the V chord) whose root–5th bass line alternates between string 5 and string 6, respectively, a reversal from the G7 and C7 voicings.

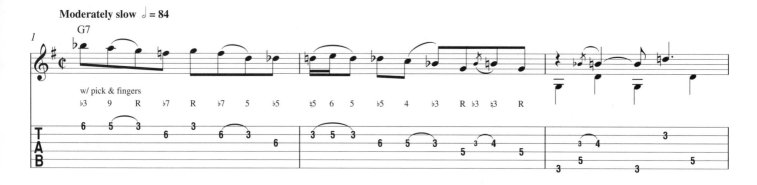

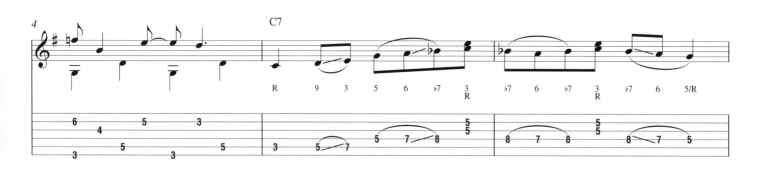

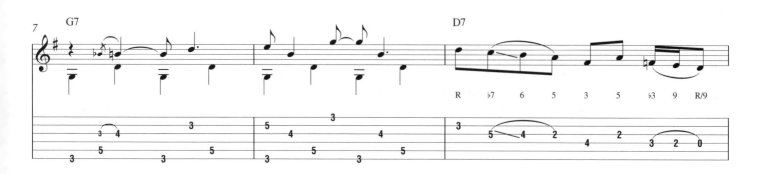

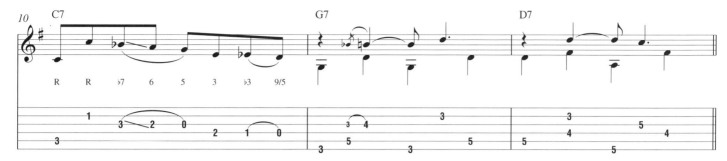

JAM #136: ONE-BAR RHYTHM/LEAD ALTERNATIONS

Like Jam #134, the alternations in this example rotate every measure, so the Chet Atkins–style picking patterns are, once again, shortened to one bar. However, the order in which the alternations are performed is reversed, resulting in rhythm/lead sequence. These alternations are maintained throughout the Jam's first 10 measures. Then, to cap the Jam, a two-measure version of the G7 picking pattern is performed in measures 11–12. Meanwhile, the lead phrases are played in several locations on neck, using a variety of note sources, including the G composite blues scale (G–A–Bb–B–C–Db–D–E–F), G major pentatonic scale (G–A–B–D–E), C Mixolydian mode (C–D–E–F–G–A–Bb), and C composite blues scale (C–D–Eb–E–F–Gb–G–A–Bb).

MEASURES 1–4: After one bar of the G7 picking pattern opens the Jam, a jump blues–style lick, derived from the G composite blues scale, is performed in measure 2. In measure 3, the G7 pattern returns for another repetition before giving way to a run up the extended form of the G major pentatonic scale (measure 4), setting up the fret hand for the forthcoming C7 picking pattern.

MEASURES 5–8: The IV-chord harmony (measures 5–6) is handled by one bar of the C7 picking pattern and a passage that descends strings 3–4 via major and minor 3rds that are diatonic to the C Mixolydian mode. On beat 4, a Bb-to-B (minor-to-major) hammer-on signals the return to the I (G7) chord in measure 7. Here, the G7 picking pattern is performed for one bar, followed in measure 8 by a G composite blues scale lick that shifts from first position to third position at its midpoint. Again, note the minor-to-major hammer-on at the end of the phrase (in the key of D, F to F♯), which anticipates the V (D7) chord harmony in measure 9.

MEASURES 9–12: Rather than jump all the way up to 10th position for the sixth-string D7 voicing, the picking pattern in measure 9 settles for a fifth-string voicing in third position—the same voicing used in the turnaround (measure 12). In measure 10, a C composite blues scale lick incorporating chromaticism (E–Eb–D), legato, and a position shift outlines the C7 harmony (IV chord). In measures 11–12, the Jam concludes with one bar of the G7 picking pattern and one bar of the third-position D7 pattern, respectively.

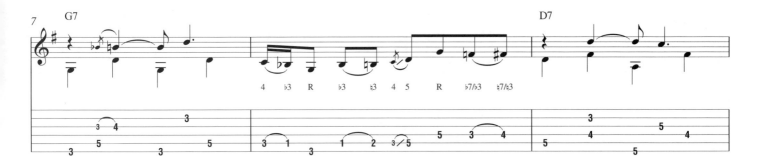

JAM #137: TWO-BAR RHYTHM/LEAD ALTERNATIONS

In this example, the rhythm/lead alternations are played in two-bar intervals—a one-bar increase from Jam #136. As a result, the treble-string melodies of the Travis-picking patterns are more extensive. The exceptions, of course, are the V- and IV-chord changes in measures 9–10, where the harmonies change every bar.

Like the rhythm parts, the lead phrases are two measures long, played in a (mostly) eighth-note rhythm. Since the IV (C7) chord is handled exclusively by its picking pattern, these licks are only played over the G7 and D7 harmonies, deriving their notes from the G composite (G–A–B♭–B–C–D♭–D–E–F) and D composite (D–E–F–F♯–G–A♭–A–B–C) blues scales, respectively.

MEASURES 1–4: The two-bar version of the G7 picking pattern sets up the Jam, followed in measures 3–4 by a two-bar G composite blues scale lick that starts off as a run up the extended form of the G major pentatonic scale before introducing tones such as the ♭7th (F) and ♭3rd (B♭), implying the former scale. In addition to outlining the G7 harmony, the scale pattern puts the fret hand in an advantageous position for the eighth-position C7 picking pattern (measures 5–6).

MEASURES 5–8: The C7 picking pattern in measures 5–6 is identical to the G7 pattern from measures 1–2, only it's voiced five frets higher. In measures 7–8, a two-bar, chromatic-laden phrase is employed to outline the G7 harmony. This phrase is a hybrid of two scale—G major pentatonic (G–A–B–D–E) and G Aeolian (G–A–B♭–C–D–E♭–F)—borrowing major qualities from the former and minor qualities from the latter. Note the phrase's final note, D, which anticipates the D7 harmony (measure 9) by half a beat.

MEASURES 9–12: In measures 9–10, one-bar version of the D7 and C7 picking patterns handle the V- and IV-chord changes, respectively, followed by a two-bar passage that shifts seamlessly from a G composite blues scale phrase (measure 11) to a D composite blues scale lick (measure 12). Note the use of the minor-to-major (F-to-F♯) hammer-on on beat 4 of measure 11 to resolve to the root of the V (D7) chord—a technique that you should be familiar with by now! The hammer-on is then restated in measure 12, where it resolves to the second-string root (fret 3). The G note that precedes the F-to-F♯ hammer-on is used to enclose, or "frame," the major 3rd, F♯.

🔊 JAM #138: RANDOM RHYTHM/LEAD ALTERNATIONS

For this final installment of the Travis-picking Jams, the alternations have been arranged randomly. What's unique about this arrangement is how few times the lead and rhythm parts actually alternate. After opening with the four-bar version of the G7 picking pattern (see Jam #133), a six-measure lead passage commences over the IV (C7) chord. This phrase then moves on to the I (G7) chord before concluding with one-bar phrases over the V (D7) and IV (C7) chords in measures 9–10. Then, to cap the Jam, the picking pattern returns in measures 11–12 for the I–V (G7–D7) turnaround progression.

The lead passage crams a lot of notes into its six measures, pulling pitches from several sources, including the C composite blues scale (C–D–Eb–E–F–Gb–G–A–Bb), G composite blues scale (G–A–Bb–B–C–Db–D–E–F), and D major pentatonic scale (D–E–F#–A–B). What makes this expansive phrase work so well is its emphasis on root notes. If you look closely, you see that, as the harmony unfolds, the root of each new chord is stated on beat 1 of that measure. As a result, the listener is better able to hear the underlying chord changes.

MEASURES 1–4: The first four measures of the Jam are entirely comprised of the G7 picking pattern. While measures 1 and 3 are identical, measures 2 and 4 contain different melodies, so be sure to vary your picking and fretting in the latter.

MEASURES 5–8: Measure 5 contains the first of six straight measures of lead playing. Here, a two-bar C composite blues scale phrase begins on the root note at fret 8 of the first string before working its way down the scale. At the end of measure 6, the phrase moves chromatically (A–A♭–G) from the 6th of C7 to the root of the G7 chord (measure 7). Here, a variation of the Lester Flatt run is employed for the first half of the I-chord harmony. Then, when the phrase reaches string 2, it reverses course and descends the G composite blues scale.

MEASURES 9–12: To outline the V (D7) and IV (C7) chords in measures 9–10, the final two bars of the lead phrase employ a descending D major pentatonic phrase and a C composite blues scale lick, respectively. On beat 4 of measure 10, the lead passage transitions to the G7 picking pattern via a chromatic (A♭–G) pull-off. This picking pattern, a restatement of measure 1, is followed by a fifth-string D7 voicing whose root–5th bass line moves from string 5 to string 6—a reversal from the G7 voicing's sixth-to-fifth string movement.

SECTION V: FUNK

CHAPTER 24: FUNK RIFF
THE RESOURCES

CHORDS

F7

1 3 1 2 1 1

B♭7

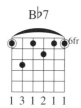

1 3 1 2 1 1

C7

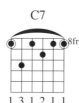

1 3 1 2 1 1

C7♯9

2 1 3 4

SCALES

F Minor Pentatonic:
F–A♭–B♭–C–E♭
(1–♭3–4–5–♭7)

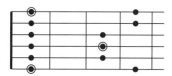

F Composite Blues Scale (Open Position):
F–G–A♭–A–B♭–C♭–C–D–E♭
(1–2–♭3–♮3–4–♭5–♮5–6–♭7)

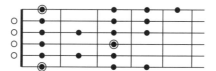

F Composite Blues Scale (2nd Position)

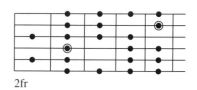

2fr

F Composite Blues Scale (Extended Form)

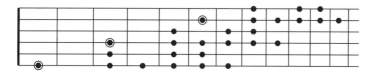

F Major Pentatonic (Extended Form):
F–G–A–C–D
(1–2–3–5–6)

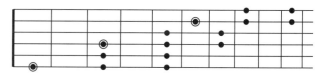

F Blues Scale (1st Position):
F–A♭–B♭–C♭–C–E♭
(1–♭3–4–♭5–♮5–♭7)

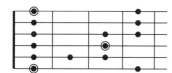

F Blues Scale (Extended Form)

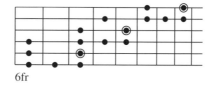

6fr

B♭ Composite Blues Scale (Open Position):
B♭–C–D♭–D–E♭–F♭–F–G–A♭
(1–2–♭3–♮3–4–♭5–♮5–6–♭7)

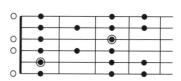

B♭ Composite Blues Scale (3rd Position)

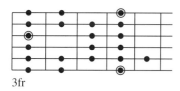

3fr

B♭ Composite Blues Scale (5th Position)

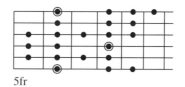

5fr

B♭ Minor Pentatonic (6th Position):
B♭–D♭–E♭–F–A♭
(1–♭3–4–5–♭7)

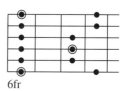

6fr

B♭ Minor Pentatonic (Extended Form)

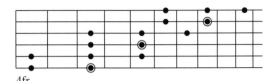

4fr

C Composite Blues Scale (2nd Position):
C–D–E♭–E–F–G♭–G–A–B♭
(1–2–♭3–♮3–4–♭5–♮5–6–♭7)

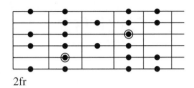

2fr

C Composite Blues Scale (5th Position)

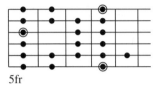

5fr

C Blues Scale:
C–E♭–F–G♭–G–B♭
(1–♭3–4–♭5–♮5–♭7)

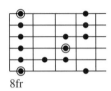

8fr

JAM #139: THE 12-BAR FORM

Funk may be the last music genre covered in *One-Man Guitar Jam*, but it's arguably the most enjoyable to play in this type of solo-guitar setting. When you're playing solo, with no other instruments available to establish the groove, it's up to you, and the riff used in the next six examples grooves in spades!

The two-bar riff is comprised entirely of single notes and is rooted in the key of F major, although multiple repetitions of the ♭7th (E♭) imply an F dominant tonality. Rhythmically, the riff fluctuates between straight eighth notes (beats 1–2) and 16th-note syncopations (beats 3–4), a staple of funk rhythm. Harmonically, the Jam is arranged as a 12-bar blues in the key of F, with dominant seventh chords substituted for basic major triads: F7 (I chord), B♭7 (IV chord), and C7 (V chord). For the turnaround (measures 11–12), the Jam follows the I (F7) chord with a funk-certified C7♯9 voicing, sending the Jam back to the top.

MEASURES 1–4: The initial four bars of the Jam consist of two repetitions of the F7 riff. On beats 1–2 of measure 1, the sixth-string root (F) is followed by an F–E♭–F sequences, which is performed on string 4 and played in staccato fashion. Then, on beats 3–4, a syncopated passaged fluctuates between a chromatic line on string 3 (A♭– A–B♭) and the root on string 4. In measure 2, beats 1–2 from measure 1 are restated, followed by a syncopated figure that pairs the fourth-string root with the open A string and the B♭ note at fret 1 of the fifth string, leading to a second repetition of the two-bar riff (measures 3–4).

MEASURES 5–8: In measures 5–6, the riff is transposed to the key of B♭ for the IV chord. You'll notice that the open A string has been replaced by a fretted D note (fret 5, fifth string), followed by the note E♭ (fret 6). At measure 7, the F7 riff returns for another repetition.

MEASURES 9–12: In measures 9–10, the two-bar riff is adjusted to accommodate the one-bar durations of the V (C7) and IV (B♭7) chords; that is, the first half of the riff is played once at fret 8 (C7) and then once at fret 6 (B♭7). The same treatment is given to the F7 riff in measure 11. When the riff begins to repeat in measure 12, the C7♯9 chord abruptly enters on beat 3 to signal a return to the top of the form. Rather than strum all four notes of the voicing, a syncopated pattern alternates between the fifth-string root and the rest of the voicing (strings 2–4).

JAM #140: ONE-BAR LEAD/RHYTHM ALTERNATIONS

This first series of funk alternations consists of one bar of lead and one bar of rhythm, a sequence that is maintained throughout the Jam's first 10 measures. At measure 11, a two-bar F composite blues scale (F–G–Ab–A–Bb–Cb–C–D–Eb) phrase enters to bring the Jam to its conclusion. To conform to the new one-bar format, the two-bar riff is shortened to one bar, using the riff's opening bar for each repetition. Meanwhile, the lead phrases are derived from a variety of sources, including the aforementioned F composite blues scale, the F minor pentatonic scale (F–Ab–Bb–C–Eb), Bb composite blues scale (Bb–C–Db–D–Eb–Fb–F–G–Ab), and C composite blues scale (C–D–Eb–E–F–Gb–G–A–Bb).

MEASURES 1–4: The Jam opens with a whole-step bend and release, which is followed by a bluesy lick rooted in the F minor pentatonic scale. The one-bar version of the F7 riff enters in measure 2 and is followed by another F minor pentatonic phrase (measure 3). This lick is relegated to the bass strings and is characterized by its syncopated repetitions of the notes Eb (b7th) and C (5th). In measure 4, the one-bar F7 riff returns for another repetition.

MEASURES 5–8: In measure 5, the Bb7 harmony is implied with an Angus Young–inspired Bb composite blues scale lick that employs a half-step bend to move from the chord's minor 3rd (Db) to its major 3rd (D). Note that the change in harmony (F7 to Bb7) is emphasized immediately, with the root (Bb) held through beat 1 (i.e., a quarter note). In measure 6, the riff is relocated to sixth position for the Bb7 harmony. In measures 7–8, the I-chord harmony is implied with an F composite blues scale lick and one bar of the F7 riff, respectively. Although played on different beats, the half-step, minor-to-major bend at the end of measure 7 is reminiscent of the one from measure 5, lending continuity to the Jam.

MEASURES 9–12: The lick in measure 9 is a variation of the lick from measure 5, although it's played two frets higher (one whole step) to accommodate the new (C7) harmony. Following one bar of the Bb7 riff (measure 10), the Jam concludes with a two-bar F composite blues scale lick that descends the scale in a rhythmic sequence that pairs 16th notes (beats 1 and 3) and quarter notes (beats 2 and 4). On the "and" of beat 2 of measure 12, the lick resolves to the C note at fret 3 of the fifth string to acknowledge the arrival of the V (C7#9) chord.

228

JAM #141: TWO-BAR LEAD/RHYTHM ALTERNATIONS

The sequence of the alternations from Jam #140 is retained in this example, although now the alternations are played in two-bar intervals. As a result, the riff is played here in its original, two-bar form. Meanwhile, the lead phrases are played over each of the chord changes—F7, Bb7, and C7—and derive their notes from the composite blues scale relative to each change: F composite (F–G–Ab–A–Bb–Cb–C–D–Eb), Bb composite (Bb–C–Db–D–Eb–Fb–F–G–Ab), and C composite (C–D–Eb–E–F–Gb–G–A–Bb).

MEASURES 1–4: The Jam opens with a two-bar F composite blues scale phrase that commences in fourth position before shifting to first position for resolution. The lick employs a variety of rhythms, including quarter notes, eighth notes, and 16th notes, as well as a touch of syncopation (see beat 3 of measure 2). At measure 3, the F7 riff enters to handle the second half of the I-chord harmony.

MEASURES 5–8: At measure 5, a two-bar Bb composite blues scale phrase, played in the vicinity of sixth position, enters for the IV-chord harmony. To emphasize the new harmony (Bb7), two chord tones, D and Bb, occupy the lick's first two beats. On beat 3 of measure 5, a flurry of scale tones descend the strings, played in a rhythm that is comprised mostly of 16th notes and 16th-note triplets. Again, note the chord tone on beat 1 of measure 6—the root of Bb7—which further highlights the IV-chord harmony. This phrase is followed in measures 7–8 by another repetition of the F7 riff.

MEASURES 9–12: In measure 9, the V (C7) chord is implied with a C composite blues scale lick that moves from its third-string root (fret 5) to the root on string 6 (fret 8). This descending phrase is followed by a lick that moves in the opposite direction, moving from its sixth-string root (fret 6) to the D note (the 3rd) at fret 7 of the third string, where is reversed direction and works its way back down the strings. In measures 11–12, the Jam concludes with one-and-a-half repetitions of the F7 riff and syncopated strumming of the V (C7#9) chord.

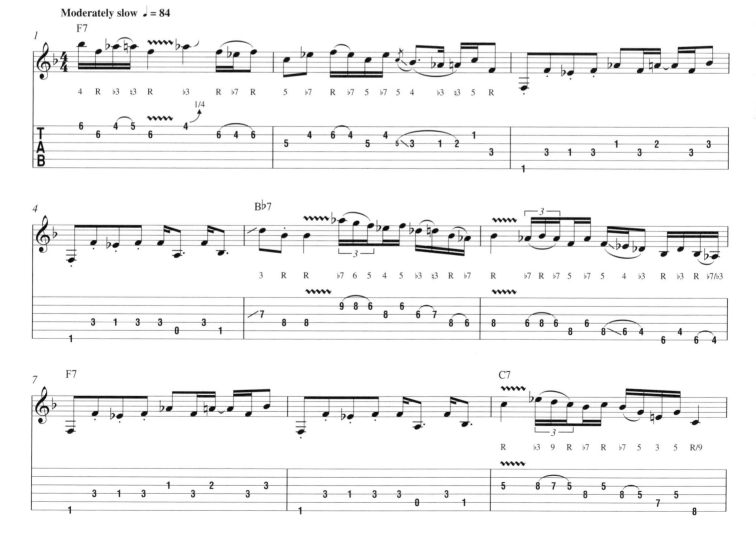

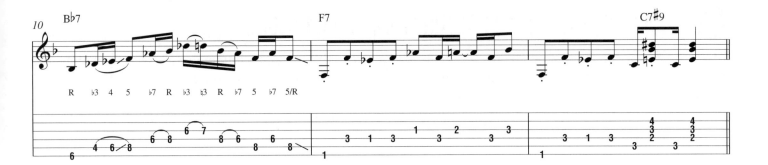

🔊 JAM #142: ONE-BAR RHYTHM/LEAD ALTERNATIONS

To accommodate the return of one-bar alternations, the rhythm parts reprise the one-bar riffs from Jam #140. These shortened riffs are continuously alternated with one bar of soloing through the Jam's first 10 measures. Then, in measures 11–12, the Jam concludes with two bars of rhythm, which consists of the F7 riff and the syncopated C7♯9 chord.

The lead parts may be brief but they make up for their brevity with a diverse group of licks. Nearly every phrase employs a new soloing concept and/or a new scale source, including F minor pentatonic (F–A♭–B♭–C–E♭), F composite blues (F–G–A♭–A–B♭–C♭–C–D–E♭), F major pentatonic (F–G–A–C–D), B♭ minor pentatonic (B♭–D♭–E♭–F–A♭), and B♭ composite blues (B♭–C–D♭–D–E♭–F♭–F–G–A♭).

MEASURES 1–4: Following one bar of the F7 riff, a string-bending motif is introduced in measure 2. Rooted in the F minor pentatonic scale, the lick opens with a whole-step bend/release figure on string 2, which is immediately mimicked on string 3. In measure 3, the F7 riff makes its second appearance, followed in measure 4 by a swift descent of the F composite blues scale. Note the efficient, whole-step (A♭-to-B♭) transition from the I (F7) chord to the IV (B♭7) chord on string 6. The A♭ functions as both the ♭3rd of F7 and the ♭7th of B♭7, while the B♭, of course, functions as the root of B♭7.

MEASURES 5–8: In measure 5, the riff is relocated to sixth position, where it implies the new, IV-chord harmony. In measure 6, the string-bending motif from measure 2 is restated note-for-note, although the source of the pitches is now the B♭ minor pentatonic scale. At the end of this phrase, a quick, five-fret jump is needed in order to get to the F7 riff at the onset of measure 7. Following one repetition of the riff, a multi-octave run up the extended form of the F major pentatonic scale is employed to put the fret hand in an advantageous position for the impending V (C7) chord (measure 9).

MEASURES 9–12: Following one bar of the C7 riff (measure 9), the B♭ composite blues scale outlines the B♭7 harmony with a phrase that commences in sixth position before utilizing major and minor 3rds to descend strings 3–4. This phrase concludes with a third-string, minor-to-major (A♭-to-A) hammer-on that resolves to the root of the I (F7) chord. Here, the F7 riff is reprised for one-and-a-half repetitions, leading to syncopated C7♯9 chord strums.

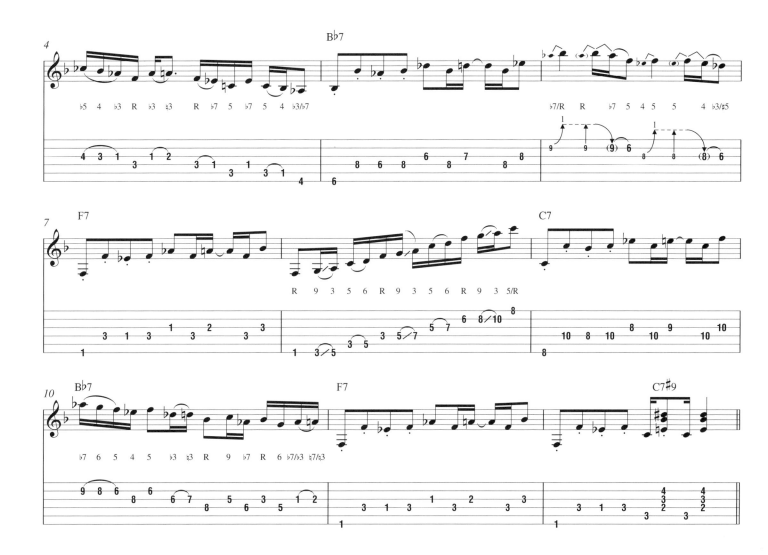

◉ JAM #143: TWO-BAR RHYTHM/LEAD ALTERNATIONS

In this example, the one-bar rhythm/lead alternations from Jam #142 have been extended to two measures. As a result, the rhythm parts are now comprised of the full, two-bar versions of the riffs—except, of course, in measures 9–10, where the one-bar versions handle the V and IV chords. Throughout the 12-bar form, the riffs are offset with two measures of lead, all of which are performed over the I (F7) chord and derive their notes from either the F blues scale (F–A♭–B♭–C♭–C–E♭) or the F *composite* blues scale (F–G–A♭–A–B♭–C♭–C–D–E♭).

MEASURES 1–4: The Jam commences with the F7 riff, which occupies both measure 1 and measure 2. In measures 3–4, a two-bar, legato-based F blues scale phrase is performed in first position. Notice that the sixth-string root is restated on beat 1 of measure 3 to further emphasize the F7 harmony. At the end of measure 4, a quick, five-fret jump must be executed to transition from the F blues scale phrase to the B♭7 riff (measure 5).

MEASURES 5–8: The two-bar B♭7 riff handles the IV-chord harmony (measures 5–6) and is followed in measures 7–8 by another F blues scale passage. This time, the phrase is derived from the extended form of the scale, starting on string 5, and moves from sixth position to 11th position as it ascends the strings in a repetitive sequence.

MEASURES 9–12: Following one-bar versions of the C7 and B♭7 riffs (measures 9–10), an F *composite* blues scale lick is employed to conclude the Jam. What differentiates this phrase, note-wise, from the previous F blues scale licks is the inclusion of the major 3rd (A)—the rest of the notes are found in both scales. After opening in fourth position, the phrase shifts to the first-position pattern of the F blues scale on beat 3 of measure 11, resolving to the root of the C7#9 chord on beat 3 of the subsequent measure.

JAM #144: RANDOM RHYTHM/LEAD ALTERNATIONS

This final installment of the funk-riff alternations involves juggling the rhythm and lead parts in random fashion. After opening with three measures of the F7 riff, the Jam unfolds with two bars of lead, two bars of rhythm, three more bars of lead, and, lastly, two bars of rhythm.

The randomness of this arrangement eliminates the structured sound of the predetermined one- and two-bar tradeoffs, giving the Jam or more improvised feel, which is the ultimate goal of *One-Man Guitar Jam*. Also, because the alternations occur randomly, some of the lead and rhythm parts must be performed *through* chord changes, rather changing *with* the harmony. That is, instead of transitioning from lead to rhythm—or vice versa—when a new chord arrives, these parts are maintained through the change in harmony. For example, the lead phrase that begins in measure 8, over the F7 harmony, is played through the V (C7) and IV (Bb7) changes in measures 9–10, as well.

MEASURES 1–4: Following one-and-a-half repetitions of the F7 riff, a descending F blues scale (F–Ab–Bb–Cb–C–Eb) lick caps the final bar of the four-bar I-chord harmony. Rhythmically, the phrase features straight 16th notes on beats 1 and 3 and syncopation on beats 2 and 4.

MEASURES 5–8: The phrase that began in measure 4 flows seamlessly to a B♭ composite blues scale (B♭–C–D♭–D–E♭–F♭–F–G–A♭) phrase. This lick (measure 5) is characterized by the minor 3rd/major 3rd (D♭/D) "rub" that occurs on beats 3–4. After your ring finger slides up to fret 6 of the third string to play the minor 3rd, your index finger will voice the major 3rd at fret 3 of the second string, followed by another articulation of the minor 3rd as the two-beat legato figure descends. In measure 6, the riff is implemented for the second bar of the IV (B♭7) chord, as well as for the return to the I (F7) chord in measure 7. In measure 8, the F composite blues scale (F–G–A♭–A–B♭–C♭–C–D–E♭) provides the pitches to a two-string ascent of the neck, putting the fret hand in an advantageous position for the forthcoming C7 lick.

MEASURES 9–12: After the C7 harmony is emphasized on beat 1 via a vibratoed root note (fret 8, first string), the lick in measure 8 descends strings 1–4 with pitches from the C blues scale (C–E♭–F–G♭–G–B♭). At the end of the phrase, the fourth-string root (C) slides down one whole step (two frets), to the root of the IV chord, B♭. Here, a jump-blues lick is culled from the B♭ composite blues scale, leading to the Jam's conclusion—one-and-a-half repetitions of the F7 lick and syncopated strums of the V (C7♯9) chord.

233

CHAPTER 25: FUNK "SKANK" GROOVE
THE RESOURCES

CHORDS

A7   D7   E7   E7#9

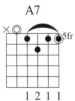 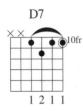 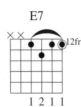 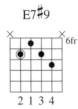

SCALES

A Composite Blues Scale (2nd Position):
A–B–C–C♯–D–E♭–E–F♯–G
(1–2–♭3–♮3–4–♭5–♮5–6–♭7)

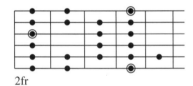

2fr

A Composite Blues Scale (4th Position)

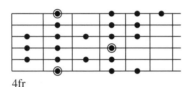

4fr

A Composite Blues Scale (Extended Form)

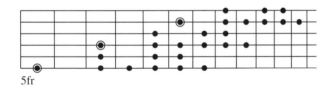

5fr

A Blues Scale (Extended Form):
A–C–D–E♭–E–G
(1–♭3–4–♭5–♮5–♭7)

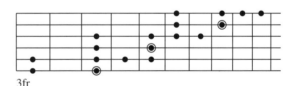

3fr

A Minor Pentatonic:
A–C–D–E–G
(1–♭3–4–5–♭7)

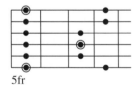

5fr

D Composite Blues Scale (Open Position):
D–E–F–F♯–G–A♭–A–B–C
(1–2–♭3–♮3–4–♭5–♮5–6–♭7)

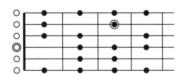

D Composite Blues Scale (2nd Position)

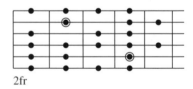

2fr

D Composite Blues Scale (4th Position)

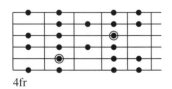

4fr

D Minor Pentatonic:
D–F–G–A–C
(1–♭3–4–5–♭7)

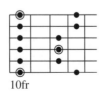

10fr

D Mixolydian (2nd Position):
D–E–F♯–G–A–B–C
(1–2–3–4–5–6–♭7)

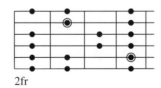

2fr

D Mixolydian (7th Position)

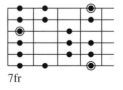

7fr

E Composite Blues Scale (9th Position):
E–F♯–G–G♯–A–B♭–B–C♯–D
(1–2–♭3–♮3–4–♭5–♮5–6–♭7)

E Composite Blues Scale (Extended Form)

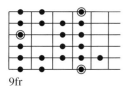

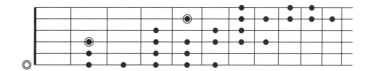

9fr

 # JAM #145: THE 12-BAR FORM

In funk music, no rhythm-guitar style is more common than the "skank" groove, no doubt due to its diversity. Skank grooves—performed with full chords, chord partials, and/or single notes—involve strumming the aforementioned in a 16th-note rhythm, alternating the chord (or single-note) attacks with percussive mutes to create syncopation.

The next six Jams feature a two-bar skank groove comprised of one bar of syncopated dyads (double stops) and one bar of syncopated single notes. The groove that is established in measures 1–4, over the A7 harmony, is then relocated to 10th and 12th positions for the D7 and E7 chords, respectively. The dyads used in the first half of the riff are comprised of the ♭7th and major 3rd of each chord change—G/C♯ for A7, C/F♯ for D7, and D/G♯ for E7—and are approached on beats 1 and 4 via a half step.

The second half of the riff is comprised of notes from the Mixolydian modes relative to the chord changes—A Mixolydian (A–B–C♯–D–E–F♯–G), D Mixolydian (D–E–F♯–G–A–B–C), and E Mixolydian (E–F♯–G♯–A–B–C♯–D)—starting on the root and moving down, stepwise, to the ♭7th and 6th. Then, on beat 4, the line slides back up to the ♭7th to further emphasize the dominant quality of the chords.

While the groove is pure funk, the progression is a standard 12-bar blues. Like previous Jams, the V chord appears in measure 12 to signal a return to the top of the form. To further enhance the funk qualities of the Jam, an E7♯9 voicing—a favorite of Jimi Hendrix—is substituted for a basic dominant seventh chord (E7). Preceded by a chromatic (D–D♯–E) line, the E7♯9 chord is played on the "and" of beat 3, lending additional syncopation to the Jam's groove.

MEASURES 1–4: The Jam opens with two repetitions of the A7 skank groove. The dyad skank is performed in measures 1 and 3 and offset in measures 2 and 4 by the single-note line.

MEASURES 5–8: In measures 5–6, the two-bar skank groove is transposed to the key of D, necessitating a five-fret shift from fifth position to 10th position. For the return of the I chord in measures 7–8, the A7 skank groove is played again.

MEASURES 9–12: Because the V (E7) and IV (D7) chords in measures 9–10 last for only one measure apiece, the single-note portion of those skank grooves is eliminated. For the turnaround, the dyad portion of the A7 groove (measure 11) is followed in measure 12 by an abbreviated single-note line. On the "and" of beat 2, a legato-based chromatic (D–D♯–E) passage leads to the V (E7♯9) chord, which is played on the "and" of beat 3.

Moderately slow ♩ = 92

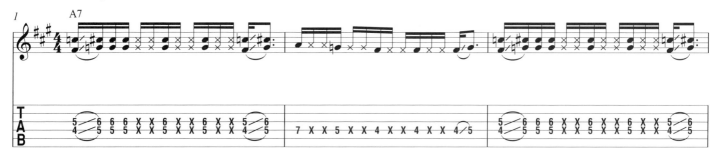

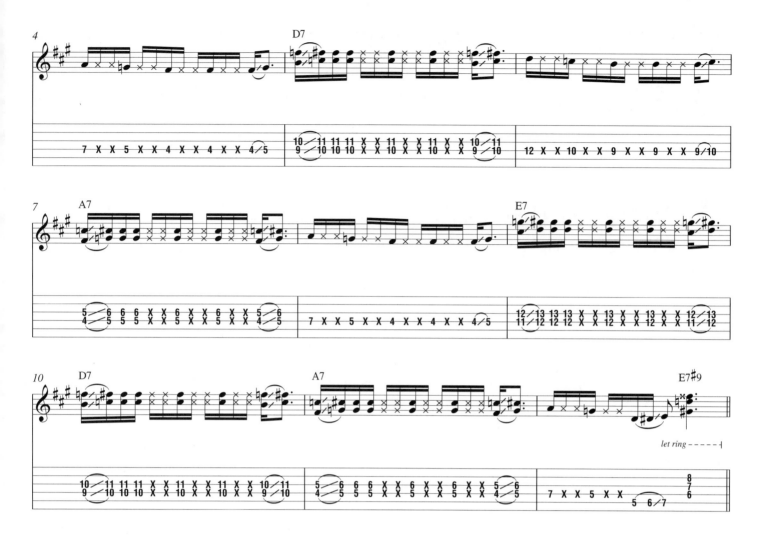

🔊 JAM #146: ONE-BAR LEAD/RHYTHM ALTERNATIONS

This first series of alternations involves one bar of lead continuously fluctuating with one bar of the skank groove. The one exception is measures 11–12, where a two-bar lead phrase is utilized for the turnaround. Also, because the alternations occur in one-bar intervals, the skank grooves are shorted to include only the dyads (the single-note lines are note used in this example). Meanwhile, the lead phrases are composed from a variety of sources, including the A blues scale (A–C–D–E♭–E–G), A composite blues scale (A–B–C–C♯–D–E♭–E–F♯–G), D composite blues scale (D–E–F–F♯–G–A♭–A–B–C), and E composite blues scale (E–F♯–G–G♯–A–B♭–B–C♯–D).

MEASURES 1–4: The Jam kicks off with a one-bar A composite blues scale lick that commences with a Chuck Berry–style phrase and ends with a minor-to-major (C-to-C♯) hammer-on that resolves to the first-string root (fret 5). In measure 2, the A7 funk groove makes its first appearance, followed in measure 3 by a run up the extended form of the A blues scale. This phrase concludes with a quarter-step bend of the minor 3rd (C), resolving to another repetition of the A7 skank groove (measure 4).

MEASURES 5–8: Rather than make a position shift after performing the A7 skank groove in measure 4, the lick in measure 5 stays in position, deriving its notes from the fourth-position pattern of the D composite blues scale to outline the IV-chord (D7) harmony. This phrase is followed in measure 6 by the D7 skank groove, requiring a four-fret position shift. In measure 7, the Chuck Berry phrase from measure 1 is restated and followed by notes that emphasizes the minor qualities of the A composite blues scale—that is, the notes also imply the A Dorian mode (A–B–C–D–E–F♯–G). Like the end of measure 3, a quarter-step bend of the minor 3rd (C) resolves to a repetition of the A7 skank groove (measure 8).

MEASURES 9–12: The phrase in measure 9 starts out as a run up the extended form of the E major pentatonic scale (E–F#–G#–B–C#); however, on beat 4, the minor 3rd (G) is introduced, implying the E composite blues scale. Following one bar of the D7 skank groove (measure 10), a flurry of notes from the A composite blues scale is performed in the vicinity of 10th position before shifting to 12th position in measure 12, where the lick resolves to the root of the V (E7#9) chord. This phrase is a case study in how to juxtapose the minor 3rd and minor 3rd over a dominant seventh chord. After multiple iterations of the minor 3rd (C) in measure 11, the major 3rd (C#) is played exclusively (three times) in measure 12.

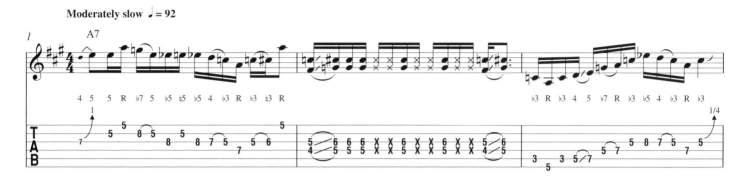

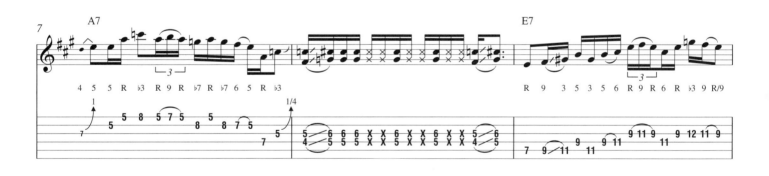

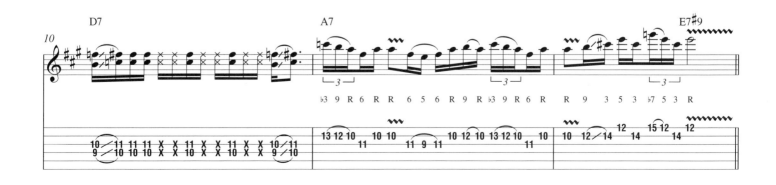

JAM #147: TWO-BAR LEAD/RHYTHM ALTERNATIONS

The alternations in this example—two-bar lead/rhythm tradeoffs—represent a clash in musical styles, albeit a sonically appealing one. Following two measures of sequenced minor-pentatonic string skipping that would feel right at home in a Paul Gilbert instructional video, the Jam transitions to two measures of the A7 funk groove. The string-skipping sequences are then transposed and restated in measures 5–6, over the IV (D7) chord, before yielding to another repetition of the A7 groove (measures 7–8). In measures 9–10, the Jam makes an abrupt departure from its previous rock and funk sounds in favor of country-flavored passages. These phrases lead to one last repetition of the A7 skank (measures 11–12), reestablishing the Jam's fundamental funk sound. Despite the presence of three disparate musical styles, the Jam maintains a cohesive 16th-note groove throughout the 12-bar form.

MEASURES 1–4: Rooted in the A minor pentatonic scale (A–C–D–E–G), the opening string-skipping sequence consists of an eight-note sequence that is repeated every other beat, starting on a lower string with each repetition. At measure 3, the two-bar A7 skank groove enters for one repetition.

MEASURES 5–8: The D minor pentatonic string-skipping sequence in measures 5–6 is a note-for-note replica of the one from measures 1–2, only played five frets higher to accommodate the new (D7) harmony. Getting to 10th position requires a large fret-hand jump, but the accuracy of your first note, F, can be improved if you focus your eyes on its fretboard location, fret 13 of the first string, sliding your pinky into place. Use a similar approach when transitioning back to the A7 skank in measure 7.

MEASURES 9–12: In measure 9, the extended form of the E composite blues scale provides the pitches for a phrase that moves incrementally down the neck, shifting from seventh position to fourth position and, finally, to second position. This phrase is followed in measure 10 by a D composite blues scale lick that matches the contour of its predecessor, although it's played entirely in second position. Note the three-note (C–B–A) pull-off at the end of the phrase, which facilitates the transition back to the A7 skank (measures 11–12). The single-note portion of the skank segues to a chromatic (D–D♯–E) line that flows into the V (E7♯9) chord, which is strummed on the "and" of beat 3.

238

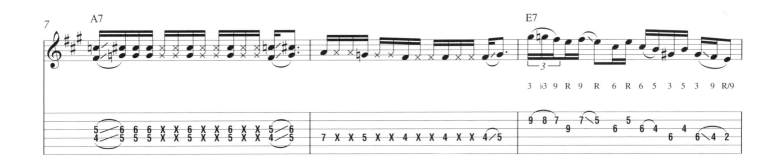

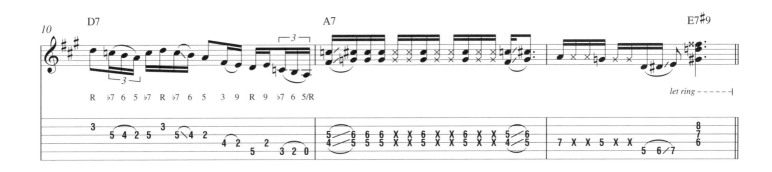

🔊 JAM #148: ONE-BAR RHYTHM/LEAD ALTERNATIONS

In this Jam, the lead and rhythm parts are flip-flopped, resulting in a rhythm/lead sequence, and the alternations are performed in one-bar intervals. As a result, the skank grooves have been shortened to include only the dyad figures, like in Jam #146. Meanwhile, the lead phrases have a distinct blues-rock feel and feature a recurring 16th-note triplet rhythm. Melodically, the licks are flavored with pitches from several scales, including A minor pentatonic (A–C–D–E–G), A blues (A–C–D–Eb–E–G), D composite blues (D–E–F–F♯–G–Ab–A–B–C), and D Mixolydian (D–E–F♯–G–A–B–C).

MEASURES 1–4: After opening with one bar of the A7 skank, the Jam transitions to an aggressive A minor pentatonic lick that features a repetitive double-stop/pull-off figure and incorporates the aforementioned 16-note triplet rhythm. For an authentic blues-rock sound, be sure to nudge the double stops up a quarter step. In measure 3, the A7 skank is reprised from one measure, followed in measure 4 by a restatement of the rhythmic motif from measure 2. Although the repetitive pattern is displaced by one beat and the double stops are absent, the notes (in order: C, A, G, and E) are the same, only played an octave higher.

MEASURES 5–8: In measure 5, the skank groove has been transposed to the key of D for the IV (D7) chord. Staying in position, a D composite blues scale phrase is employed in measure 6 to handle the second half of the IV-chord harmony. Note the last note of the phrase, A, the root of the impending A7 chord, is slid down string 5 to facilitate the transition to the A7 skank (measure 7). In measure 8, the A blues scale supplies the notes to a speedy, repetitive pull-off figure that, like the licks in measures 2 and 4, incorporates 16th-note triplets.

MEASURES 9–12: In measure 9, the skank groove handles the V-chord (E7) harmony, followed in measure 10 by a seventh-position D Mixolydian phrase, which outlines the IV (D7) chord. In measures 11–12, the Jam concludes with one-and-a-half bars of the A7 skank, followed by a chromatic (D–D♯–E) approach to the turnaround chord, E7♯9, which is struck on the "and" of beat 3.

🔊 JAM #149: TWO-BAR RHYTHM/LEAD ALTERNATIONS

The one-bar rhythm/lead alternations from Jam #148 have been extended to two measures in this example. As a result, the skank grooves in the first half of the Jam are performed as their original, two-bar versions, which include both the dyads and the single-note lines. To further enhance the Jam's syncopated feel, the initial lead phrase (measure 3) opens with a highly syncopated rhythmic motif, which is restated in the Jam's second lead passage (measure 7). These syncopated lines are bookended and contrasted with phrases that feature uninterrupted streams of 16th notes and 16th-note triplets. Melodically, the leads are constructed from a variety of scales relative to the I (A7) chord, including A minor pentatonic (A–C–D–E–G), A blues (A–C–D–E♭–E–G), and A composite blues (A–B–C–C♯–D–E♭–E–F♯–G).

MEASURES 1–4: Following two bars of the A7 skank groove (measures 1–2), the first syncopated phrase commences (measure 3). This lick is rooted in the A minor pentatonic scale and shifts to third position on beat 4. In measure 4, the phrase returns to fifth position and incorporates the ♭5th (E♭) on beat 3, implying the A blues scale.

MEASURES 5–8: At measure 5, the skank groove is relocated to 10th position for the IV (D7) chord. Following the single-note skank (measure 6), the rhythmic motif is restated in measure 7. Like its predecessor, this lick is rooted in the A minor pentatonic scale. In measure 8, the phrase segues to a flurry of notes from the A composite blues scale, resolving to the fourth-string root (fret 7) on beat 4.

MEASURES 9–12: In measures 9–10, one-bar versions of the skank grooves handle the V (E7) and IV (D7) chords, followed by an A composite blues scale lick that vacillates between 12th and 10th positions before resolving to the root of the V (E7#9) chord on beat 3 of measure 12. This lick is similar to the one at the end of Jam #146; however, this time, the major 3rd (C#) is featured in the first half of the lick, rather than the minor 3rd (C), which now occupies the second half of the phrase.

JAM #150: RANDOM RHYTHM/LEAD ALTERNATIONS

For this final funk Jam—and the last Jam of the book—the alternations have been arranged randomly, with emphasis on lead playing. In fact, eight of the Jam's 12 measures are devoted to soloing—a 2-to-1 ratio.

The skank grooves are played over the I (A7) chord exclusively and shortened to one bar (one exception is the turnaround). Meanwhile, the lead phrases incorporate two distinct soloing concepts: single-note lines and sliding 6ths. The single-note lines constitute a majority of the phrases and are derived from either the A blues scale (A–C–D–Eb–E–G), A composite blues scale (A–B–C–C♯–D–Eb–E–F♯–G), or D composite blues scale (D–E–F–F♯–G–Ab–A–B–C). Although the sliding 6ths are not performed within the confines of specific scale patterns, they do extract their notes from the Mixolydian modes relative to the E7 and D7 chord changes: E Mixolydian (E–F♯–G♯–A–B–C♯–D) and D Mixolydian (D–E–F♯–G–A–B–C).

MEASURES 1–4: The Jam commences with a one-bar A composite blues scale phrase that shifts from fifth position to third position as it descends strings 4–6. However, at the lick's midpoint, it shifts back up to fifth position, where it concludes with a quarter-step bend of the minor 3rd (C). In measure 2, the A7 skank appears for one bar to establish the Jam's funky syncopation before giving way to a bluesy phrase that, over the course of two bars, incorporates all six of the guitar's strings and eight of the A composite blues scale's nine tones.

MEASURES 5–8: The phrase that began in measure 3 continues, unabated, in measures 5–6. Note the voice leading implemented at the end of measure 4, where the A7 harmony's minor 3rd (C) is hammered onto the root of the D7 chord, which is held for half a beat to emphasize the new harmony. This two-bar, country-flavored phrase works its way up the D composite blues scale before jumping to string 1 at the onset of measure 6. Here, the phrase reverse course and begins to work its way back down the scale. In a maneuver borrowed from measure 10 of Jam #147, a three-note (C–B–A) pull-off facilitates the transition to the A7 skank groove in measure 7. Following one bar of skank, an A blues scale lick, reminiscent of the phrase from measure 3, bridges the I (A7) and V (E7) chords.

MEASURES 9–12: In measures 9–10, sliding major and minor 6ths are employed over the V (E7) and IV (D7) chords. Using notes from the E Mixolydian and D Mixolydian modes, the shapes emphasize the major qualities of the chords on beat 1 (via the chords' major 3rds) and the dominant qualities on beat 4 (via the b7ths). Pluck the 6ths with a combination of your pick and middle finger, paying close attention to the syncopated rhythms. In measures 11–12, the A7 skank makes its final appearance and is punctuate with a syncopated strum of the V (E7♯9) chord.

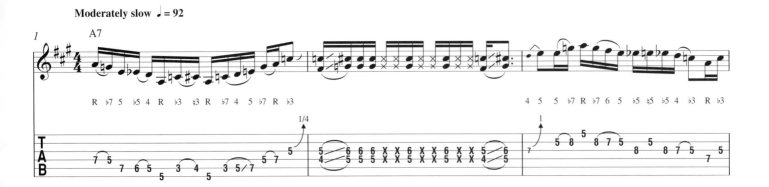

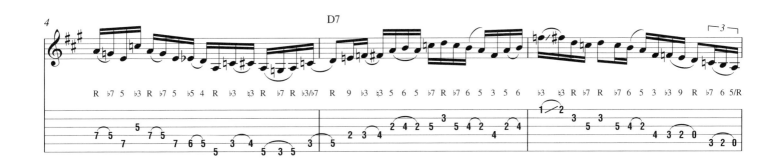

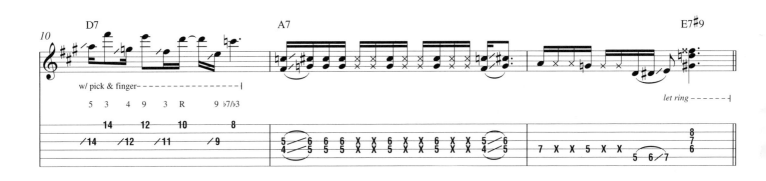

ABOUT THE AUTHOR

Troy Nelson is the author of *Rhythm Guitar 365*, *Fretboard Freedom*, and the #1 bestseller *Guitar Aerobics* (all published by Hal Leonard). He's also the former editor-in-chief and senior editor of *Guitar One* and *Guitar Edge* magazines, respectively.

A 25-year veteran of the guitar, Nelson initially gravitated toward the instrument because of his love of rock, metal, and blues. Later, he studied jazz in college, where he discovered guitarists Wes Montgomery and Johnny Smith and saxophonists John Coltrane and Charlie Parker—all of whom profoundly influenced and inspired his playing style. Seeking new challenges and growth as a musician, Nelson has spent the past several years immersed in country music.

Nelson earned an associate's degree in occupational music from Milwaukee Area Technical College and a bachelor's degree in sports management from the University of Georgia, where he graduated summa cum laude. Nelson currently resides in Nashville, Tennessee, with his wife, Amy, a former record-label executive, and twin daughters, Sophie and Claire.

GUITAR NOTATION LEGEND

Guitar music can be notated three different ways: on a *musical staff*, in *tablature*, and in *rhythm slashes*.

RHYTHM SLASHES are written above the staff. Strum chords in the rhythm indicated. Use the chord diagrams found at the top of the first page of the transcription for the appropriate chord voicings. Round noteheads indicate single notes.

THE MUSICAL STAFF shows pitches and rhythms and is divided by bar lines into measures. Pitches are named after the first seven letters of the alphabet.

TABLATURE graphically represents the guitar fingerboard. Each horizontal line represents a string, and each number represents a fret.

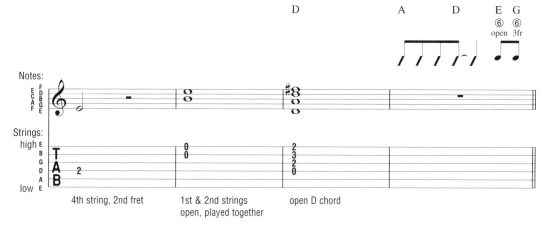

4th string, 2nd fret

1st & 2nd strings open, played together

open D chord

Definitions for Special Guitar Notation

HALF-STEP BEND: Strike the note and bend up 1/2 step.

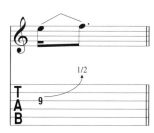

WHOLE-STEP BEND: Strike the note and bend up one step.

GRACE NOTE BEND: Strike the note and immediately bend up as indicated.

SLIGHT (MICROTONE) BEND: Strike the note and bend up 1/4 step.

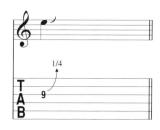

BEND AND RELEASE: Strike the note and bend up as indicated, then release back to the original note. Only the first note is struck.

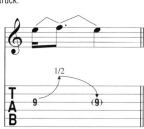

PRE-BEND: Bend the note as indicated, then strike it.

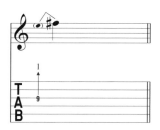

PRE-BEND AND RELEASE: Bend the note as indicated. Strike it and release the bend back to the original note.

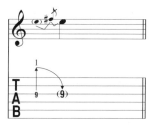

UNISON BEND: Strike the two notes simultaneously and bend the lower note up to the pitch of the higher.

VIBRATO: The string is vibrated by rapidly bending and releasing the note with the fretting hand.

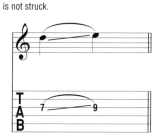

WIDE VIBRATO: The pitch is varied to a greater degree by vibrating with the fretting hand.

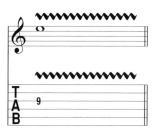

HAMMER-ON: Strike the first (lower) note with one finger, then sound the higher note (on the same string) with another finger by fretting it without picking.

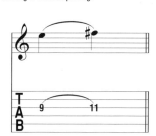

PULL-OFF: Place both fingers on the notes to be sounded. Strike the first note and without picking, pull the finger off to sound the second (lower) note.

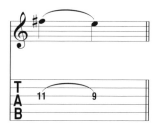

LEGATO SLIDE: Strike the first note and then slide the same fret-hand finger up or down to the second note. The second note is not struck.

SHIFT SLIDE: Same as legato slide, except the second note is struck.

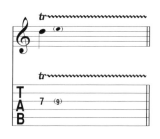

TRILL: Very rapidly alternate between the notes indicated by continuously hammering on and pulling off.

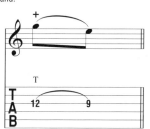

TAPPING: Hammer ("tap") the fret indicated with the pick-hand index or middle finger and pull off to the note fretted by the fret hand.

NATURAL HARMONIC: Strike the note while the fret-hand lightly touches the string directly over the fret indicated.

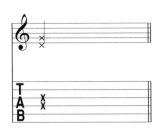

PINCH HARMONIC: The note is fretted normally and a harmonic is produced by adding the edge of the thumb or the tip of the index finger of the pick hand to the normal pick attack.

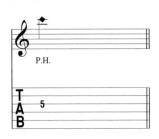

HARP HARMONIC: The note is fretted normally and a harmonic is produced by gently resting the pick hand's index finger directly above the indicated fret (in parentheses) while the pick hand's thumb or pick assists by plucking the appropriate string.

PICK SCRAPE: The edge of the pick is rubbed down (or up) the string, producing a scratchy sound.

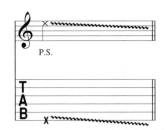

MUFFLED STRINGS: A percussive sound is produced by laying the fret hand across the string(s) without depressing, and striking them with the pick hand.

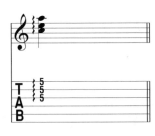

PALM MUTING: The note is partially muted by the pick hand lightly touching the string(s) just before the bridge.

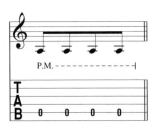

RAKE: Drag the pick across the strings indicated with a single motion.

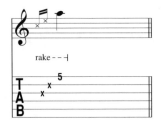

TREMOLO PICKING: The note is picked as rapidly and continuously as possible.

ARPEGGIATE: Play the notes of the chord indicated by quickly rolling them from bottom to top.

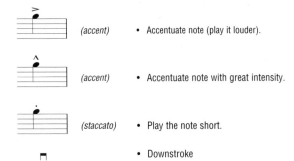

VIBRATO BAR DIVE AND RETURN: The pitch of the note or chord is dropped a specified number of steps (in rhythm), then returned to the original pitch.

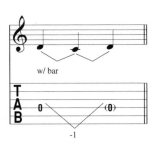

VIBRATO BAR SCOOP: Depress the bar just before striking the note, then quickly release the bar.

VIBRATO BAR DIP: Strike the note and then immediately drop a specified number of steps, then release back to the original pitch.

Additional Musical Definitions

 (accent) • Accentuate note (play it louder).

(accent) • Accentuate note with great intensity.

(staccato) • Play the note short.

⊓ • Downstroke

ᐯ • Upstroke

D.S. al Coda • Go back to the sign (𝄋), then play until the measure marked *"To Coda,"* then skip to the section labelled **"Coda."**

D.C. al Fine • Go back to the beginning of the song and play until the measure marked *"Fine"* (end).

Rhy. Fig. • Label used to recall a recurring accompaniment pattern (usually chordal).

Riff • Label used to recall composed, melodic lines (usually single notes) which recur.

Fill • Label used to identify a brief melodic figure which is to be inserted into the arrangement.

Rhy. Fill • A chordal version of a Fill.

tacet • Instrument is silent (drops out).

• Repeat measures between signs.

• When a repeated section has different endings, play the first ending only the first time and the second ending only the second time.

NOTE: Tablature numbers in parentheses mean:
    1. The note is being sustained over a system (note in standard notation is tied), or
    2. The note is sustained, but a new articulation (such as a hammer-on, pull-off, slide or vibrato) begins, or
    3. The note is a barely audible "ghost" note (note in standard notation is also in parentheses).

Get Better at Guitar

...with these Great Guitar Instruction Books from Hal Leonard!

101 GUITAR TIPS
INCLUDES TAB

STUFF ALL THE PROS KNOW AND USE

by Adam St. James

This book contains invaluable guidance on everything from scales and music theory to truss rod adjustments, proper recording studio set-ups, and much more. The book also features snippets of advice from some of the most celebrated guitarists and producers in the music business, including B.B. King, Steve Vai, Joe Satriani, Warren Haynes, Laurence Juber, Pete Anderson, Tom Dowd and others, culled from the author's hundreds of interviews.

00695737 Book/CD Pack.........................$16.95

AMAZING PHRASING
INCLUDES TAB

50 WAYS TO IMPROVE YOUR IMPROVISATIONAL SKILLS

by Tom Kolb

This book/CD pack explores all the main components necessary for crafting well-balanced rhythmic and melodic phrases. It also explains how these phrases are put together to form cohesive solos. Many styles are covered – rock, blues, jazz, fusion, country, Latin, funk and more – and all of the concepts are backed up with musical examples. The companion CD contains 89 demos for listening, and most tracks feature full-band backing.

00695583 Book/CD Pack.........................$19.95

BLUES YOU CAN USE
INCLUDES TAB

by John Ganapes

A comprehensive source designed to help guitarists develop both lead and rhythm playing. Covers: Texas, Delta, R&B, early rock and roll, gospel, blues/rock and more. Includes: 21 complete solos • chord progressions and riffs • turnarounds • moveable scales and more. CD features leads and full band backing.

00695007 Book/CD Pack.........................$19.95

FRETBOARD MASTERY
INCLUDES TAB

by Troy Stetina

Untangle the mysterious regions of the guitar fretboard and unlock your potential. *Fretboard Mastery* familiarizes you with all the shapes you need to know by applying them in real musical examples, thereby reinforcing and reaffirming your newfound knowledge. The result is a much higher level of comprehension and retention.

00695331 Book/CD Pack.........................$19.95

FRETBOARD ROADMAPS – 2ND EDITION

ESSENTIAL GUITAR PATTERNS THAT ALL THE PROS KNOW AND USE

by Fred Sokolow

The updated edition of this bestseller features more songs, updated lessons, and a full audio CD! Learn to play lead and rhythm anywhere on the fretboard, in any key; play a variety of lead guitar styles; play chords and progressions anywhere on the fretboard; expand your chord vocabulary; and learn to think musically – the way the pros do.

00695941 Book/CD Pack.........................$14.95

GUITAR AEROBICS
INCLUDES TAB

A 52-WEEK, ONE-LICK-PER-DAY WORKOUT PROGRAM FOR DEVELOPING, IMPROVING & MAINTAINING GUITAR TECHNIQUE

by Troy Nelson

From the former editor of *Guitar One* magazine, here is a daily dose of vitamins to keep your chops fine tuned! Musical styles include rock, blues, jazz, metal, country, and funk. Techniques taught include alternate picking, arpeggios, sweep picking, string skipping, legato, string bending, and rhythm guitar. These exercises will increase speed, and improve dexterity and pick- and fret-hand accuracy. The accompanying CD includes all 365 workout licks plus play-along grooves in every style at eight different metronome settings.

00695946 Book/CD Pack.........................$19.99

GUITAR CLUES
INCLUDES TAB

OPERATION PENTATONIC

by Greg Koch

Join renowned guitar master Greg Koch as he clues you in to a wide variety of fun and valuable pentatonic scale applications. Whether you're new to improvising or have been doing it for a while, this book/CD pack will provide loads of delicious licks and tricks that you can use right away, from volume swells and chicken pickin' to intervallic and chordal ideas. The CD includes 65 demo and play-along tracks.

00695827 Book/CD Pack.........................$19.95

INTRODUCTION TO GUITAR TONE & EFFECTS

by David M. Brewster

This book/CD pack teaches the basics of guitar tones and effects, with audio examples on CD. Readers will learn about: overdrive, distortion and fuzz • using equalizers • modulation effects • reverb and delay • multi-effect processors • and more.

00695766 Book/CD Pack.........................$14.99

PICTURE CHORD ENCYCLOPEDIA

This comprehensive guitar chord resource for all playing styles and levels features five voicings of 44 chord qualities for all twelve keys – 2,640 chords in all! For each, there is a clearly illustrated chord frame, as well as *an actual photo* of the chord being played! Includes info on basic fingering principles, open chords and barre chords, partial chords and broken-set forms, and more.

00695224...$19.95

SCALE CHORD RELATIONSHIPS
INCLUDES TAB

by Michael Mueller & Jeff Schroedl

This book teaches players how to determine which scales to play with which chords, so guitarists will never have to fear chord changes again! This book/CD pack explains how to: recognize keys • analyze chord progressions • use the modes • play over nondiatonic harmony • use harmonic and melodic minor scales • use symmetrical scales such as chromatic, whole-tone and diminished scales • incorporate exotic scales such as Hungarian major and Gypsy minor • and much more!

00695563 Book/CD Pack.........................$14.95

SPEED MECHANICS FOR LEAD GUITAR
INCLUDES TAB

Take your playing to the stratosphere with the most advanced lead book by this proven heavy metal author. *Speed Mechanics* is the ultimate technique book for developing the kind of speed and precision in today's explosive playing styles. Learn the fastest ways to achieve speed and control, secrets to make your practice time really count, and how to open your ears and make your musical ideas more solid and tangible. Packed with over 200 vicious exercises including Troy's scorching version of "Flight of the Bumblebee." Music and examples demonstrated on CD. 89-minute audio.

00699323 Book/CD Pack.........................$19.95

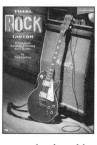

TOTAL ROCK GUITAR
INCLUDES TAB

A COMPLETE GUIDE TO LEARNING ROCK GUITAR

by Troy Stetina

This unique and comprehensive source for learning rock guitar is designed to develop both lead and rhythm playing. It covers: getting a tone that rocks • open chords, power chords and barre chords • riffs, scales and licks • string bending, strumming, palm muting, harmonics and alternate picking • all rock styles • and much more. The examples are in standard notation with chord grids and tab, and the CD includes full-band backing for all 22 songs.

00695246 Book/CD Pack.........................$19.99

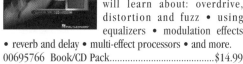

TAB+

Accurate Tabs
Gear Information
Selected Pedal Settings
Analysis & Playing Tips

The Tab+ Series gives you note-for-note accurate transcriptions in notes and tab PLUS a whole lot more. These books also include performance notes to help you master the song, tips on the essential gear to make the song sound its best, recording techniques, historical information, right- and left-hand techniques and other playing tips – it's all here!

TAB. TONE. TECHNIQUE.

25 TOP ACOUSTIC SONGS

Big Yellow Taxi • Can't Find My Way Home • Cat's in the Cradle • The Clap • Closer to the Heart • Free Fallin' • Going to California • Good Riddance (Time of Your Life) • Hey There Delilah • A Horse with No Name • I Got a Name • Into the Mystic • Lola • Losing My Religion • Love the One You're With • Never Going Back Again • Norwegian Wood (This Bird Has Flown) • Ooh La La • Patience • She Talks to Angels • Shower the People • Tequila Sunrise • The Weight • Wild Horses • Wish You Were Here.

00109283 .... $19.99

25 TOP CLASSIC ROCK SONGS

Addicted to Love • After Midnight • Another Brick in the Wall, Part 2 • Aqualung • Beat It • Brown Sugar • China Grove • Domino • Dream On • For What It's Worth • Fortunate Son • Go Your Own Way • Had to Cry Today • Keep Your Hands to Yourself • Life in the Fast Lane • Lights • Message in a Bottle • Peace of Mind • Reeling in the Years • Refugee • Rock and Roll Never Forgets • Roundabout • Tom Sawyer • Up on Cripple Creek • Wild Night.

00102519 .... $19.99

25 TOP HARD ROCK SONGS

Back in Black • Best of Both Worlds • Crazy Train • Detroit Rock City • Doctor, Doctor • Fire Woman • Hair of the Dog • In My Dreams • In-A-Gadda-Da-Vida • Jailbreak • Nobody's Fool • Paranoid • Rock Candy • Rock of Ages • School's Out • Shout at the Devil • Smoke on the Water • Still of the Night • Stone Cold • Welcome to the Jungle • Whole Lotta Love • Working Man • You've Got Another Thing Comin' • Youth Gone Wild • The Zoo.

00102469 .... $19.99

25 TOP METAL SONGS

Ace of Spades • Afterlife • Am I Evil? • Blackout • Breaking the Law • Chop Suey! • Cowboys from Hell • Down with the Sickness • Evil • Freak on a Leash • Hangar 18 • Iron Man • Laid to Rest • The Last in Line • Madhouse • Mr. Crowley • Psychosocial • Pull Me Under • Raining Blood • Roots Bloody Roots • Sober • Tears Don't Fall • Thunder Kiss '65 • The Trooper • Unsung.

00102501 .... $19.99

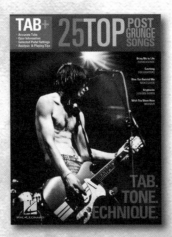

25 TOP POST-GRUNGE SONGS

All Star • Bawitdaba • Blurry • Boulevard of Broken Dreams • Bring Me to Life • Closing Time • Devour • Du Hast • Everlong • Far Behind • Hero • How You Remind Me • I Hate Everything About You • I Stand Alone • It's Been Awhile • Kryptonite • Metalingus • My Own Summer (Shove It) • One Last Breath • One Week • The Reason • Remedy • Sex and Candy • Thnks Fr Th Mmrs • Wish You Were Here.

00102518..$19.99

HAL•LEONARD®
CORPORATION
7777 W. BLUEMOUND RD. P.O. BOX 13819
MILWAUKEE, WISCONSIN 53213

www.halleonard.com

Prices, contents, and availability
subject to change without notice.